THE ESSENTIAL GUIDE TO
Decorating

THE ESSENTIAL GUIDE TO
Decorating

Vinny Lee

projects devised and written by Jane Davies
photography by Ray Main and Graeme Ainscough

THUNDER BAY
P·R·E·S·S

San Diego, California

Contents

Introduction

This book is an informative and illustrated guide to all aspects of decorating your home, introducing the basics such as planning your decorative scheme, explaining the main techniques that you may need, and providing you with ideas and inspiration for every room. Armed with this book and a little imagination, you can create the interior that you have always longed for.

Above: *When planning a room's overall scheme, it is important to think about how functional and decorative objects will work together.*

Opposite: *The white walls of this contemporary interior are accented by the strong colors of the sofa and accessories such as pillows and paintings. The wooden floor adds a touch of warmth to the room.*

A changing world

Interest in decorating has become increasingly popular recently due to changes in both our approach to home life and our response to personal environments. Where colors were once dictated by what was available in the local stores or by a limited palette of standard shades produced by a few commercial paint manufacturers, it seems now that the sky is the limit. For example, paint colors can be blended to match fabrics exactly and created to suit your whims and wishes.

Available to all

The growth of interest in do-it-yourself home improvement, inspired by numerous television programs and magazine articles, has brought the world of the professional decorator, painter, carpenter, and other craftspeople out into the open. Large home-improvement stores offer everything you could need, from lights and kitchen sinks to specialty wallpapers and paints. Even items that once had to be made-to-order are now available instantly.

Because decorating has become such a readily accessible and popular activity, there is a growing need for good, basic information on how to create a successful decorating scheme and the elementary techniques involved. Knowing some professional tricks of the trade is also invaluable in understanding the terminology and practical aspects of decorating. Advancements in the technology of paints and other finishes means that there is an increasingly wide choice of products available, so practical guidance on making basic choices is extremely useful when making your selection.

Using this book

Before embarking on any decorating project, it is important to get the basics right, so the book begins by looking at the different choices available to you and the techniques required. Each area of the home is then looked at in turn, examining the individual requirements of each area before moving on to the styling of each room. Devising a new decorating scheme should be an exciting and creative experience, so we discuss where you can find inspiration and how to focus your taste to suit your lifestyle. Throughout the book you will find many inspiring projects that you can re-create in your own home. The projects vary in difficulty and size, so there is something for everyone to tackle, from the cautious beginner to the more confident, advanced decorator. Written in easy-to-follow language, they incorporate clear, step-by-step photographs.

This comprehensive guide to decorating is aimed at all home-improvement enthusiasts—those in permanent or temporary accommodation, in large or small homes, and in urban or rural locations. It is a practical and informative guide to making the most of your own space as well as an inspirational book that will show you how to create your own style.

Creating your own environment

Tailoring your surroundings to suit the layout, style, and shape of the building, as well as your personal tastes, is what makes a house into a home. Home is a fixed residence, a place where you return to; it is familiar and should be designed to accommodate your needs and requirements.

The home itself has become an important part of our daily life—it is no longer just a place to wash, eat, and sleep. Although these functions are important, the home is also a place where you can express yourself—your tastes, interests, and personal style. It can be a gallery or showcase for things you admire and enjoy, such as artifacts and objects that you have found on local walks, on vacation, or on extended travels. Home is a place to unwind and relax as well as to party and entertain friends. It may also be a place where you work or exercise, which means that many different functions have to be incorporated into the basic domestic agenda.

Below: Your home should be an expression of your own style. Here, dark colors are twinned with bold accessories to create a dramatic look.

Finding your own style

Because of the increasing choice of materials available to us, it is now easier to tailor our environment to our own individual taste. As such, your home and the way it is decorated says a lot about you. Some may decorate in an aspirational classic period style; some may opt for a look that is practical and easy to live; others may choose to follow a fashion or trend.

The most important thing is to create a space that you are comfortable living in. Strong, fashionable trends often hit the headlines and make the pages of leading interior magazines, but although these may have an

influence on the interiors market for a time, they may not be right for you. Although a particular look may appeal, you may have to dilute or adapt it to suit your space and lifestyle.

For example, the minimalist style of the work of the architect Claudio Silvestrin, a master of the spiritually clean environment, is a purist's dream. His interiors are almost monastic, made up mainly of white and linear spaces, but Silvestrin happily admits that his look is not for everyone—you have to be disciplined to live with it and appreciate the thought that goes into achieving the balance of space and light.

But you can admire the perfection of Silvestrin's work without having to follow it slavishly. Start with the principal features—the clean lines and beautiful shapes—and then make use of ample storage space, editing down your possessions. In time, you may find you are throwing out more and buying less, slowly becoming a follower of the minimalist regime.

You might find yourself inspired by a photograph of the inside of a fantastic house in a glossy book or magazine. The room shown would have cost a great deal of money and taken many months or even years of dedicated work to achieve—that may all be way beyond your means and inclination. The key here is to think practically, analyze the pictures or photographs, and extract the elements that really appeal to you.

Ask yourself what it is that draws you to that particular room. Is it the color of the walls? The style and arrangement of the furniture? The floor covering or the aspect of the room? Once you have figured out exactly what it is, then think through whether it is a practical style for you and how it can be re-created. Will it work in your room and suit your lifestyle? Most importantly, is it just a fad that you will tire of?

Personalizing your space

The eminent French designer Philippe Starck once said: "It is important to inject love into the place where you live. It is not healthy to rent an interior designer to create a home for you because it is not good to live in another person's fantasy. People should select for themselves and stamp their own identity on a place. They should mix and match everything to make their own cocktail."

When embarking on decorating your home, think about your lifestyle and how and where you live. Do you have a room in a shared house? Are there communal living areas shared by others? You might be a student paying rent for the use of a single room in a house, a teenager living in a family home, or an adult in your own apartment.

The degree of personalization of a space may vary. For example, your bedroom may be the place where you can truly express yourself, but a shared area such as a sitting room or dining area may need to be a compromise scheme that works around the likes and dislikes of others who are using the space, too.

In a shared room, a neutral decor may the most suitable, with a background of simple wall and floor coverings that can be enlivened by accessories. In shared utility areas, such as a kitchen or bathroom, the priority is most likely to be practicality— surfaces that are durable and that can be easily, regularly, and thoroughly cleaned will be the best option.

You may also choose to keep "public" rooms, such as living and dining areas where people outside the family circle are admitted, in a looser style of decoration so that there are some personal elements but you have not created an overpowering or overly intimate space that visitors will find uncomfortable.

Changing tastes

Your own tastes generally change over time. Your childhood likes and dislikes will probably not have been the same as those you had in adolescence. Similarly, after you left home (an environment that was influenced by your parents and their choice of decor), you will have started to experiment with

your own schemes. The compromise will have started again when you met a partner and set up home together. Then, if you have a family, your ideas and style will have had to be modified to accommodate their needs, too. Time and circumstances, as well as fashions, trends, and even the location of your home, will all have an effect on the way you live and decorate your space.

Above: *Glass can be used to create the illusion of space, such as in this stunning contemporary stairwell.*

Color and texture

Color and texture are important ingredients in the overall appearance of a room. Color helps to define the mood and ambience, and can be used to disguise or accentuate features. Texture will add highlights and interest, not just to wall surfaces but also to furniture and accessories.

Finding inspiration

Bringing together a color palette for a room's overall scheme will depend on the style or type of decoration that you opt for, and the key to deciding this is inspiration. You may start by finding a fabric that you like and the colors in the pattern will lead you into a scheme, or it might be a painting, a piece of furniture, or a handmade piece of craftwork that triggers your ideas.

Below: This yellow vase is shown against an orange wall. Yellow and orange are compatible colors within the same "family."

Inspiration now comes from all over the globe thanks to movies, television, and increasing worldwide travel. This means that the subtle blues and greens of a traditional Scandinavian home can be found in a New York apartment, the art of a remote African village may be displayed in all its glory in a chic studio in Paris, and the sun-washed walls of an Italian villa can be re-created in a kitchen in London.

Themes, such as a collection of Asian china or African masks, can be the basis and inspiration for a whole decorating scheme. If artworks are not your thing, then explore the wealth of materials and finishes available. Be brave and experiment with unusual materials to create a unique look.

Color theory

There are many different options when it comes to planning a color scheme. These include choosing colors that are part of the same family (have a similar base color), colors that are opposites, or tonal colors. The easiest way to see these choices is to look at a color wheel. The color wheel is like the rainbow, but the colors are laid around in a circle rather than in an arc. The primary colors—red, yellow, and blue—are the spokes of the wheel, and between them you get colors that are made from a mixture of the primaries. This means that between red and yellow you will find a red with a hint of yellow, then a true orange, followed by yellow with a hint of red. Between yellow and blue the colors are yellow with a hint of blue, true green, and blue with a hint of yellow.

Colors that belong to the same family are those that contain one of the same primaries, so red, yellow, and orange are of the same family as red, purple and blue. Opposite or contrasting colors are those that lie opposite each other on the color wheel, so red and green, orange and blue, and yellow and violet are opposites. Tonal schemes select a single color such as red and use darker and lighter shades of it rather than mixing other colors.

Choosing your colors

Choosing color is very personal and people react differently to various shades, so you should choose colors that you and your family feel comfortable with. For example, one person may find red a warming color but to another person it could be overpowering.

Neutral colors have long been popular—magnolia, beige, soft yellows, and off-whites are all favorites because they are easy to live with and make a room look light and bright.

There is a standard decorating guideline that says that dark colors make surfaces advance and light colors make them recede, but there are exceptions to the rule. Dark colors can be effective in making a ceiling seem farther away—for example, a well-lit, shiny deep blue will make the ceiling seem infinite, like a sky at night. Like texture, dark colors can also be used to disguise or camouflage uneven surfaces and architectural imbalances.

For impact and drama, bold colors are the best. Many people are wary of using them and of making such a definite statement when decorating their home, but if you take the plunge, the effect can be rewarding. It may take time for your eyes to get accustomed to rich, dark shades, so you can always take it step by step, building up gradually to a really deep shade. Paint one wall in a strong shade and live with it for a few weeks until you get used to it, or start with an basecoat of a paler shade and add a top layer of the darker color later, so that you have time to adapt and become familiar with the change.

Also remember that when you first see the bare walls painted in a dark color, they may appear strong and even overwhelming, but as soon as you have added carpets, furniture, pictures, lights, and soft furnishings to the room, the effect will be reduced.

Tone-on-tone schemes

You could use the interior designers' trick of tone-on-tone schemes—this involves using a variety of different shades of the same color. For example, if you paint your walls in a mid-coffee brown and put a paler, light brown carpet on the floor, you can use a patterned upholstery fabric that contains both those shades and perhaps add a deeper tone of

furniture to make a stronger statement. The accessories can then consist of lighter and darker tones of the same base color so that all the shades have the same harmonious ground note. However, you should take care to ensure the scheme does not look dull. To avoid this, add glass, brass, gold, or silver and plenty of patterns and textures.

Texture

The type of finish that you choose for the walls will also influence the overall effect. A matte surface will make a dark tone seem duskier and softer, or even silky. It will absorb light, making the effect a little darker. A shiny gloss surface will emphasize the depth of color, and because the surface is light-reflective, can double the impact of natural or artificial lighting.

Texture is important not only in your wall finish but also in the combination of fabrics that you use—a room full of soft, smooth surfaces will look flat to the eye, but introduce a few pillows covered in a richly textured chenille and you will add variety.

Top: *Furniture or a painting against a strong-colored wall lessens the impact.*

Above: *This heavily textured rug provides contrast in a room that has lots of smooth surfaces.*

Mood boards

Mood boards are used by professional decorators to show their clients a selection of materials, paint colors, wallpapers, trimmings, and floor coverings, so that the textures and colors can be seen together. Mood boards are a way of showing all the ingredients of the recipe before it is prepared.

Opposite: A mood board encapsulates your ideas for a decorative scheme, including your chosen colors, textures, patterns, and fabrics.

Below: When you have created your mood board, you can re-create the ideas in your home.

A mood board is a way of gathering together elements of decorating materials so that you can see and touch them, and mix and match until you find your perfect scheme. Trying to explain to someone verbally, or imagine in your mind's eye, how colors and textures work together is almost impossible. One person will say that they are looking at a cream color while someone else may describe it as yellow or golden. The word "fringe" can be used to describe all sorts of different trimmings and finishes, but only one will be the right one for your lampshade or valance, so to see an actual sample is important.

The mood board also gives you the chance to play around with various samples and see how they relate. For example, if you like a warm cream paint and have found a fabric with a similar color, then you can try them with different highlighting colors, such as red or green, to see which works best.

Making a mood board

To construct a mood board, you need a large sheet of thick, white cardboard. Start by thumbtacking small swatches and samples to it. As you update or modify the board, remove and discard the older or replaced pieces. Eventually, when you have arrived at a final selection, glue them in place to ensure that none of the pieces falls off and becomes lost.

Although the board is primarily a visual guide, always keep references of the manufacturers of any items you attach to it—it would be extremely frustrating to finalize your choice and then be unable to source a product.

The mood board is also a useful way of seeing how the colors and fabrics react in different lights. You can take it to a window and see if the colors look good together in daylight, then at night look at them under an electric light to see if they are compatible and if any tonal alterations occur.

You should make a separate board for each room in the house—do not try to squeeze two or three schemes onto one board or it will become confusing. It can also be helpful to take the board with you when you go to choose furnishings, floor coverings, or other finishes because it will give both you and the supplier a point of reference.

Items for mood boards

Some items on the board can be temporary—for example, you may find a leaf or a candy wrapper that is just the right color for a paint or fabric you want. Keep the paper or leaf and pin it to the board until you can find the paint color to match. You may also find some inspirational pictures or postcards that show a room or piece of furniture that has the right features or is an interesting shape—you can pin any of these to your mood board to remind you of what you are looking for. Remember, inspiration is all around you.

Style and period

You can create your own unique style by mixing antique and modern schemes or old and new furniture. You may choose a period design that is appropriate to the age of your home or one that you admire. Whatever elements you decide on, try to use a cohesive color and fabric scheme to tie them together.

Finding your style

Past, future, and current trends can influence your decorating scheme. The building you live in may be of a certain period or style that relates to a range of colors and a certain type of furniture, and this may inspire you to echo those elements in your decor. For example, a block of apartments built in 1950s or 1960s would be the perfect setting for retro-style furniture with geometric-print fabrics. An early 20th-century house may still have original features such as plaster cornicing and marble fireplaces—these may take you in the direction of a more classic collection of furniture and fabrics.

Even if the building in which your home is located does not have a tangible style, there may be periods of history or eras that you have a nostalgic feeling for or enjoy. For example, you may favor Art Deco and the Jazz Age, with their angular, boxy furniture, champagne-tinted mirrors, and feeling of opulence and decadence. Or perhaps the Shaker style is more to your taste—restrained and wholesome with an emphasis on craftsmanship and utility.

Asian influences in interior style tend to be cyclical—the black and red lacquer furnishings and Zen-style simplicity are both currently fashionable, but during the early 1900s a more decorative Asian style was in vogue. The fashion was for chinoiserie and richly embroidered silks, ornately painted and inlaid furniture, and large vases and painted bowls. So although the inspiration was derived from the same source, this influence was interpreted in different ways.

Re-creating period style

Tastes in style and period living vary widely, too. Some people choose to ignore the style of the building or apartment in which they live. They may remove cornicing details and block out door panels so that they are left with a blank canvas on which to create their own individual look. Others spend a great deal of time, effort, and money trying to restore elements of the original decor of their home, searching through antiques markets and visiting specialty suppliers to find just the right period fireplace, and often employing master craftspeople to copy old plaster details.

Whichever path you choose to follow, it is important to be 100 percent committed to it. If you are going to restore a place to its original period style, then do your research into the colors and fabrics that were available at that time. For example, there is no point in using synthetic fabrics such as nylon in a turn-of-the-20th-century room because nylon was not invented until the 1930s. Large pictorial printed fabrics featuring Chinese urns and cranes will look equally out of place in a 1960s-inspired apartment.

All decorative elements, from drapes and carpets to wall colors and furnishings, should be harmonious—they do not have to

Below: This shieldback chair is a classic period feature that would also look effective in a modern setting.

be from exactly the same year but should have a common theme.

When re-creating a particular period, start with the basics, such as paint. There are now many paint companies that specialize in historically accurate paint colors and finishes, so it should be easy to find a period paint color. Some companies even emulate the old matte and chalk effects within their paints.

With the current revival of interest in wallpaper, it is also easier to find the geometric 1950s- and 1960s-style prints, many of which have had a 21st-century adaptation in coloring. Designers such as Todhunter Earle have used 1960s-style shapes in their collection of wallpapers, but in subtle rather than garish tones. For the more fun cartoon-style prints, Cath Kidston has created a delightful range of nostalgic floral prints and cowboy designs.

An eclectic mix

For those who opt for a more eclectic and easygoing style, it is, however, simple enough to mix the old and the new together. You do not have to stick rigidly to every decorating rule in order to create a successful interior, so feel free to experiment with what you already have.

Many people inherit pieces of furniture from family and friends, or build up a collection over the years from different homes. Not all the pieces will necessarily be of the same period or style, so if you have an eclectic selection, you have to find a way to link them by some other means. In this case, the background elements play an important role in bringing all the pieces together. For example, the walls, floor covering, and drapes should be of a similar or contrasting but compatible palette.

The larger pieces of furniture, such as sofas and armchairs, can be linked by using the same upholstery fabric on them. Another option is to cover some pieces of furniture in a patterned fabric and then to pick out individual colors from the pattern for the seats and covers on the other pieces of furniture. Throw pillows can also be used to create a conformity among diverse styles and shapes of furniture.

There are many timeless pieces of furniture that fit into almost any scheme or design of room—they stand alone like pieces of sculpture or art. For example, the Eames Model 670

rosewood-faced chair with leather-covered cushions and matching footstool first went into production in 1956 and is still being manufactured today. This chair can be seen in many different styles of contemporary home, from bare white minimalist surroundings and retro 1950s style to the eclectic mix of the average home.

Other classics include the Corbusier recliner, Sori Yanagi Butterfly footstool, Thonet bentwood chairs, and original Lloyd Loom chairs, all of which will sit comfortably in any home as long as a fairly classic or neutral style of decor has been adopted.

Above: Timeless pieces, such as this chrome and wood table, fit into any scheme.

Seasonal living

Seasons and cycles of time bring different needs and requirements. For example, we often long to be cool in the height of summer and warm in the depths of winter—our surroundings should be arranged so that they are adaptable enough to cope and make us comfortable with these extremes.

After the long, dark days of winter, spring is a welcome change, bringing buds, brightness, and a feeling of freshness and renewal. This is a good time to open windows and blow away the hibernal cobwebs. As spring turns into summer and the weather warms, flowers are abundant and succulent fruits come into season, which can add zesty freshness and color to your rooms.

The fall is a rich time of harvest and changing colors. Russet reds, bronze, and copper colors abound. As winter comes around again, we settle down to rest in our cozy homes and await the arrival of the next burst of spring.

Seasonal fabrics

In recent times, the trend for replacing the summer surface dressings of a room with winter ones has become popular. This may be because soft furnishings have become less expensive and easier to buy, so there is huge choice and availability. Also, having two sets of covers spreads the wear and tear on the fabrics and leaves one set free for repairs, cleaning, or washing.

If you want to change the appearance of a room significantly, start with the windows. Take down heavy, dark-colored winter drapes and replace them with pale or white

sheer voile curtains for spring and summer. Then swap the covers on throw pillows from richly textured, jewel tones and ornate patterns to crisp cotton, linen, and slub silk in pastel shades and light checks or prints. Finally, replace woolen throws and blankets with waffle or textured cotton. You are not changing the furnishings, just the dressings, but you will feel a noticeable difference in your surroundings inside as the seasons change outside.

Covers for headboards on beds and highback dining chairs are simple ways of acknowledging seasonal changes. Purchase rich, warm-colored covers for the winter and fall, and fresh, zesty ones for the spring and summer. Covers also help to preserve the fabric underneath and are easily removed for washing if they become stained or marked.

Seasonal changes can also give a cosmetic lift to your surroundings, creating a welcome change that echoes the cycles of

Below and right: Yellow is an adaptable color. It can be strong, warm, and sunny or pale and refreshing.

Natural seasonal features

Colors can be highlighted with the addition of seasonal blooms, and what better way to emphasize the periodic changes than with plants and flowers.

In winter, glossy green pot plants such as holly and ivy can be used in arrangements when flowers are scarce or expensive. You may also add scented bowls of woodchips or pinecones, and orange pommanders decorated with cloves. Springtime is a season for vivid yellow, bright green, and fresh flowers—cut flowers can be bought but will last much longer if grown from bulbs. Summer is a time when flowers are abundant in gardens and meadows. Indoors you can echo the feeling of heat and sun with an arrangement of small cacti or exotic flowers such as orchids. Fall sees the leaves dropping from the trees and the rich mellowness of orange, red, and rust in parks and pathways. You could collect some leaves, dry them, and arrange them in a decorative bowl.

Left: *These deep purple flowers are enhanced by being placed in polished silver or glass containers.*

Above: *Bright green and white flowers are ideal to bring a breath of spring air to a room.*

Below: *Roses complement any interior throughout the spring and summer.*

nature and the landscape outside. It can also be beneficial to your health and outlook. For example, you probably change your bedding from a winter-weight feather or down comforter to a light cotton blanket between winter and summer, so why not change to a linen sheet or cover during the hottest months?

Reversible fabrics are useful for seasonal changes. For example, drapes with a dark side and a light side could be used with the pale side to the front in the summer and the more colorful side to the fore in the winter.

Seasonal mood changes

Removable covers also give you the opportunity to change the pace or style of your home—for example, one set of covers and soft furnishings could be classic or neutral and the other modern or bright, so that it is not only a seasonal change but also a mood or style change as well.

Variety is the spice of life, so changing the emphasis of color and/or pattern in your home will alleviate any staleness or

boredom with your surroundings. The changes do not have to be radical to have an effect.

By linking color and pattern, subtle but impressive changes can be made. For example, imagine a room with pale to mid-blue walls. For the winter, you could use accessories from the darker end of the spectrum, such as navy and midnight blue. Then inject warmth with mulberry and burgundy, which have a blue base note but also a warm red element that heats up an otherwise cool color. In the spring and summer, the blue could be made cooler with the addition of silver gray, white, and icy blue accessories, to enhance blue's cold trait.

A neutral room with white, pale cream or beige walls offers a whole range of opportunities when it comes to seasonal accessorizing. For example, spring and summer could be a time for vivid, zesty colors such as orange, green, and lemon, but in the winter you could add the mellow tones of mink, mouse, toffee, and coffee for a snug, relaxing, and cozy environment.

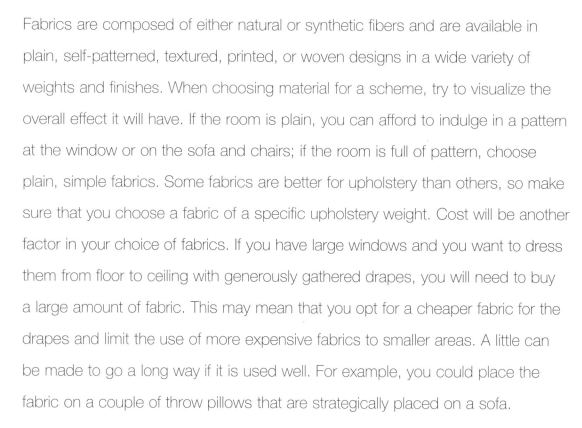

Fabrics

Fabrics are composed of either natural or synthetic fibers and are available in plain, self-patterned, textured, printed, or woven designs in a wide variety of weights and finishes. When choosing material for a scheme, try to visualize the overall effect it will have. If the room is plain, you can afford to indulge in a pattern at the window or on the sofa and chairs; if the room is full of pattern, choose plain, simple fabrics. Some fabrics are better for upholstery than others, so make sure that you choose a fabric of a specific upholstery weight. Cost will be another factor in your choice of fabrics. If you have large windows and you want to dress them from floor to ceiling with generously gathered drapes, you will need to buy a large amount of fabric. This may mean that you opt for a cheaper fabric for the drapes and limit the use of more expensive fabrics to smaller areas. A little can be made to go a long way if it is used well. For example, you could place the fabric on a couple of throw pillows that are strategically placed on a sofa.

CLOCKWISE FROM TOP LEFT:

Long-pile fabrics are more suitable for throw pillows and small areas rather than larger upholstery requirements.

Trimmings and braids can lift and embellish a plain pillow or drape—these small glass beads add to the opulence of the shiny pillow cover.

The fabrics that you choose will have a lasting effect on the overall feel of a room. This sheer fabric with floral velvet embellishment will add a sense of romance wherever it is placed.

Sheer voile is an effective window dressing because it lets in plenty of light.

A blanket does not need to be monochrome—here, the blanket is rich mixture of blue, brown, and cream colors.

For drapes and shades, choose materials that are soft and that hang well. A stiff or rigid fabric will hang awkwardly in lumps and ridges instead of soft furls and pleats.

Try using rich velvets and chenilles on throws and pillows to add a feeling of luxury to a room.

Vivid colors and geometric patterns can be used on rugs to create a dramatic floor area.

Thick chenille like this is well-suited to all general upholstery needs.

Fur made from synthetic fibers is fun to use, but always check that it has a flame-retardant label to ensure that it is also safe.

Loose-weave fabrics, like this knitted mohair, is decorative rather than practical. It may be used as a throw over the back of a chair or sofa or as a wall hanging.

Intricately woven, patterned fabrics with no surface pile or loops are good for upholstery and drapes.

Light, colorful materials with fresh summery prints can help to lift a dark or basement room where natural light is restricted.

Classic patterns, such as this cheerful check, never seem to decline in their popularity.

Planning your home

Before you start work on a new property or making alterations to an existing home, take time to plan and discuss your aims. Ask yourself what it is you want and how this can be achieved. It is easier and less costly to spend time and effort on planning than to rush in and make errors that will need to be fixed later.

Opposite: Ensure that adjacent areas are decorated in a complementary fashion.

Below: Before you decorate, draw a detailed plan that includes fixed features such as fireplaces and alcoves, and furniture such as tables and chairs.

Drawing out your plan

The first thing to do when tackling decorating is to look at the overall layout of your home. Write down a list of the activities that take place in each room. If you are decorating a small apartment or you use a room for more than one function, such as a home office/ guest bedroom, you will need to devise a scheme that will work around the various activities. If you have a larger home, there will be rooms that have only a single purpose and the decoration can be focused on that activity.

Once you have made a list of functions, figure out the allocation of space. Even in a sole-purpose room, you will need to define areas for storage and larger pieces of furniture. With a pencil, draw a room plan to scale on squared paper. Include any fixed features and immovable objects, such as windows, doors, fireplaces, and chimney breasts.

When you are happy with the plan, draw over the outline with a permanent marker pen.

Once the room plan is finished, make small, scaled cutouts of the larger movable pieces of furniture, such as bookcases, sofas, and beds. Place these on the floor plan of the room and move them around until you think you have the right configuration. It is much easier to move small pieces of paper around than to lift and move heavy furniture.

Planning each room

There is a logical procedure for laying out furniture. Think of the way the room is used—imagine walking into it and carrying out the activity appropriate to the space, such as working, bathing, or cooking. For example, in a study area, the desk should be near the phone and light sockets and by a window to use natural light.

In a bedroom, try to keep electrical appliances to a minimum, and avoid keeping computers and work items here. If you have a single-room apartment, place a screen in front of the work area to create a barrier between the sleeping and working parts of the room.

Kitchens and bathrooms are usually located according to the layout of waste and water pipes, which will be placed so that they connect with main sewers and drains. In some homes, these rooms become dual purpose due to their size. For example, if you have a small kitchen and a large bathroom, consider putting the washing machine in the bathroom. If the bathroom is small but drying space is needed, place a retractable drying line over the bath.

In a large bathroom, you may want to keep a yoga or exercise mat as well as weights or other equipment so that you can do exercise routines there.

If so, you will have to allot adequate storage space for these items on your plan.

The kitchen is increasingly becoming the main living area of the home, with dining and seating areas adjoining the cooking space. When planning the decoration of an area like this, keep certain constraints in mind. The kitchen sink or main section of worktop is best placed by a window so that most of the natural light will be focused on one of the primary working areas.

Include some form of barrier between the kitchen and dining areas—this is especially useful in households with young children. A breakfast bar or similar mid-height divider will enable an adult working in the kitchen to monitor small children playing nearby as well as form a protective barrier

that will make it easier to confine children to a safe distance away from the heat and dangers of the kitchen (see box, page 214).

Decorating the utility areas, such as bathrooms and kitchens, usually centers on the need for durable and waterproof materials. Both rooms require good ventilation, but the surfaces and materials used within the space should also be easy to clean. Ceramic tiles have long been a favorite material for use behind sinks and handbasins, but now reinforced glass, stainless steel, and cement are often used.

Bathrooms, shower rooms, and separate toilets are sometimes windowless, dark, and box-like rooms, so a decorative scheme should counteract this by making the place appear light, colorful, and spacious.

(see box, page 214).

Making the most of natural light

According to Asian traditions, you should wake facing the sunrise and go to sleep in the direction of the sunset. Organizing your home on this axis has many practical advantages, since you start the day and spend the morning in rooms that make the most of the natural daylight, but as the light fades, your activities move to other rooms where light is not as readily available but may not be as necessary. You may find that by removing or creating openings in internal walls, you get a better and more effective flow of light from one side of the building to the other.

Basic
techniques

Getting started

Before you start decorating, take time out for research and preparation. Do some research into the materials so that you can choose the right finish for the right area. Next, do any preparatory work. The more preparation you put in, the better the end result will be. All that filling and sanding, washing and stripping, will seem worthwhile when you see the final, smooth painted ceiling or papered wall. Once this is done, you can start decorating—this chapter explores the basic techniques, from painting and wallpapering to tiling and flooring, and looks at ways of using architectural features to their best advantage.

This chapter will provide you with a thorough grounding in all the basic decorating techniques. After a brief introduction to each method of decorating, the book focuses on the range of materials available and the tools and applicators that are recommended. The practical step-by-step sections take you through all the essential groundwork (such as filling holes and stripping wallpaper), as well as covering more complex techniques (such as laying a tongue-and-groove wood floor or making a fire surround).

For those already competent in home-improvement skills, this information is a good way of refreshing the memory, whereas for the beginner it is aimed to be instructive as well as helpful. Even if you are not going to be tackling the decorations yourself, this will help you to plan a timescale and enable you to check on the progress of the work.

Preparing a room

To prepare a room for decoration, you should empty it as much as possible. Take out all the furniture, pictures, fabrics, and fittings that

Above: *Preparation is the key to a successful finish. Here, a wood floor is being sanded before a finish is applied.*

Right: *Any cracks and holes in walls need to be filled before you can decorate.*

you can. Anything that has to stay behind and is not being decorated should be protected against any splashes or spills. Floors should be protected with lots of old newspaper or a large, heavy-duty plastic sheet.

Very large pieces of furniture may need to be moved to the center of the room and protected with drop cloths or old bed sheets. You can buy roller bases—extendible metal brackets with rollers at each end—that make it easier to maneuver large cupboards and chests around.

Be very careful when moving furniture. Never try to do it single-handedly or you may risk injury; ask a couple of friends to help you instead.

Order of work

Unsightly features may need to be camouflaged, and this is the time to plan how and where it will be done. Water pipes, telephone cables, and other household wiring are best boxed in or hidden behind a window seat or some other piece of built-in furniture. In some cases, wiring can be laid under floorboards or put under the edge of a wall-to-wall carpet.

If you are embarking on a radical redecoration, this is the time to have any basic repair work or major jobs done. For example, if you have contemplated underfloor heating, install it now when carpets and furniture are out of the way and you have easy access to the uncovered floor. Try to think from the underneath out, so that all the work is carried out in logical stages before the paint or paper is put in place.

Removing varnish or paint finishes off a wooden floor should be done well before any paint pot is opened. The microfine dust generated by an electric sanding machine and even handheld sandpaper will take time to settle

and will only be thoroughly removed after being wiped a couple of times with a damp cloth. Even lifting a carpet will cause dust to rise, so mats, rugs, and carpets should be removed before walls and paintwork are wiped down.

Do not be tempted to start jobs in the wrong order. For example, sanding the window frames while the wall paint is drying elsewhere in the room is not a good idea because the dust from the frames will stick to the wet wall paint and damage the surface and finish of the wall. Always think through the order of your jobs before starting them.

Preparing the surfaces

Unless you are moving into a recently completed conversion or a newly built home, you will have to prepare the walls and ceiling before any decoration takes place. Even in newly built homes, you may need to fill cracks. Fresh plaster shrinks as it dries, and if it dries quickly in a room where central heating is in use, then fine hair line cracks will appear where

the plaster has been used over joints in wallboard or in corners. There is also a certain amount of what is known as "settling," when bricks and boards adjust to their resting places.

In an older building or room that has been previously decorated, you will most likely need to strip off the existing paper. This is a laborious task but you can rent steamers from commercial rental stores that will make the job much easier.

It is well worth spending time on preparation, even filling in small holes where nails for hanging pictures have been, because the effort put into the groundwork will ensure that the final finish is good. It is pointless putting up sheets of expensive wallpaper over a badly prepared surface because they will not adhere properly, and when the paper dries the surface will be bumpy and uneven. Surfaces painted in a solid color also need to be well-prepared because any blemish or mark will be particularly noticeable in the finished surface because there is no pattern to distract the eye.

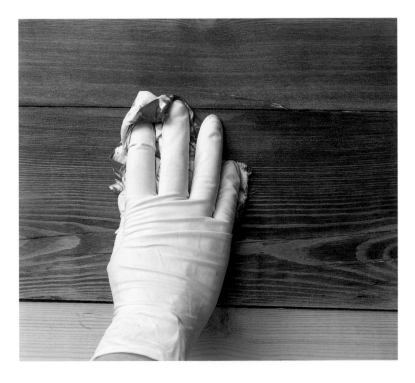

Left: *Before you start decorating your home, make sure that you have all the necessary protective clothing such as these gloves, which will protect your hands when applying woodstain.*

Choosing your paint

Paint is one of the most versatile and easy finishes to apply—it can look plain, smooth, and matte or rough and textured. Patterns can be painted over a basecoat, block-printed, or stenciled. Paints can also be used to create many different effects, such as making the wall look like marble or wood.

Early paint sources

In early times, pigments came from natural sources such as earth—for example, the color sienna is named after the red Tuscan earth from which it was made. Plants, leaves, and mosses were frequently used to obtain green colorings, and red was often made using animal blood or crushed insects. Blue used to be extracted from the woad plant, which is a member of the mustard family, and indigo, most commonly known as the color of denim jeans, came from the *Indigofera* plant and was introduced into Europe from the East in the 16th century.

History of paint

Paint is usually a liquid, made up of a pigment that is dissolved in water or oil. Many centuries ago, pigments used to come from natural sources (see box, left). These early paints were expensive because they took time and trouble to prepare, and the basic ingredients had to be imported from far away. Therefore, wall paints tended to be confined to the homes of wealthy city dwellers and would be mixed on site by master craftspeople.

The industrial revolution had an effect on paint—carbon or gas black was a by-product of the incomplete combustion of natural gas. Some discoveries are relatively recent. For example, the earliest synthetic dye, mauve, was obtained at the end of the 19th century, while the vivid greens of forest and emerald were not developed until 1938.

Even though the dyes and pigments themselves have advanced, many people prefer to look to the past for inspiration. There is an increasing interest not only in traditional colors but also in old techniques, such as pickling and the use of distemper, which with some modifications can produce a more stable and durable finish than when it was originally in use.

Choosing a color

The best way to get an idea of the range of colors available is to get some paint chips. These are strips of paper showing a range of shades of one color and they are available from most paint and home stores. Take some paint chips home and see how they look next to furniture and fabrics. Isolate one or two of the tones that you feel comfortable with, then buy a small tester pot so that you can try out the colors in your own home without buying a lot of paint. You can either paint

Right: Consider applying bands of different colors to a single wall to create a striking look.

the color directly onto an area of the wall or paint a piece of lining paper or cardboard that can be temporarily stuck to the wall.

This trial patch will give you a chance to see a volume of color and to study it in different lights. Look at the paint patch during the day in natural light and then again in the evening in artificial illumination because colors can vary. What appears to be a muted ocher yellow in daylight may look sad and sludgy by electric light.

When building up a strong wall color from a pale base, you may well be advised by the paint manufacturer to choose a colored basecoat that complements the final paint color. A colored basecoat will help build up the

depth of color. Conversely, if you are going to use a lighter color over a dark base, apply a basecoat of white or beige first to block out the strong tones as completely as possible, before applying the actual color.

Many manufacturers now produce a range of "one-coat" paints, which claim that they will cover walls in a single application, on a prepared wall without a basecoat. This does work well if you are applying a color with a similar strength of tone as the color already on the wall. However, when it comes to painting a much lighter color over a dark base color, then you may still have to apply two coats.

There are many different paint effects you can try (see pages 38–9), and these can look good in moderation if skillfully carried out. In a period setting, they can be used to create panels of interest in a long corridor or to mimic the effect of expensive wallpapers or woods. But the fashion for paint effects has also spread to wallpapers, and you can now buy papers printed with rag-rolled effects, for example, that may be a simpler alternative for you.

The paint finish that you choose will also affect lighting. Dark, matte surfaces absorb light, whereas light and shiny paint surfaces reflect it. Textured surfaces are also more light-absorbent than smooth finishes.

Above: *Dark, matte paint colors, such as this deep-blue decorative scheme, tend to absorb light and therefore work well in rooms that have ample natural lighting.*

types of
paint

Paint is one of the most inexpensive but effective ways to finish and seal a surface. It protects against wear and tear as well as adding color and disguising any surface imperfections. To achieve a durable finish, it is important to choose the correct formulation for the surface. Paint manufacturers are responding to consumer demands for paint that is odor-free, pleasant to use, and easy to clean up. As a result, the range now available is vast.

Common paint types

There are many types of paint to choose from and each gives a slightly different finish. The most common is latex.

Latex paint

This water-based paint formulation is commonly used on internal walls and ceilings. It is available in different finishes such as matte, eggshell (semi-gloss), and satin. Paint with a matte finish has no sheen, whereas eggshell (semi-gloss) finishes have a slight gloss, and satin has a slight sheen and is formulated to cope with moisture and heat in bathrooms and kitchens. Satin may also be used in busy hallways because it dries to a wipeable finish so that marks can easily be sponged off.

Matte finish This type of paint has a flat, matte finish that is suitable for use in most areas in the house—it will mark and show fingerprints but can be carefully wiped down with a damp sponge, although other types of stain are more difficult to deal with. There are many "period-style" paints now available for purchase that claim to produce an extra-matte finish. These paints have been specially formulated to appeal to period property owners who

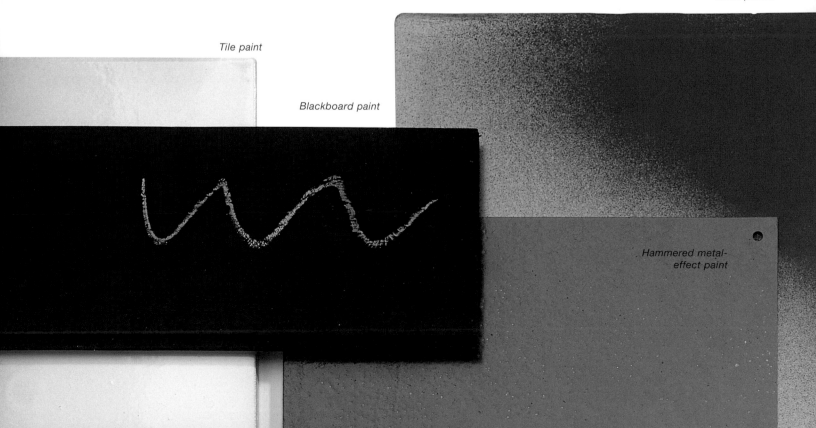

Metal primer

Tile paint

Blackboard paint

Hammered metal-effect paint

want to achieve a dead-flat, nonreflective finish that is reminiscent of a traditional distemper finish.

Eggshell (semi-gloss) finish

Eggshell is a traditional paint that gives a hard, semi-matte finish and is available in water- and oil-based formulations. It can be used for walls and woodwork.

Satin finish This paint produces a fairly robust surface finish with a slight sheen. It is easily wipeable and therefore suitable for heavy-traffic areas such as hallways. It can also be used in kitchens and bathrooms. Many types of satin paint claim one-coat coverage.

Kitchen and bathroom paint

Many manufacturers now produce latex paint that has been specially formulated for use in areas that are prone to condensation and steam. This paint contains fungicides to prevent the development of mold and mildew, which can be a problem in areas with high moisture levels such as bathrooms or kitchens.

Multisurface paint

This is a fairly recent development in paint technology—a mid-sheen formulation that can be used on walls, ceilings, woodwork, and metal. Although it tends not to be as durable as an oil-based gloss or satinwood paint, this will still give a perfectly good finish. It is relatively odor-free and therefore is particularly good for use in children's rooms. It is also ideal for people with allergies such as asthma who may be adversely affected by paint fumes.

Gloss paint

This tough, oil-based formulation is ideal for interior and exterior woodwork and metalwork. It is traditionally used on wood surfaces such as built-in bookcases, windowsills, and baseboards. Gloss is extremely durable and easy to clean, with a high shine finish. It is available in quick-drying and one-coat formulations, which make it practical to use.

Recently, many professional interior decorators have used gloss on walls as well as wood and metal. When used in this way, it produces a lacquer-like surface and is particularly effective in the darker, richer tones of green, red, brown, and black.

Satinwood paint

This mid-sheen paint is an alternative to gloss for interior woodwork and metalwork and, is gaining in popularity because it is available in both water- and oil-based formulations.

Specialized paints

These paints are formulated to solve specific problems.

Radiator paint

This paint formulation for use on radiators withstands temperature change—standard gloss and satinwood paints tend to yellow slightly when they are exposed to high temperatures.

Paint maintenance

Many types of durable paint have been developed in recent years—tough, water-based paints are available for interior woodwork and metalwork, while oil-based formulations are essential for exterior paintwork to withstand changes of temperature and harsh weather conditions. However, all painted finishes that are subject to wear and tear need to be maintained periodically. A light sanding down and recoating of interior and exterior paintwork every couple of years will stop you from having to do more time-consuming stripping and refinishing.

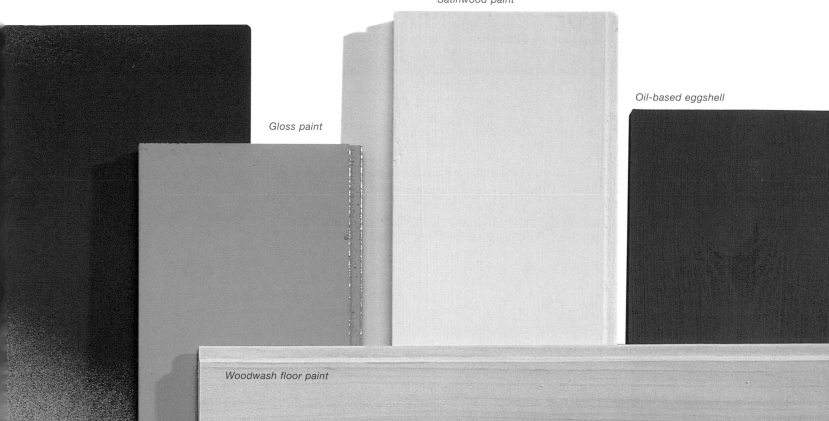

Satinwood paint

Gloss paint

Oil-based eggshell

Woodwash floor paint

Preparing gloss paint surfaces

Gloss surfaces such as windowsills, baseboards, and doors need to be rubbed down with a piece of sandpaper before a new coat of paint can be applied. The gloss of the old surface has to be taken back to a smooth, matte finish so that the new gloss paint can be applied to a surface to which it can grip or adhere.

When using gloss, remember to put just a little amount of paint on the brush and then to work it in really well. If you apply heavy brushfuls, you will end up with drips and an uneven finish.

Radiator paint is available in white as well as a range of other colors.

Tile paint

This is a tough, enamel formulation that can be cleaned like normal tiles when applied to ceramic surfaces.

Floor paint

There are various formulations of paint available for use on different types of flooring, including wood floorboards, vinyl flooring, tiled floors, and concrete floors. These types of paint are extremely durable, and in most cases, they do not require an additional coat of varnish.

Melamine paint

This is a paint formulated to adhere to shiny, nonporous, melamine surfaces such as kitchen cabinets, self-assembly, and built-in furniture.

Metal paint

This tough enamel paint inhibits rust on interior and exterior metalwork and is available in a smooth or hammered finish. It comes in a wide range of colors.

Preparation

When applying paint, it is often necessary to apply a basecoat or primer. This prepares the surface and reduces the absorption of the final coat of paint. It is important to check the compatibility of the basecoat with your chosen finish. Oil-based paints require oil-based primers, and water-based paints need water-based primers.

Multisurface primer

This primer is suitable for use on most sound surfaces, including wood, metal, and melamine.

Oil-based primer and basecoat

This has been specially formulated to reduce the lengthy preparation time for gloss finishes on bare woodwork. It is a simple one-step preparation for raw wood.

Water-based primer and basecoat

This primer is a quick-drying formulation and should be applied to raw wood before applying the coat of paint.

Metal primers

There are many different metal primers available for ferrous and nonferrous metals, and some are specially formulated to prevent rust. They all provide a key (rough surface) for the paint to adhere to.

Tile primer

This primer provides a key so that paint adheres to all types of glossy ceramic surfaces.

Melamine primer

This type of primer provides a key for paint to adhere to this shiny, nonporous material.

Paint applicators

There are several different tools you can use to apply paint, including paintbrushes, rollers, and paint pads. The one you choose will depend on personal preference.

Paintbrushes

There is a huge number of different paintbrushes available in a wide variety of sizes. The best-quality "professional" brushes are relatively expensive but produce the best results. The bristles remain flexible, hold a large quantity of paint, and do not shed. Cheaper brushes can ruin a paint finish because the bristles can fall out.

Choose a large brush for big areas and a smaller brush for "cutting in" or painting around the edges of a ceiling or wall and painting woodwork. Generally, synthetic bristles perform better when painting with gloss paints, while natural bristles are more absorbent with latex paints.

Specialized brushes are also available for creating particular types of paint effects—they tend to be fairly costly because they are made of animal hair, but if they are well looked after, they will last a lifetime.

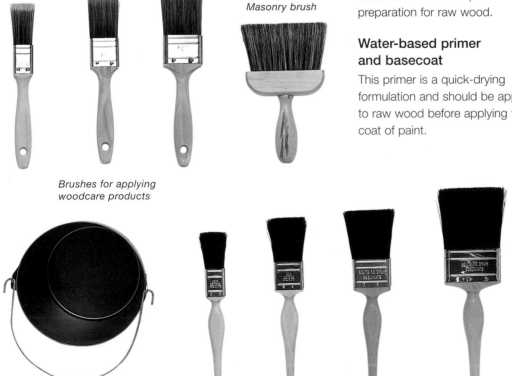

Masonry brush

Brushes for applying woodcare products

Metal paint bucket

Various-sized brushes for applying latex and gloss paint

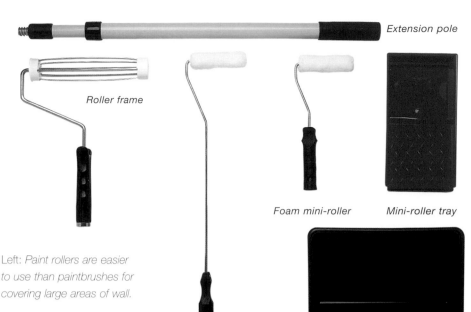

Extension pole

Roller frame

Foam mini-roller

Mini-roller tray

Radiator roller

Left: *Paint rollers are easier to use than paintbrushes for covering large areas of wall.*

Roller tray

Short-pile roller cover

Long-pile roller cover

Paint scraper

Paint rollers

A variety of different removable roller covers are available for applying different types of paint.

Rollers are usually the quickest method of applying paint and they can be attached to extension poles. This is particularly useful for painting difficult-to-reach areas such as ceilings.

Foam rollers should be used for applying gloss and satinwood paints to large areas such as doors because they provide smooth, even coverage without brushmarks. Long-pile rollers should be used to paint textured surfaces such as exposed brickwork and textured wallpaper because the long hairs carry more paint, which can be worked into the crevices. Mini-rollers with long handles are also available for painting awkward areas such as behind radiators.

Paint pads

Paint pads are a relatively recent invention—the absorbent spongy pads are held on plastic or wood handles. They are widely available in a variety of different shapes and sizes to suit different areas.

Care and maintenance of painting equipment

Paintbrushes

Professional painters and decorators recommend soaking brand-new brushes overnight— this loosens any bristles that will otherwise be shed while you are painting.

Paintbrushes should be cleaned immediately after use—water-based paint should be removed with water and a little liquid detergent if required. Oil-based paint should be removed with mineral spirits or a special brush-cleaning solution.

Concentrate on the area of the brush where the bristles meet the handle because paint gets lodged there. Never allow paintbrushes to soak for too long unsupported because the bristles will bend.

Some paintbrushes are sold with holes through the handles. This allows them to be threaded onto a thin length of wood dowel or wire and then suspended in water or mineral spirits over a paint bucket without ruining their bristles. Some paint buckets are sold with plastic clips around the edges so that you can suspend the brushes in the liquid.

Rollers

Paint rollers are a great way of covering a large wall area quickly. They are, however, notoriously difficult to clean because of their absorbency. To clean them successfully, soak them under a running faucet and then work a little detergent into the pile until the water runs clear. Make sure that all the air bubbles are squeezed out from the roller after washing. Otherwise, the next time that you use it, you will get a mottled effect on your paint surface.

For really stubborn paint, you can buy an attachment for an electric drill onto which you fix the roller. This is then spun in a high-sided bucket and the paint is gradually removed using centrifugal force.

Paint pads

These pads can be cleaned by immersing them in a bucket or bowl of warm water with a little mild detergent.

painting techniques

The most important thing you can do when you decide to paint is to prepare the surfaces well. Assess the quality of your walls honestly before you begin to use any paint at all. Identify the current finish and try to discover any problems that may lie beneath it before you begin. This may result in your needing to fill holes or cracks in plasterwork or around piping, but the effort you put in right at the start will make all the difference to the look of your paintwork when you are finished.

When do you need to strip wallpaper?

If the room you intend to paint is papered in pale-colored wallpaper that is in good condition, it is possible to paint over it. This will provide a good, smooth surface for the paint finish to be applied to.

Strongly colored wallpaper, vinyl wallpaper, textured wallpaper, or wallpaper in a bad condition should, however, be removed before painting. Some vinyl wallpapers are designed to peel cleanly off the walls to leave a backing paper in place that can then be painted in a similar way to lining paper.

If you do not have any backing paper, you should line the walls before painting. This will also prevent a buildup of paint on plaster, which becomes difficult to remove after several coats have been applied to it.

Preparation methods

If you want to achieve a professional-looking finish, there is no escaping preparation—getting a surface ready for paint can take longer than the painting itself, but the results will be worth it. Take your time—it can be tempting to rush through the preparation so that you can start painting, but the overall finish will be affected if fail to do a thorough job.

Stripping wallpaper

Wallpaper should be stripped using a sponge and warm water or a steam stripper. For the perfect finish, line the walls.

Tools and materials

Implement to score wallpaper such as a wire brush
Electric steam stripper
Metal scraping knife
Sponge and warm water

1 Use the wire brush or other scoring implement to make slits all over the surface of the wallpaper.

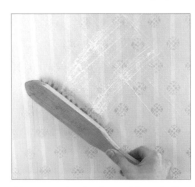

Use a scoring implement to cut slits into the existing wallpaper.

2 Fill the electric steam stripper with water to the level that is indicated on it, and then switch the power on.

3 Hold the plate of the steam stripper carefully over one section of the papered surface until you can see the paper begin to blister and bubble.

Once it is hot, hold the plate of the steam stripper over the wallpaper.

4 Slide the scraping knife underneath the bubbling paper. Then carefully remove the paper in strips—it should come away easily by this stage.

Remove the bubbling wallpaper with a scraping knife.

5 Finish by removing any residue that is left on the wall. To do this, soak a sponge in warm water and wipe the surface down.

Filling small holes or cracks in plaster walls

Tools and materials

Scraper
Multipurpose or masonry spackle
Putty knife
Fine-grit sandpaper and block, or flexible sanding block

1 Remove any loose debris and dust from the hole or crack in your wall with a scraper and cut it back to form a V-shaped groove, which will give the spackle a stronger surface to which to adhere.

First, remove any dust and debris from the hole or crack.

2 Apply spackle with a putty knife so that it is slightly raised above the hole in the wall. It is important to do this because it will eventually shrink back slightly when it begins to dry.

Use a putty knife to push spackle into the crack.

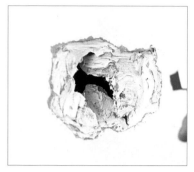

Use a spray gun to apply plenty of water to the crumbling plaster.

Filling small holes in wallboard

Tools and materials

Small knife

Pair of scissors

Self-adhesive plaster repair tape (fiberglass)

Putty knife

Spackle

Fine-grit sandpaper and block, or flexible sanding block

3 Once the filler has completely dried (after about 20 minutes), sand the surface smooth by using medium-grit sandpaper wrapped around a sanding block.

2 Wearing safety gloves, apply the expandible foam spackle. Only fill the hole halfway because the spackle will expand when it comes in contact with the water.

1 If you are filling a small hole in wallboard, begin by using a knife to cut away any loose areas of plaster that are crumbling away.

Use a sanding block to smooth the spackle level with the wall.

Half-fill the hole with expandible foam spackle.

Use a small knife to cut away the loose areas of plaster.

4 Deep holes, such as those that will be left when plastic wall anchors are removed, can be filled with scrunched-up newspaper and then spackle.

Filling large holes in plaster or around pipework

Tools and materials

Spray gun and water

Expandible foam spackle

Safety gloves

Sharp knife

Multipurpose spackle

Fine-grit sandpaper and block, or flexible sanding block

1 Brush away any remnants of loose and crumbling plaster and wet the area by spraying it with water from a spray gun.

3 Spray water onto the repair while you work to ensure that it remains moist enough for the spackle to expand. Allow to dry.

4 Use a sharp knife to trim off any excess spackle until it is level with the surface of the wall. Sand to a smooth finish.

2 Use scissors to cut the repair tape into a number of small pieces. Then apply the repair tape to the hole in overlapping layers so that they completely cover the hole.

3 Apply spackle over the repair tape. Allow to dry, then sand.

Remove any excess spackle by trimming it with a sharp knife.

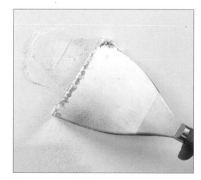

Use a putty knife to apply spackle, working from the center outward.

Hollow walls

Hollow or stud partition walls are made up of a sandwich of studs or joists between wallboard panels; these are the most common types of internal wall in modern houses. The studs run vertically from ceiling to floor at regular intervals (usually 1-ft. intervals). Wallboard walls are not as robust as brick-built walls and can easily be damaged (often by furniture legs).

Repairing large holes in wallboard

Although large holes in hollow walls made from wallboard can look daunting, they are relatively easy to repair.

Tools and materials

Craft knife

Scraps of wallboard

Wallboard nails and hammer

Self-adhesive repair tape

Finishing plaster

Plasterer's trowel

1 Use a sharp craft knife to cut out a neat, regular-shaped piece of wallboard around the damaged area, back to the nearest studs. You need to cut the wallboard back until it slightly overlaps the stud, which will give you an anchor for your repair patch.

Use a craft knife to cut a neat shape around the damaged area.

2 Cut a repair patch of new wallboard, using the damaged piece as a guide.

Cut out a new piece of wallboard using the old piece as a guide.

3 Nail the repair patch along the studs using galvanized wallboard nails at regular intervals.

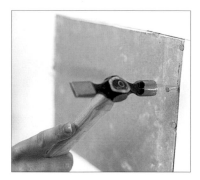

Hammer the new piece of wallboard into place.

4 Use self-adhesive repair tape to cover over the joints completely.

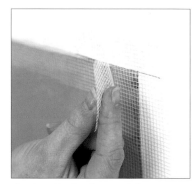

Apply self-adhesive repair tape over the joints.

5 Mix the finishing plaster, and apply it in a sweeping movement using the trowel to work it into the edges. When the plaster is almost dry, smooth the surface with the trowel and apply another layer if required.

Apply plaster to the whole repaired area using a trowel.

Filling gaps around door casings and baseboards

The areas where woodwork meets plaster are prone to developing gaps because of the way the different materials expand and contract. Large gaps are ugly and allow heat to escape. Tackle them before decoration.

Tools and materials

Craft knife

Painter's caulk

Caulk gun

Damp cloth

1 Use a craft knife to cut the plastic nozzle off the top of the painter's caulk. Load the canister onto the caulk gun. Use a slow squeezing movement to apply the caulk in a long bead along the baseboard or casing.

Apply the caulk along the length of the baseboard.

2 Wrap a damp cloth around your finger and smooth it along the bead of caulk, forcing the caulk gently into the gap.

Use a damp cloth to force the caulk into the gap.

Painting ceilings

Once you have completed the preparation, you are ready to start painting.

Order of work

Rooms should be painted from the top downward to avoid spoiling areas you have just painted. Start with the ceiling, followed by the walls, then the woodwork, which will take longer to dry, and finally the floor if your are painting it. If you are sanding floorboards, do this after painting the walls but before painting the baseboards because they are likely to get marked.

For perfect, professional results, bare plaster ceilings should be papered before painting. If you prefer not to, then the bare plaster should be sealed with a suitable general-purpose primer. Primer is used to seal the porous surface and prevents the plaster or paper from absorbing excess paint. Special primers and paints are available for problem areas, such as damp, nicotine, or water stains. Flexible ceiling paint is also available for use on ceilings prone to fine, hairline cracks, often caused by movement in rooms above—its special formulation flexes with the ceiling. It is also possible to buy nondrip paints that are less messy to use than standard ones.

Most people prefer to paint their ceilings a light color. This is a matter of personal preference and there are no hard-and-fast rules, but ceilings that are lighter than the surrounding walls tend to give the illusion of height and reflect a lot of light back into the room. Dark-painted ceilings can look dramatic but do give the illusion of a lower ceiling. This can, of course, be a useful device to employ if you are trying to make a room with high ceilings and large dimensions feel cozier.

Dealing with previously painted ceilings

If painting a previously painted ceiling, wipe it down first with a strong cleanser using a sponge or long-handled mop. Seal stubborn stains with primer.

Tools and materials

Drop cloths

Masking tape

Paintbrushes and paint

Small screwdriver (optional)

Rollers

Roller trays

Roller extension rod

Suitable ladder or work platform (optional)

1 If possible, clear the room of all its furniture and protect the floor with a fabric or plastic drop cloth. If necessary, tape this to the baseboard with masking tape to stop it from moving. Begin by "cutting in" with a small paintbrush. If you have coving, do not worry if you overpaint the edges slightly because coving is usually finished in satinwood or gloss paint, so this will be painted over later anyway. If you have an unpainted plaster cornice, you can protect it with masking tape.

2 Mask off pendant light fittings and paint around them. If you are having difficulties painting close to the fitting, switch off the electricity

Mask off your light fittings and then paint around them.

supply and then use a small screwdriver to remove the plastic cover from the light fitting (this will expose the wiring, so it important to switch off the electricity).

3 When cutting in is complete, fill in the remaining ceiling area with a roller or a large brush. Fix an extension rod onto a standard roller in order to reach high ceilings, or use a stepladder. Allow the first coat to dry before applying a second coat.

Use a roller on an extension rod to paint the majority of the ceiling area.

Safety tip

When painting awkward areas such as stairwells, it is possible to rent ladders and platforms that can be erected to give a level platform over stairs. Never use ladders on your own, and always inspect older ladders carefully before using them. Rental stores will be able to advise you on the safest ladder for the job you have to complete.

Below: You can paint your ceiling in a darker shade of the predominant color in your scheme. Remember, however, that painting a ceiling dark can make it look lower.

Painting walls

Walls should be carefully prepared before repainting (see page 32). Flaws and imperfections should be filled and sanded, and ideally bare plaster should be sized and papered. If you prefer to paint directly onto new plaster, then seal it first with a multisurface primer to prevent it from absorbing excess paint. Previously painted surfaces should be wiped down with a strong cleansing solution to remove dirt and grease, and any rough patches or holes should be filled and sanded. Strong, dark paint colors and highly patterned wallpapers are particularly difficult to cover with lighter paint colors. It is advisable to apply a coat of white multipurpose primer before painting on the new color in such cases. Painting rooms in different color combinations is a very popular look. Many people like to pick out "feature walls," such as those with chimney breasts or alcoves, in different colors. Internal corners where two colors meet can be difficult to paint neatly, particularly if the walls are not completely perpendicular. It is best to wait for one color to dry, then mask it off with low-tack masking tape, and paint the second color.

Tools and materials

Cleansing solution and sponge

Paintbrushes and paint

Paint bucket (optional)

Masking tape

Rollers

Roller trays

1 Prepare previously painted walls by washing them down with a strong cleanser.

Always wash down previously painted surfaces.

2 Load a small paintbrush (2-in. wide, for example) by dipping the bristles about halfway into the paint and then wiping off the excess on the edge of the paint bucket. Cut in around the edges of the room. Treat each wall as a panel, working the color into the corners. Mask off the top of the baseboards if you do not feel confident about painting freehand up to the edge. Use masking tape around obstacles such as light switches to protect them.

Paint each wall, using masking tape to protect items such as baseboard.

3 Use a roller or large brush to fill in the main area of the wall, painting one wall at a time. You may find it easiest if you work from the top to the bottom and to start in the top righthand corner, which will stop you from brushing against areas that you have just painted (reverse this if you are lefthanded). This is not a hard-and-fast rule, however. Allow the paint to dry, then apply a second coat using the same method.

Use a roller to paint over each expanse of wall.

Right: *Bright colors, such as the warm yellow on these walls, will require at least two coats of paint.*

Painting baseboards (and woodwork)

Tools and materials

Flexible sanding block
Damp cloth
Plastic sheet and masking tape
Piece of cardboard
Paintbrushes and gloss or satinwood

1 Prepare previously painted baseboards by rubbing down with a flexible sanding block—this will give the surface a key to help the new paint adhere properly. Use a damp cloth to wipe away dust before applying new paint.

Sand the baseboard before you paint it.

2 Protect the floor with a sheet of plastic taped to the floor just below the baseboard (if the room is carpeted, slip a piece of stiff cardboard between the carpet and baseboard). Use a piece of cardboard held against the wall while you paint the baseboard using a small paintbrush.

Hold some cardboard against the wall to protect it while you paint.

Painting radiators

Radiators are awkward to paint and they also make it difficult to paint the wall behind them.

Painting behind a radiator

The farther the radiator is from the wall, the easier it is to paint. The quickest way to paint behind a radiator is to use a long-handled mini-roller so that you can reach down the back of the radiator.

Use a long roller to apply paint to hard-to-reach areas behind radiators.

Spray painting a radiator

Radiators must be painted with special heat-resistant enamel paint. If you use standard gloss paint, the heat from the radiator will make it yellow with time.

Tools and materials

Plastic sheet and masking tape
Cleansing solution and sponge
Flexible sanding block
Spray paint for radiators or radiator enamel

1 Remember to switch off the radiator and allow it to cool down first. Mask off the area behind the radiator by taping a plastic sheet to the wall. Clean the radiator thoroughly with a strong cleansing solution to remove any grease and grime, then sand lightly to key the surface.

2 Shake the can of paint thoroughly and then spray paint in even sweeps from a distance of approximately 12 in. Allow the first coat of paint to dry thoroughly before applying a second coat of the spray paint using the same method as before.

Hold the can upright and apply the paint in even sprays.

Using a paintbrush to paint a radiator

Instead of spray painting a radiator, you could use a special brush with an angled head to help you to reach the awkward areas. If you are painting an old-fashioned radiator, then you should work from the inside out. A standard panel radiator can be painted with a brush or a sponge roller.

Below: Baseboards should be painted in colors that complement the wall and floor.

types of
paint effects

There is a huge variety of paint effects to try out that allow you to create all sorts of finishes within your home. Some involve manipulating glaze, while others create a textured surface. There is something out there for everyone. If you are attempting a paint effect for the first time, however, it would be a good idea to practice on a piece of masonite. This will allow you to get a feel for the materials and experiment with color before committing your effect to the walls.

Paint effects

The various types of paint effects available today are described in detail below.

Broken color finishes

These techniques are generally applied onto large, flat surfaces and are ideal for walls. They involve the manipulation of "glaze." This is a translucent veil of color that is applied over an opaque basecoat. Areas of the basecoat are then exposed.

Effects such as colorwashing, dragging, rag-rolling, stippling, and sponging all fall into this category. Many paint effects have their roots in earlier centuries and seem to come in and out of fashion. They do provide quick cover-ups for less-than-perfect plastering, or can distract the eye from textured surfaces that would be costly to remove. Most paint effects can appear new and fresh if interpreted in a subtle way using fresh, contemporary colors.

Faux finishes

These finishes were historically used to mimic expensive materials such as marble, stone, exotic

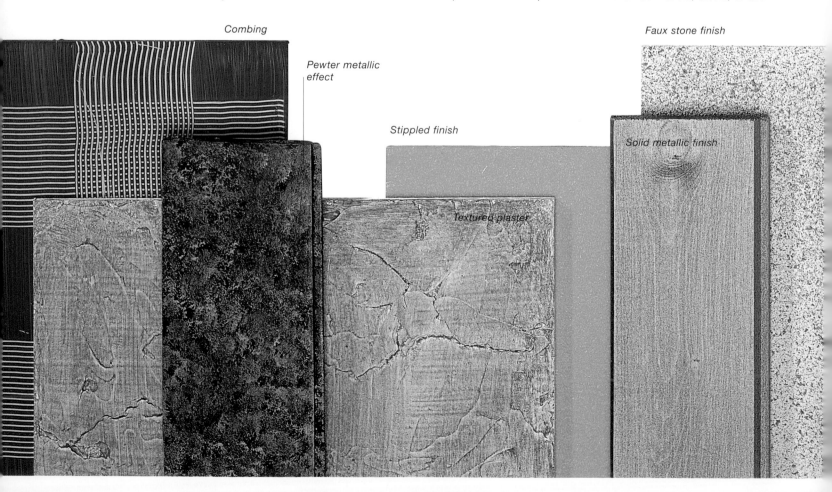

Combing

Pewter metallic effect

Stippled finish

Textured plaster

Faux stone finish

Solid metallic finish

hardwoods, and semiprecious stones that added grandeur to interiors. Many of these finishes are suitable for smaller items of furniture and accessories but some can also be applied to internal walls and doors.

Textured finishes

These finishes add three-dimensional texture as well as color to internal walls. They can be achieved in a number of ways, either by adding particles such as sand and sawdust to paint or by applying a textured substance to the walls before painting.

Metallic and pearlescent finishes

The various finishes that come under this heading add a touch of glamour to an interior. Some are achieved in the traditional way by applying thinly beaten metal leaf directly to the wall, while others involve metallic, iridescent, or pearlescent particles suspended in paint or glaze. These effects can be subtle, showing up when the light hits them a certain way.

Tools and materials

In order to achieve these paint effects, you will need to invest in specialist tools and materials.

Glazes

These are available in water-based or oil-based formulations and form the basis of broken color effects. They come in a colorless form that can be tinted with artist's paints, latex paints, or powder pigments, or in ready-mixed colors. When painted over a flat basecoat, they add a transparent veil of color that can be built up or taken off in layers. Many paint effects depend on manipulating the glaze, and rely on its "open" time. This refers to the length of time that the glaze can be moved around before it dries. Water-based glazes have a shorter "open" time than oil-

based glazes, but many people find that they are more pleasant to use because they do not have a strong odor.

Basecoats

This is the first coat of any paint effect and provides the base onto which the glaze is applied. Latex

Softener brush

Stencil brushes

Dragging brush

Stippling brush

Hints and tips

When starting a paint effect, make sure that you have mixed up enough colored glaze to complete the job because it is almost impossible to reproduce exactly the same color a second time. It is also worth storing a jar of the colored glaze in case you need to touch up areas of paintwork at a later date.

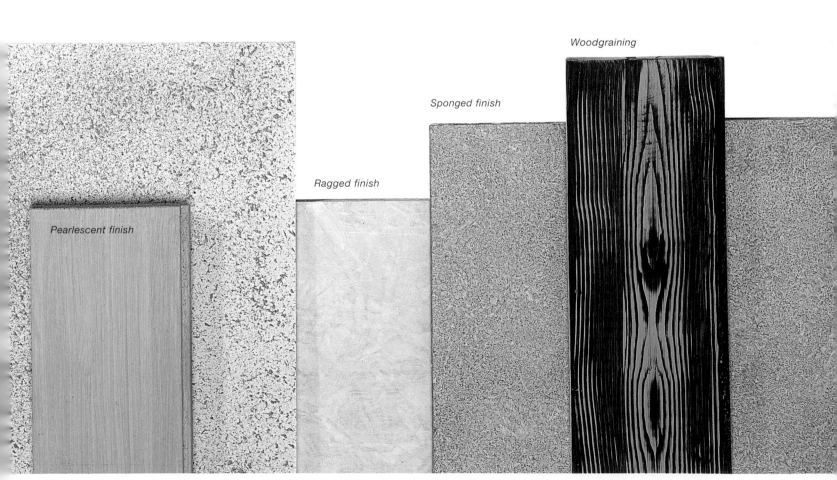

Pearlescent finish

Ragged finish

Sponged finish

Woodgraining

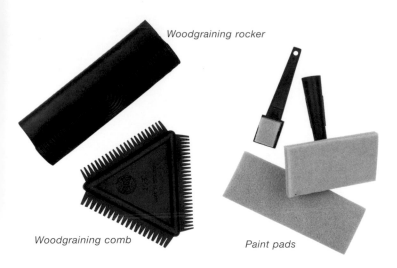

Woodgraining rocker

Woodgraining comb

Paint pads

Natural sponge

Chamois leather cloth

satin paint is often chosen because its shiny surface covers surfaces well and the slippery finish it produces makes the glaze easy to move around. White latex satin can be tinted by adding artist's acrylic paints or colorizers, or you can buy a ready-mixed color of your choice. The basecoat is usually a neutral or complementary color to the glaze. It shows through the glaze in places and affects the final look considerably.

Specialized paintbrushes

These are high-quality brushes designed to create particular effects in wet glaze. Because most of them are handmade with natural-hair bristles, they are fairly expensive, but they are well worth the investment if you are going to use them a lot. If not, then experiment with different-sized standard paintbrushes, trimming the bristles if necessary.

Softener brushes These are used for eliminating brushmarks from water- and oil-based glazes by gently dusting the bristles over the surface of the glaze. The most costly and traditional type of softener brush is made from badger hair. In more recent times, less expensive hog-hair softener brushes have been used.

If you do not want to purchase a softener brush, it could be substituted with a less costly lily-bristled dusting brush or another type of soft-bristled painter's dusting brush.

Dragging brushes These brushes have extra-long, straight bristles that are used for dragging through a glaze to produce regular and long brushstrokes.

Woodgraining tools These include rockers, which are rubber tools that are pulled through a glaze using a slight rocking motion to produce a woodgrain effect similar to pine. Rubber combs, on the other hand, have special teeth spaced at different intervals. They are pulled through the glaze to produce the effect of woodgrain or other patterns.

Liner brushes These brushes are specially designed to paint decorative lines on furniture— their long, thin bristles can be heavily loaded with paint to achieve continuous lines.

Stencil brushes These brushes have a blunt, stubby appearance and are used for stippling paint through stencils. They should be used in an upright position.

Stippling brushes These broad brushes contain groups of bristles for creating tiny dots in wet glaze.

Sponges and cloths

These are used in broken color techniques, particularly sponging and rag-rolling. Natural sponges give the softest appearance; synthetic sponges are cheaper but should only be used if they have had pieces picked out of them to give a more irregular, natural look. Many types of cloth can be used, from chamois leather to scrunched-up paper, each giving a different result.

Masking tape

This adhesive paper tape is used for masking off areas that you do not want to paint. Low-tack tape is less likely to damage previously painted surfaces. Flexible masking tape is available that allows you to mask off curved areas.

AT-A-GLANCE TOOLS AND MATERIALS

Paint effect	Tools	Materials
Colorwashing	Large brush, softener brush	Glaze, basecoat
Dragging	Dragging brush	Glaze, basecoat
Stippling	Stippling brush	Glaze, basecoat
Ragging	Clean cloths	Glaze, basecoat
Rag-rolling	Clean cloths	Glaze, basecoat
Sponging	Natural sponge	Glaze, basecoat
Marbling	Feather, liner brush	Glaze, basecoat, artist's oil or acrylic colors
Woodgraining	Graining comb or rocker	Glaze, basecoat
Crackling	Standard brushes	Glaze, basecoat, top coat
Combing	Flexible comb	Glaze, basecoat
Distressing	Steel wool	Wax, basecoat, top coat
Metallic finish	Standard brushes	Metallic paint or powder

paint effect techniques

Paint effects can completely transform a space, but unfortunately a badly applied technique or an unwise choice or color can make it ineffective. At worst, it can make the room look worse than it was originally. Take time to familiarize yourself with the tools and materials before embarking on a whole room. If you are unsure of a technique, practice on an appropriate surface such as a sheet of masonite or begin with a small test patch in an area that will not be seen.

Broken color finishes

These finishes are all applied over a basecoat. The effect is achieved by disturbing the surface of the glaze with a variety of different tools, allowing the basecoat to show through.

Colorwashing

This is one of the most popular paint effects. It is popular for creating a rustic Mediterranean look and is ideal for producing a deliberately distressed look on walls that are less than perfect.

Tools and materials

Paint buckets

Paintbrush or roller and tray

Large paintbrush

Satin and matte latex paints

Water-based glaze

Natural-bristle softener brush or other soft-bristled brush

1 Apply the basecoat of satin latex to the prepared walls and allow to dry.

Use a paintbrush or roller to apply the basecoat to your walls.

2 Mix the matte latex with the glaze and a little water until you have a liquid the consistency of light cream. Take a large paintbrush and apply the mixture using sweeping, random, and crisscrossing strokes, working on an area of about 1 sq. yd. at a time.

Apply the glaze to the walls using a large brush.

3 Go back over the area of the glaze with a softener brush, only lightly touching the surface so that you slightly blur the brushstrokes. Clean the brush on a cloth to avoid a build-up of glaze.

Work over the glaze using a softener brush to blur the brushstrokes.

Dragging

This technique is often used to mimic woodgrain or woven fabric and adds a subtle texture to flat surfaces. It relies on keeping the brush lines perfectly straight, so it looks most effective when applied to a limited area rather than over a complete wall.

Tools and materials

Paintbrush or roller and tray

Paint bucket

Latex paint and water-based glaze

Dragging brush or long-bristled paintbrush

Cloths for wiping brushes

Varnish (optional)

1 Apply the basecoat with a brush or roller and allow it to dry. Mix up the colored glaze and paint it onto the wall.

Mix up the glaze and then paint it over the basecoat.

2 Using a dragging brush, hold its bristles up against the glaze and then pull it carefully downward through the glaze,

Hints and tips

If you are trying to cover a large area, it is easier to work with somebody else so that one person applies the glaze and the other softens the effect. This will avoid obvious joint marks. In heavy-wear areas such as children's rooms and hallways, a couple of coats of matte water-based varnish applied over the paint effect will give it better durability.

keeping it straight until you reach the baseboard. After each stroke, wipe the brush on a cloth to avoid a build-up of glaze, then line the brush up for the next stroke. Repeat until the whole area is covered. Varnish if required.

Pull the dragging brush gently down through the glaze.

Stippling

This is a useful, subtle effect that works well on flat surfaces and on molding, giving an aged appearance. It can also be used for mimicking stone, providing a subtle, mottled effect.

Tools and materials

Paintbrush or roller and tray

Satin latex paint

Water-based glaze and artist's acrylic colors

Stippling brush or large, flat household scrubbing brush

Varnish (optional)

1 Apply the basecoat and allow to dry. Paint on the glaze to give even coverage.

Paint the glaze over the basecoat and allow it to dry.

2 Use the stippling brush to mark the glaze, using short, stabbing movements that will leave a mottled finish but with no brushstrokes. Allow the surface to dry and then varnish over the top if a tough finish is required.

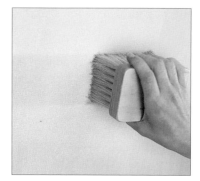

Mark the glaze by stabbing the surface with the stippling brush.

Textured finishes

These finishes can be made subtle by adding fine grains of sand or sawdust to latex basecoats, or more dramatic by using textured plaster colored with pigments and applied with a plasterer's trowel to the wall. Because textured finishes are hard to eradicate, it is best to apply them to walls that have been lined with heavyweight lining paper. This will make them easier to strip if you want to change them. Textured finishes can also be applied through stencils to give a three-dimensional look.

Subtle textured finish

Tools and materials

Matte latex paint and sand

Paint buckets

Paintbrushes

Tinting pigments

Water-based glaze

1 Mix some matte latex and sand together in a paint bucket and apply the mixture to the wall using a paintbrush. Allow the surface to dry.

Apply the paint-and-sand mixture to the walls with a paintbrush.

2 Mix up a colored water-based glaze and then brush it randomly over the textured surface in order to highlight the irregularities.

Randomly brush the glaze over the textured surface.

Rough plaster finish

Tools and materials

Paint bucket

Textured plaster

Latex paint and water-based glaze

Plasterer's trowel

Standard and masonry paintbrushes

1 In a paint bucket, mix up the textured plaster to a thick, smooth consistency and apply it to the walls using the smooth edge of a plasterer's trowel. Go back over the surface with a large paintbrush, adding extra peaks and troughs or smoothing down any rough areas until you have created a finish that you are happy with. Allow the surface to dry overnight.

Use a large brush to add additional peaks and troughs if required.

2 Paint the surface with your basecoat color and allow it to dry. Then use a large, dry masonry paintbrush to apply the glaze over the textured finish, picking out the irregularities in the surface.

Use a dry masonry brush to apply glaze over the textured wall.

Metallic and pearlescent finishes

Metallic and pearlescent glazes are applied over complementary basecoats to produce fairly realistic metallic effects. Glitter can also be added to glaze to create a sparkling wallcovering, which is particularly suitable for use in children's rooms.

Using pearlescent finishes

Tools and materials

Complementary basecoat

Paintbrush or roller and tray

Pearlescent top coat

Matte water-based varnish

1 Begin by applying the basecoat using a paintbrush or roller and allow to dry thoroughly (for about an hour) before you apply the top coat.

Apply the basecoat and allow to dry thoroughly.

2 Apply the top pearlescent coat carefully. Make sure that you work in one direction only in order to avoid brushmarks.

Use even brushstrokes in the same direction to apply the top coat.

3 Allow to dry, then varnish with a couple of coats of matte water-based varnish.

Apply a couple of coats of water-based varnish to finish.

Using metallic finishes

Tools and materials

Basecoat

Paintbrushes

Metallic top coat

1 Begin by applying your choice of basecoat using a paintbrush.

Apply a coat of basecoat evenly to the whole wall.

2 When the basecoat is completely dry, apply a top coat of metallic paint, taking care not to leave any brushstrokes.

Apply the metallic paint, taking care not to leave any brushstrokes.

Painting abstract shapes

Effects covering whole rooms are diminishing in popularity and are now being replaced with subtler bands of colors or shapes on feature walls that give the feeling of abstract works of art. The different shapes can be combined with any of the paint effects already described.

Horizontal bands

Horizontal bands around a room will give the illusion of greater width, particularly if painted in pale tones. Dividing up a room horizontally will add interest in a large room. Traditionally, rooms used to have chair and picture rails dividing them, which allowed the use of different bands of color. For a contemporary look, divide the room into bands of varying thickness.

Tools and materials

Level and metal ruler

Pencil

Low-tack masking tape

Latex paint

Paintbrushes or rollers and trays

1 Measuring up from the baseboard or down from the ceiling will often give you a line that is not perfectly horizontal because floors and ceilings are not always level with each other. If you want a true horizontal line, use a level on top of a long metal ruler to keep the line level. Mark the line around the room lightly in pencil. Mask off with low-tack masking tape.

2 Use a paintbrush or roller to apply the band of color, pulling off the masking tape before the paint has dried. Once it is completely dry, apply the masking tape to the painted section and repeat.

Vertical lines

Vertical lines around a room help to give the illusion of greater height. They can look overpowering in small spaces but work well when used sparingly on a feature wall. For a contemporary look, vary the widths of the lines and try to use harmonious tones or different shades of the same base color.

Tools and materials

Chalk line

Low-tack masking tape

Soft cloth

Latex paints

Paintbrushes or rollers and trays

1 Use a chalk "snap" line to mark a straight vertical line quickly. You will need two pairs of hands; one person should hold the line at the top of the wall, the other should hold it taut at the bottom. Then "snap" the line sharply to leave a pale vertical chalk line on the wall. This can then be masked off with tape and the chalk line erased with a cloth.

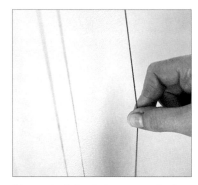

Use a chalk line to leave a vertical chalk mark on the wall.

2 Paint using a paintbrush or roller—remember to remove the masking tape before the paint has dried. Allow it to dry completely before reversing the process, applying masking tape to the finished area to paint the adjacent line.

Paint the area that has been surrounded with masking tape.

Painting circular features

Painted circles is a good way to introduce accent colors and decorative features.

Tools and materials

Hammer and nail

String and pencil

Quick-drying spackle

Paint and paintbrush

Flexible masking tape

1 Hammer in a nail at the point where you want the center of the circle to be. Tie one end of a piece of string to the nail and knot the other end around a pencil. The length of the string should equal the radius of the circle. Hold the string taut and pull the pencil around to form a circle on the wall. Remove the nail and fill the resulting hole with spackle.

Keeping the string taut, pull the pencil around to draw a circle.

2 Paint the circle, starting with the outline. You can mask off the line with flexible masking tape first.

Now paint the circle, starting with the outline.

Lettering and numbers

Lettering is a popular form of decoration and can be achieved in several different ways. Lines of poetry or quotations work particularly well in bathrooms; try recipes in kitchens and numerals in home offices. Experiment with different sizes and typefaces to achieve different styles.

Using plastic lettering

Tools and materials

Level

Pencil

Plastic letters

Latex paint and small paintbrush

1 Use a level to draw a faint horizontal pencil line in the place where you want the lettering. Use large plastic letters to draw around.

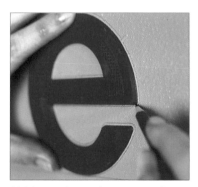

Hold your chosen letters up to the wall and draw around each one.

2 Fill in with paint. If needed, make a brush-rest using a cane with some batting wrapped in cotton.

Use a small paintbrush to paint the inside of the letters on the wall.

Using a projector

Rent or borrow an overhead projector. Write freehand or photocopy the writing of your choice onto acetate, then project the writing onto the wall where you want to paint the letters. Draw around the letters with a soft pencil, then fill in with paint (see recipe wall project, pages 220–1).

Using stencils

Tools and materials

Level

Pencil

Stencil

Masking tape

Paint and large stencil brush

Varnish (optional)

1 Use lettering stencils to spell out your chosen words along a straight pencil line on the wall. Apply the paint by dabbing sparingly through the stencils using a large, blunt stencil brush.

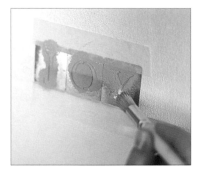

Dab the paint through the stencils to color in your chosen words.

2 Remove the stencil carefully by peeling it away and then varnish over the whole surface if necessary to finish.

Once the paint has dried, peel off the stencil from the wall.

Left: If you do not want to use letters, then experiment with other shapes, such as this natural vine-leaf design.

Choosing your wallpaper

Wallpaper adds softness to a wall and can help reduce echoes and the emptiness of a large room. Papers can be very decorative with a large all-over pattern, striped, or even printed to look like a paint effect such as marbling, so that you get the effect without ever having to dip your brush in a pot.

History of wallpapering

Wallpaper was developed for the middle and upper classes as an inexpensive alternative to wood paneling, tapestry, and cloth hangings, which were favored up until the 17th century. But even as a less expensive alternative, it was still a luxury item, printed with hand-applied blocks and intricately carved and color-separated rollers. There are still a few specialty wallpaper manufacturers who produce luxurious, often hand-colored tableaux panels and papers that are close to the original quality and craftsmanship of the earlier varieties.

Wallpaper grew in popularity in the 19th century, when mechanized engraved cylinders and continuous rolls of paper were produced. The Arts and Crafts period saw it reach new heights with the artist William Morris producing many highly colored designs that are still in production today.

Other older styles of paper, such as anaglypta and lincrusta, have also seen something of a revival with people restoring period homes. These papers first became popular in Victorian times and have a stamped pattern that stands out in relief against the background. They were commonly used on ceilings and below chair rails, for example, between the baseboard and waist height. They are sometimes painted today with gloss paints for a high-shine, wipeable finish or sometimes even with matte finishes in order to create a chalky appearance.

During the 1950s and 1960s, further advances in the production of wallpaper took place. Coatings, such as a fine layer of plastic, saw the introduction of vinyl papers, which were better able to cope with the extremes of temperature

Right: Floral patterns work well in a traditional bedroom. If you are using an elaborate pattern, then consider papering just the top half of the wall above the chair rail.

and moisture in bathrooms. Metallic-backed papers with silvery backgrounds and iridescent finishes were also produced at this time.

Other wallcovering options include textured woodchip papers, which were popular in the 1950s and 1960s but have been in decline for some time now. They do have some advantages, though. These thick, textural papers cover over and disguise a multitude of sins, such as cracks and bumps on uneven wall surfaces.

During the 1980s and early 1990s, the popularity of wallpaper began to wane, with paint becoming the primary wallcovering, but in the late 1990s a new vogue for papers began to arise once more.

Choosing wallpaper

The wallpaper that you choose will depend on a number of different factors, including the shape, size, and function of the room that is to be decorated. If the walls are uneven, you may want to choose a thicker paper. In rooms with a lot of pictures and paintings, a simple, quiet design will probably be the best option to choose.

The next step is to look through as many sample books of wallpaper as possible. Some of these have very helpful pictures of interiors decorated with various wallpapers.

The current trend for wallpaper is to use it as a panel or on one wall rather than on all four walls. This is mixed with painted surfaces and becomes a highlight or feature of a room rather than a complete covering.

Lining paper that is left unpainted is another slightly obscure but attractive finish that has been in vogue for a number of years. The paper, which is off-white when applied, "ages" in sunlight and takes on a yellow, almost parchment-colored hue. Ordinary brown wrapping paper has also been used to great effect, especially in small rooms such as studies. Good-quality brown paper has a slight stripe in it, and therefore it needs to be hung carefully to ensure that all the lines run in the same direction.

Hessian, silk, and grass have all been applied to paper backings and are still popular in parts of northern Europe and France.

types of

wallpaper

Before you choose your wallpaper, you must decide what type of paper to use. There is a wide variety of different types of paper available for purchase today. They are manufactured in a number of ways and produce different effects on your wall. As such, it is important to bear in mind the decorative style that you are trying to achieve when choosing your paper—for example, a heavily embossed paper will look fine in a period setting but may be at odds with a minimalist contemporary design.

Wallpaper

Standard wallpaper

Standard printed rolls are 20¾ in. wide. They come in an enormous variety of colors and designs, usually with a matte finish.

Hand-blocked/printed wallpaper

These have standard dimensions but the designs have been printed by hand, making them much more expensive than standard varieties.

Vinyl wallpaper

These designs consist of a paper backing with a printed vinyl top coat. They are easy to hang and strip, and are also very durable and resistant to scuffing. They can look shiny.

Textured/embossed papers

These papers are ideal for using on walls that are slightly uneven because their raised surface pattern disguises minor imperfections. They are hung in the same way as standard wallpapers but often require longer soaking.

Anaglypta and lincrusta

Anaglypta is an embossed paper that was first used by the Victorians. It is made from a combination of cotton and paper pulp. This is passed through patterned rollers when wet, which press out the design onto the paper. It is particularly popular for areas such as hallways because it is resilient against knocks and bumps. It comes uncolored so you can paint it to match your color scheme. It can also be used as a base for creating a number of broken color paint effects because the glaze sits in the recesses and highlights the pattern. Lincrusta is an embossed wallcovering like anaglypta but is made from a linoleum mixture— it is extremely durable.

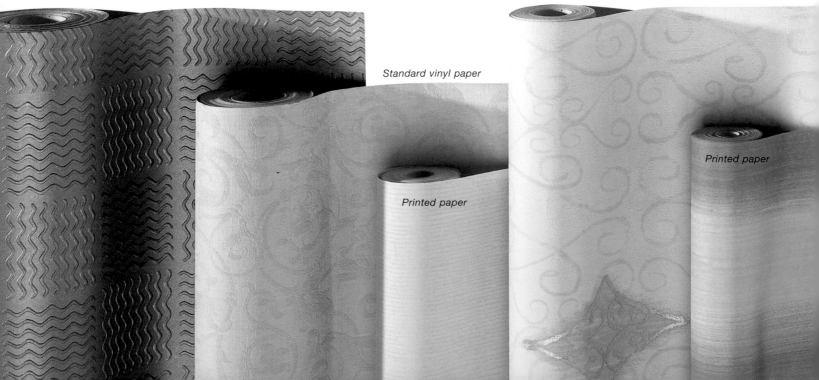

Textured vinyl paper

Standard vinyl paper

Printed paper

Printed paper

Printed paper

Woodchip wallpaper

This is a favorite in the refurbishment trade because the small "chips" of wood can hide a multitude of sins, giving walls a porridge-like texture. Take great care when removing woodchip because it may well be holding the plaster behind it together—by removing it you run the risk of exposing a wall that may need replastering professionally.

Blown vinyl wallpaper

This is a vinyl paper with a raised pattern created by a special printing process: on heating, the printed area expands, giving a three-dimensional effect. Designs used to be fairly old-fashioned, but recently they have expanded to include mosaic tiles, metal treadplate, and natural fibers.

Tools

Pasting table

These light, folding tables are inexpensive to buy and make wallpapering much easier because they are just wider than a roll of paper and long enough to spread paste without creasing the paper.

Smoothing brush

This is a wide, slim brush used for smoothing down paper once it has been hung.

Paste brush

This large, synthetic-bristled brush is used for spreading paste over paper. It is worth getting one that includes a plastic hook to stop it from falling into the paste and making a mess.

Plumb lines

The simplest form is a weight that hangs from a string, enabling you to mark a perfectly vertical line. It is also possible to buy versions that include a chalk reservoir. This chalks the string, enabling you to "snap" it against a surface to produce a chalk line.

Seam roller

This small tool has a revolving roller and is used to roll over the seams of wallpapers and borders for a flat joint.

Steam stripper

These electric machines can be bought or rented and are useful when you are stripping large areas of wallpaper. They are filled with water that is then heated to boiling point. The steam then travels up a rubber or plastic tube to a plate that is held against the wall—the steam gets under the paper and loosens the adhesive.

Scissors

Long-bladed scissors are used for cutting wallpaper in a straight line. They should have shaped, blunt ends for use when creasing the wallpaper as a guide to cutting.

Wallpaper paste/adhesive

This comes in ready-mixed or powder form for all types of wallpaper. There is also an adhesive that comes in squeezable tubes and is useful for sticking down paper edges.

Paste brush

Pasting table

Seam roller

Smoothing brush

Scissors

Printed paper

Standard vinyl paper

Printed paper

Printed paper

Anaglypta

Standard vinyl paper

wallpapering techniques

Many people are wary of using wallpaper because there is a persistent belief (mainly among those who have never tried) that it is incredibly difficult to put up. In fact, hanging wallpaper is not only straightforward if approached in a methodical manner, but also immensely satisfying and fun to do. The next few pages will take you through the basic wallpapering techniques and help you with the more awkward jobs, such as papering around corners and obstacles.

Preparation

Strip the walls of any existing paper and patch up any cracks or holes in the plaster (see pages 32–4). Before painting or wallpapering the walls, size them with diluted wallpaper paste, which gives them "good slip" so that the paper can be moved about. Then line the walls with lining paper. This is available in different weights—the heaviest gives the best coverage and the smoothest surface to work on. If you are painting the walls, hang the lining paper vertically— fill and sand any small gaps between the joints first and follow the instructions for normal wallpapering (see opposite).

Cross-lining walls with lining paper

If you are wallpapering you should "cross-line" the walls— this means hanging the paper horizontally. The reason for doing this is to avoid the joints of the lining paper and wallpaper lining up. If you do not feel confident about cross-lining, hang the lining paper vertically but take care when positioning the wallpaper on top of it, making sure that the joints do not align.

Tools and materials

Tape measure
Level
Soft pencil
Scissors
Wallpaper paste
Old paintbrush
Lining paper
Paste brush
Smoothing brush
Putty knife
Craft knife

1 Measure the width of the lining paper, and using a tape measure, mark this measurement at intervals, starting at the top of the wall. Use a level to draw horizontal lines across the room with a soft pencil. Measure the length of each wall and calculate the number of lengths of lining paper that you need to cut (allow several inches excess paper at each end).

2 Measure and cut the lengths of lining paper. Paste the first length, taking care to cover the edges. Once pasted, fold the paper into a concertina shape (paste against paste) and allow to soak for the recommended time. Paste the second length while the first is soaking.

Fold the paper into a concertina shape, ready to hang on the wall.

3 Start hanging the paper in the top righthand corner of the room, easing it into the corner with a smoothing brush. When you reach the other end of the room, trim the paper to fit.

Draw a horizontal line around the room, using a level and pencil.

Hang the concertina of lining paper, gradually smoothing it across the wall.

4 Hang the second length of paper, butting it up to the first piece. Continue around the room, one wall at a time. When you reach the baseboard, use a putty knife to push the paper into the angle between the baseboard and the wall. Hold firmly in place and trim using a sharp craft knife.

Starting points

Traditional advice recommends starting the run of wallpaper by centering it at a focal point such as a fireplace. This makes sense if you are using a paper with an obvious pattern because it will make the design look balanced. However, if it is your first attempt at wallpapering, there is no harm in starting with the longest wall that does not have any obstacles. This will give you confidence to handle other obstacles as you work your way clockwise around the room.

Butt the top edge of the second piece up to the bottom edge of the first.

Hanging wallpaper

Tools and materials

Tape measure

Level

Wallpaper

Scissors or craft knife

Pasting table and paste brush

Wallpaper paste

Plumb line

Metal straightedge

Smoothing brush

1 Measure the height from the ceiling to the baseboard and add about 1 in. to both the top and bottom to provide an overlap. If you are working with patterned wallpaper, take the repeat into account. Cut the first few lengths of paper and lay them on the pasting table. Paste carefully, from the center of the paper outward, with the edge overlapping the table slightly to avoid getting paste on the face of the paper.

Apply paste from the center out toward the edges.

2 Making sure that the first piece of wallpaper is hung straight is vital, and because most walls are not completely square, you will need a plumb line. Choose a point in the room that is close to the darkest corner and measure just under a width of the wallpaper away from the corner. Hold the string at the top of the wall, let the plumb fall to the baseboard. When it has stopped moving, mark with a pencil at intervals along the string. Join up the line with a metal straightedge.

Use a plumb line to make sure that you hang your paper straight.

3 Starting at the top, smooth the paper onto the wall, allowing an overlap of about 1 in. Work down the length of the paper using a smoothing brush to smooth the paper from the center outward, squeezing out any air bubbles. The paper should be worked well into the corner and overlap the adjacent wall by about ½ in.

Use a smoothing brush to squeeze out any air bubbles.

4 Use the rounded tip of a pair of long-bladed scissors to crease the paper carefully at the point where it meets the ceiling. Slowly pull the wallpaper away from the wall at the top and use the scissors to trim away the excess. Then carefully smooth the paper back down the wall using the smoothing brush. Repeat the process at the point where the wall meets the baseboard.

Make a crease in the paper where the wall meets the baseboard.

5 Hang the second drop of paper by carefully aligning it with the edge of the first drop and sliding it up against it to achieve a "butt" joint (the two edges should meet without any trace of a gap). If you are using a patterned wallpaper, then you will need to slide the paper along the wall until the two halves of the pattern meet up at the correct position.

6 Trim the top and bottom of the paper as shown in step 4. Repeat the process around the whole room. Make sure that the last drop of paper overlaps the corner by approximately ½ in. and is pushed well into the corner using the smoothing brush. Finally, finish off by wiping away any wallpaper paste that may have been left on the ceiling or coving and baseboard, using a clean, damp sponge.

Buying wallpaper

When buying wallpaper, remember to take with you the dimensions of your room and the height of the ceilings—the store should be able to advise you on the number of rolls to buy. Always buy a couple more than you will need because these can be stored in case you need to make any repairs. Check that all the rolls of wallpaper are from the same "batch" or print run—this should be marked clearly as a batch number on the side of the packet. If you run out of paper and need to buy more, make sure that you get the same batch because colors on different batches always vary slightly because of the printing process.

Papering around corners

Once you have mastered a straight run of wallpapering, turning corners should not be a problem. The key is to allow ½–1in. overlap.

Internal corners

Tools and materials

As for Hanging wallpaper
(see page 51)

1 When you have hung the last length of paper before reaching the corner, stop and measure the width of the next section. Do not assume that the wall is completely square—measure the gap at the top, bottom, and middle and add about 1 in. to the largest measurement in case of error.

Measure the width of the section you will need to reach the corner.

2 Lay the paper on the pasting table, and using a straightedge, mark the paper and cut with scissors. Make sure that the cut edge is the one nearest the corner. Paste and allow to soak. Reserve the cut-off section of paper if it is a reasonable size.

3 Hang the paper as above, making sure that it is pushed well into the corner with the smoothing brush. If the paper creases where it turns the corner, make a few snips along the edge with scissors and smooth into place.

If the paper creases at the corner, snip into the edge with scissors.

4 Use the cut-off section of wallpaper to cover the other side of the corner if it is large enough; if not, begin with a fresh length. Measure the width of the paper and hang a plumb line at this distance from the corner on the new wall. Paste, soak, then hang in position over the overlap, flush with the corner and with the cut edge nearest the corner. Continue the process around the room.

Hang the next piece so that the cut side is nearest the corner.

External corners

External corners are usually found in rooms with fireplaces. If you have started papering in the middle of a chimney breast, cut the section of wallpaper that will be applied to the wall up to the corner so that it is wide enough to wrap around the corner with about 1 in. spare as an overlap. If you are approaching an external corner from an alcove, however, then use the following steps to hang the wallpaper.

Tools and materials

As for Hanging wallpaper
(see page 51)

1 Measure the depth of the chimney breast at three points, then cut a length of paper that width plus 1 in. (this will be wrapped around the corner). Paste, soak, then hang as described above, using the brush to smooth the cut edge gently around the external corner.

Use the smoothing brush to ease the paper around the corner.

2 Measure the cut-off section of paper and draw a plumb line on the new wall as described above. Paste, soak, then smooth in place, covering the overlap. Trim off the top and bottom.

Put the cut-off paper in place on the new wall, covering the overlap.

Papering around obstacles

The same principles apply to papering around most obstacles. The key is to crease the paper carefully around the object to indicate where to cut.

Papering around a fireplace

Tools and materials

As for Hanging wallpaper
(see page 51)

1 Smooth the length of wallpaper down toward the top of the fireplace, stopping about 1 ft. above it. Use the brush to smooth the paper carefully into the corner where the edge of the fireplace meets the wall.

Use the smoothing brush to push the paper into the corner.

2 Use a sharp craft knife or pair of scissors to make a horizontal slit along the center of the mantelshelf from the point where the fireplace meets the wall.

Use scissors to cut a series of slits in the wallpaper.

3 Smooth the wallpaper down above the mantelshelf, and trim as described above. Use your fingertips to press the paper gently around any molding below the mantelshelf and trim using a sharp craft knife.

Smooth the paper, trimming around any molding on the fireplace.

Papering around a recessed window

Tools and materials

As for Hanging wallpaper
(see page 51)

1 Make sure that the final length of wallpaper is wide enough to cover the depth of the recess when cut. Smooth down the paper over the window, then carefully cut horizontal slits across the top and bottom of the window to the corners of the recess. Fold the resulting flap over into the recess and trim but do not smooth down.

2 Cut a small length of paper 1 in. deeper and wider than the area left at the top of the recess and smooth it in place under the previous piece of paper. Cut a small triangle off the corner of the paper to fold it neatly over the edge of the recess. Smooth the long piece of wallpaper in place over the smaller piece.

Papering around a door (or window without a recess)

1 Cut a length of wallpaper that will hang over the door and apply paste to it, avoiding the area that will be cut away. Hang it loosely over the door and cut away the area over the door, leaving around a 2-in. overlap. Use a smoothing brush to push the paper into the recess between the door casing and the wall.

Make a small diagonal slit in the wallpaper to the corner of the door casing.

2 Use the smoothing brush to ease the paper around the frame and trim using a craft knife.

Papering around light-switch and electrical-output plates

Tools and materials

As for Hanging wallpaper
(see page 51)

1 Hang the paper loosely over the plate and use the brush to locate its position through the paper. Using a craft knife, cut two diagonal slits from corner to corner.

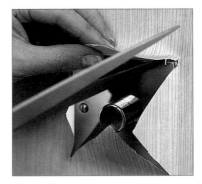

Locate the switch plate and then cut diagonal slits in the paper.

2 Fold back the paper triangles and smooth the paper around the switch plate with the brush. Use a craft knife to trim the triangles as close to the plate as possible.

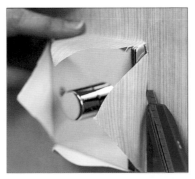

Fold the triangles back and then trim them as neatly as possible.

Alternative method

There is an alternative method for papering around light-switch and electrical-outlet plates. Switch off the power at the main supply and unscrew the front of the plate just far enough to allow you to push the excess paper underneath.

Choosing your tiles

Tiles have long been a standard wall covering for bathrooms and restrooms, as well as backsplashes and other surfaces in the kitchen. The advantage of using glazed or fired ceramics is that they are waterproof, durable, easy to wipe clean and dry, and they come in numerous different colors.

History of tiling

Although these days tiles are machine-made in many materials, originally they would have all been ceramic, handcrafted from local clay, and baked in a fire, or later, a kiln. Ceramic tiles are made in virtually every country in the world and the ceramic tradition dates back thousands of years. Among the most widely found base for tiles is terra-cotta, a low-fired red clay. In its basic form, this tile can be simply glazed or waxed to cover the porous surface, but in more sophisticated realms it can be highly decorated. The Greeks and Romans both used this type of decorated tile in the interiors of their homes, and examples of fine mosaic patterns made from hundreds of tiny colored tiles can be seen in ancient sites throughout the world.

Other tiles were made with an earthenware base. During the 16th century, this type was favored by the craftspeople in the town of Delft, in southern Holland, where the tiles were glazed with a white background and decorated with patterns in various depths of blue. For over 400 years, this blue-and-white configuration has been popular, and tiles are still made to this scheme.

Choosing your style

There is a wide variety of tiles to choose from and you should select yours to suit the size of the room you are decorating as well as to complement your scheme.

In a large bathroom, walls of tiny mosaic tiles may look incohesive and lost; conversely, in a small room large ceramic panels may make the room feel smaller.

Right: Small mosaic tiles are very popular in bathrooms today. Mix and match colors to create a pattern.

Far right: These matte-finish tiles are made in very subtle, neutral coloris that provide a sense of calm.

Therefore, you should make sure that you choose the right size of tile to be in proportion to the setting. In most bathrooms, it is usual to panel the area above the bath and handbasin with tiles in order to protect the immediate surrounding wall from water splashes and dampness. The walls, and even the ceiling and floor, of a shower stall may also be covered in tiles for the same reason.

Tiles can be chosen to be plain and innocuous so that they are simply a background, or you can select them to enhance and endorse a particular design. For example, in a Moorish bathroom, tiles will be a feature—they are not only popular in the indigenous decoration of the country and are therefore appropriate when re-creating such a style, but they are also colorful, incorporating dramatic, geometric patterns.

Small mosaics tiles can be used to form patterns or create pictures. Some of the popular patterns made using these small tiles include the ombré or shadow effect, which is a graduation of a single color that starts with dark-toned tiles near the floor and gradually fades to the palest shade near the ceiling. If you are using blues, you can create an underwater effect, so that when lying in the bath, it is as if you are at the bottom of a lagoon looking up to the sky above.

Larger, traditional tiles (4 x 4 in.) can be laid in regular lines parallel to the surface or floor, or set on their points to form a diamond pattern. You may also mix two or three shades of the same color, or contrasting shades such as black and white or blue and orange, to form a checkerboard effect.

Another way of dividing up a large expanse of tiles is to create a frieze or border. This can be

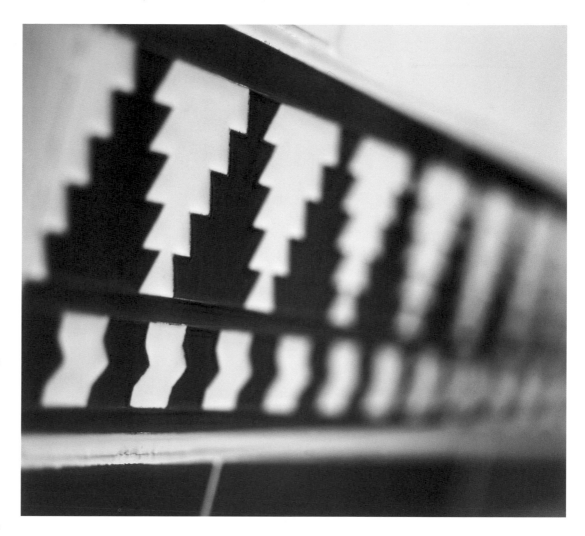

done by introducing a narrow band of smaller tiles such as mosaics, a contrasting line of narrow, linear tiles, or a slightly raised feature tile that will form a divide between the upper and lower levels on the wall. The lower level may be in one color or size of tile, while above there may be a deeper shade, different pattern, or even paint or paper.

Most ceramic tiles are machine-made so that they are exactly the same size, thickness, and color, which makes them easy to lay and provides a uniform finish. But for more rustic or bohemian settings, there are also handmade tiles and those that are manufactured so that they appear handmade. The surface of these tiles is uneven, slightly undulating, and the colors vary a little, too.

Matte-finish tiles are extremely popular today. These tiles date back to Victorian times when they were manufactured as encaustic tiles. They were especially favored by architects such as Pugin, who used them in grand civil buildings such as the the Palace of Westminster, in London, England.

The pattern on these original, and now reproduction, Victorian tiles is made by inlaying contrasting colors of clay into the surface of the tile. This is fired and the colors fused and set. Some matte-finish tiles have a sandstone appearance, and can be used in conjunction with other natural tiling material such as stone, slate, and even cement in more contemporary-style settings.

Above: *This is an example of a strong, colorful Moorish bathroom tile design. Why not try incorporating such tiles in your own bathroom scheme and make a feature of them?*

types of
tiles

Tiling is the most popular choice for protecting the walls in kitchens, bathrooms, and other areas where water is in use. When tiles are properly applied to a wall, they provide a water-resistant barrier that is easy to clean and maintain. Tiles of different sizes, made from many different materials, are now widely available. Tiling a small, regular-shaped area is a fairly easy job, although you should be aware before beginning that you will need to leave sufficient drying time between tiling and applying grout.

Types of tiles

Handmade tiles

These ceramic tiles are made by hand from pieces of clay, which gives them their characteristic individual appearance. Slight differences in thickness and size will be noticeable, and because they are glazed and fired in small batches, colors will vary. They are more expensive than mass-produced equivalents because they are labor-intensive.

Machine-made ceramic tiles

These tiles are made in large batches, often using liquid clay poured into a mold to ensure the right consistency. Many have a printed surface decoration that mimics expensive materials such as marble and stone.

They come in a large variety of different shapes and sizes, from conventional squares to large rectangles. Some manufactured tiles have a raised surface decoration that is applied before firing. Some have an undulating surface and uneven edges to mimic handmade tiles.

Mosaic tiles

Mosaic tiles, or "tesserae," come in a wide variety of materials, including glass, ceramic, and stone. The most expensive tesserae are made from a thin layer of gold leaf sandwiched between two pieces of glass. Most often associated with swimming pools, their versatility has made them increasingly popular in homes over the last few years. Although mosaics appear in ultra-contemporary interiors, they have been used since Roman times in elaborate floor designs. Tesserae are much smaller than conventional tiles, and are often supplied on a paper or mesh backing sheet. Mosaic tiles can also be purchased in loose form.

Mesh-backed mosaics

Machine-made ceramic tiles

Paper-backed mosaics

New materials

Designers are constantly exploring new materials that can be made into tiles. Metal tiles or tiles with a metallic glaze have become a popular choice to complement stainless steel and industrial-style kitchens. Resin tiles are available in a wide range of colors and have an opaque quality that suits contemporary interiors. Glass artists have developed a range of tiles that fuse clear glass with other decorative materials. Printing techniques can also be used to apply a photographic image to your tiles.

Tools and equipment

Tile-cutting tools

A variety of methods can be used for cutting tiles. The cheapest and simplest is a handheld tool that scores through the glaze of the tile, which will then snap along the line when pressure is applied. A sturdy version of the same tool incorporates a measuring gauge for accurate cutting and has a lever-operated snapping tool that grips the tile. For thicker tiles, including quarry tiles, it is worth buying or renting an electric tile cutter, which incorporates a water reservoir, making cutting easier.

Profile gauge

Tile nippers

Tile-cutting tool

Tile nippers and tile saws can be used for cutting irregular shapes from tiles, but both methods require practice.

Tile spacers

These small plastic crosses act as spacers, ensuring that each tile is an equal distance from the next. Different sizes are made to suit wall and floor tiles. They are pressed into the tile adhesive, making sure that they are below the surface of the tile so that when grout is applied they are hidden.

Grout and adhesive

Adhesive is spread directly onto the wall surface with a notched trowel, which is often supplied with the adhesive. Tiles are pressed into the adhesive, which is allowed to dry before grout is applied. Grout is applied over the tiles with a smooth-edged tool that forces the grout into the spaces between the tiles. It is important to choose the correct adhesive and grout for the situation. Areas that will get very wet, like shower stalls, should be tiled using waterproof adhesive and grout, which will prevent water from seeping through the grout lines into the wall. Areas like kitchen backsplashes, which will only occasionally be splashed with water, do not require a waterproof grout and adhesive. Grout is available in a variety of colors— you can also buy touch-up pens to refresh worn grout.

Tile saw

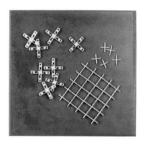
Tile spacers

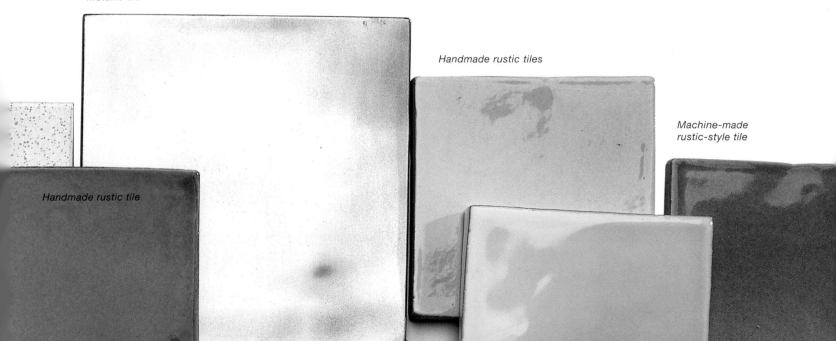

Metallic tile

Handmade rustic tiles

Machine-made rustic-style tile

Handmade rustic tile

tiling techniques

To achieve a perfectly tiled surface, plan your tiling scheme carefully to avoid awkward cuts and joints in obvious places. Make sure that you have bought sufficient tiles for the job—always buy around 10 percent extra to allow for any breakages. It is also a good idea to keep some spare tiles anyway for future repairs, safely stored and labeled. Another vital tip is to always use a sheet of squared paper to plan complicated tile designs before you begin.

Cutting tiles

To cut tiles into regular shapes, score and cut with a tile cutter. To cut away irregular shapes, follow the instructions below.

Tools and materials

Tile cutter

Tile nippers

1 Score the glaze with a series of crosshatched lines.

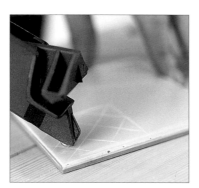

Score the glaze with the scoring part of the tile-cutting tool.

2 Use a pair of tile nippers to "bite" away the pieces of unwanted tile.

Tiling difficult areas

If you are tiling difficult-to-reach areas such as the wall above a bath or worktop, it is important to check that it is square with a level before you begin tiling. Also, make sure that you take time to plan the spacing before you begin, so that you can avoid awkward tile cuts.

Use tile nippers to break away the unwanted pieces of the tile.

Tiling a wall

Tools and materials

Level

Wood batten (optional)

Nails

Hammer

Notched trowel

Tiles and spacers

Adhesive

Grout

Flexible grout spreader or squeegee

Cloth

1 If you are tiling onto a bare wall, you should first establish a horizontal line by using a level and nailing a batten onto the wall. This will be your starting point.

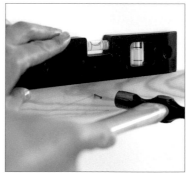

Nail a batten to a wall in a straight line to provide a starting point.

2 Use a notched trowel to apply an even layer of tile adhesive to the wall, spreading it evenly across the surface. It is best to work on an area measuring 1 sq. yd. at a time—any larger and the adhesive will dry before you can apply all the tiles.

Use a notched trowel to apply adhesive to the wall.

3 Apply the first row of tiles so that they butt up against the batten. Then remove one prong from each spacer to form a "T" shape and push into position at the base of each tile. If you need to use any half tiles or cut tiles, make sure that you position these in the darkest corner of the room where they are least likely to be seen. Before positioning the second row of tiles, push whole spacers in place at the top of each tile to ensure that they are evenly spaced. Allow the adhesive to dry thoroughly overnight.

Position spacers between each tile to ensure they are evenly spaced.

4 Use a flexible spreader to apply the grout, pushing it well into the gaps between the tiles. Remove any excess with a damp cloth and allow to dry. Polish to remove any remaining film.

Use a flexible spreader to apply grout between the tiles.

Tiling a kitchen worktop

If you are tiling an awkwardly shaped object, such as a kitchen worktop, ensure that the top is perfectly horizontal with a level before you begin. If it is not perfectly flat, you may have to fit a piece of plywood to the top before you begin tiling.

Tools and materials

PVA solution
Paintbrush
Tiles
Notched trowel
Adhesive
Spacers
Grout
Tile cutter
Cloth

1 To ensure the best finish, it is worth laying the tiles out dry before applying any adhesive. By doing this you can plan the design and figure out the ideal places to use cut tiles. It is best to begin with full tiles along the front edge of the work surface, so that any cuts can be planned to appear along the back junction with the wall. Likewise, if the work surface includes a corner,

it is best to start with a full tile in the corner, and build up the rest of the design from this point.

2 To make the tiling easier, apply a coat of PVA solution (1 part PVA to 5 parts water) to the plywood surface. This helps to seal the wood, making it easier to spread adhesive. Allow the plywood to dry before tiling.

3 Use a notched trowel, ideally a large one, to spread adhesive evenly across the plywood surface. Do not spread more than about 1 sq. yd. at a time. Use the notches to maintain a consistent depth of adhesive, which helps to ensure a consistent tile level in the finished worktop.

Apply adhesive to the surface using a notched trowel.

4 Apply the tiles, pressing them down into the adhesive with a slight twisting motion. Since the tiles are applied to a horizontal surface, there is no risk of them slipping down, but you should still be vigilant. If rows of tiles are allowed to go out of "square," this will affect the finish and lead to some unsightly tile cutting. So take time to position the tiles correctly, and use spacers to keep all gaps consistent. Spacers will also be required, although temporarily, along the junction between the edge tiles and the wooden edge strip, to ensure the lines of tiles are kept consistent.

Use spacers to make sure that the gap between tiles is even.

5 Once the adhesive has dried completely, grout the tiled surface with an epoxy grout. This type of grout is more durable than standard grout, and more hygienic for surfaces upon which food will almost certainly be prepared. It is best to concentrate on small areas at a time because epoxy grout can be difficult to work with and also tends to dry extremely quickly. Make sure that you force the grout firmly into every joint, removing any excess as quickly as possible with a damp sponge before it has had a chance to dry.

Spread the grout, taking care to force it into the joints.

6 Wait until the grout has completely dried, then give the tiled surface a final wipe over before polishing with a cotton cloth. This will help to remove any remaining grout residue and will leave a clean and bright finished surface.

Choosing your flooring

Flooring comes in a wide range of finishes, from natural wood and stone to the woven fibers of coconut husks and jute stems that form coir and sisal. These surfaces can be plain or decorative, rough or smooth—whichever you choose, be sure that it has the durability required for your room.

History of flooring

The earliest homes had beaten mud floors covered with grass or rushes, but as time went by flagstones were hewn and laid and mats woven of rush became more commonplace. Clay tiles were used in Egypt and the Romans developed concrete for their decorative mosaic floors.

Wood has also been popular for centuries, from the simple straight plank arrangements to the more ornate herringbone, parquet, and even inlaid floors dating back to the Tudor and Stuart periods. In the early 18th century, woven carpets were popular in grand homes. Less expensive painted canvas floorcloths were also popular in the United States and Britain at this time.

Animal skins and hides have also been used as floor coverings through the ages, and like a woolen mat or rug, can be used to bring warmth and softness to an area of hard stone or tile covering. Although pile carpets were developed in India before the 12th century, most floor coverings in the West were flat-woven until the 19th century.

In the 1840s, a revolution started that brought the luxury of carpets and rugs to a far wider audience, when a steam engine was used to power a loom. By the 1950s, the high-speed tufting machine was developed and the rug and carpet industry took on the mass market. With the ability to manufacture carpet by the mile, new, cheaper synthetic fibers were also introduced. These fibers, such as nylon and acrylic, brought the prices down even further.

Choosing your style

When choosing flooring, make sure that you incorporate the floor coverings into the overall decorative scheme. As a general rule, it is best to have a mixture of patterned and plain areas in a room. For example, plain walls look good with a patterned floor, as does a plain floor with patterned walls. Avoid using pattern on all surfaces because it can be overwhelming. It may also be appropriate to consider the style and period of your home and the furniture that is to be used in the room where the floor covering is to be fitted.

Choosing the right floor for each room

Different areas of the home will require different types of flooring to suit the demands of the room. For example, kitchen and bathroom floors have to be easy to wipe clean and capable of coping with water splashes and drips. In a bedroom, the floor covering should be warm and comfortable under bare feet. Hallways may be carpeted, but if you want to protect the main pathway, you could lay a runner or rug over the wall-to-wall floor covering.

Right: *Neutral-colored natural-fiber floor coverings can tie in with any color scheme.*

Natural floor coverings have become increasingly fashionable and include wood, cork, coir, stone, and terra-cotta and brick tiles. Wood generally has a warm coloring, is pleasant to walk on, and when polished reflects light back into the room. When installed in large rooms or areas, it softens sounds and is less likely to cause echoing than harder surfaces such as stone. As a rule, wood improves with age because the color mellows and becomes richer. Dents and marks only add to its character, and in fact some contemporary floor suppliers "distress" their new wood floors to give them a worn and vintage appearance. Wood is also a good canvas—it can be stripped, sanded, and stained. Paint decorative borders around the edge or opt for an all-over pattern.

Another natural floor covering is natural matting, which is made from coir, sisal, and jute. Some have patterns woven or printed onto the edges, creating a traditional carpet effect, and colored bindings of leather or woven wool can be used to link in to the color theme of the room.

Marble, granite, limestone, and slate have natural decoration in the veins and striations of their formation. Stone floors tend to be expensive but withstand hard treatment and are easy to clean. To soften hardness and reduce echoing, use kelims and mats to break up large areas.

The rich red coloring of brick and terra-cotta tiles adds warmth to any room. Brick comes in a variety of shades, from yellows through to browns and reds, and these colors can be used to create patterns. Alternately, single-colored bricks can be laid to form an attractive herringbone design. These surfaces are ideal for hallways, kitchens, restrooms, and sunrooms.

Above: *Limestone floors look stylish and are also easy to look after.*

Left: *The expanse of these large white tiles has been broken up by using small black tiles.*

types of

flooring

When deciding on the flooring for each room of your home, it is important to consider the amount of wear and tear that each area will receive and choose a floor type accordingly. Flooring falls into several categories, ranging from soft flooring, which includes carpets and rugs, to hard flooring, which includes wood, stone, and tile at the other extreme. Semihard flooring is the in-between category, which includes materials such as vinyl, linoleum, and rubber.

Soft flooring

Carpet

Carpet is one of the most comfortable and luxurious floor coverings. The best-quality carpets have a high wool content—wool fiber repels dirt naturally, is soft underfoot, and has a long lifespan. Synthetic fibers take color well and can be treated to make them resistant to stains. They are often combined with wool to produce durable carpets for areas of heavy wear. Common types of carpet pile are twist and velvet—twist pile is denser and more suitable for heavy-wear areas, while velvet pile is longer and softer, making it the ideal choice for bedrooms.

Coir, sisal, and jute

Natural floor coverings have become increasingly popular in recent years. Natural matting made from coir, sisal, and jute can be wall-to-wall like a carpet or used in bound squares or runners for hallways, stairs, or as a central panel over a wood or stone floor.

Most natural-fiber floor coverings have a latex rubber backing and should be laid by professionals. Some combine the toughness of natural fibers with the softness of wool carpet on a hessian backing. There are also unusual woven-paper floor coverings available that are tough and durable due to the tightness of the weave. These come from renewable sources and are therefore environmentally sound, but because it is a dried material, it is not advisable to use natural

Wood veneer tongue-and-groove flooring

Terra-cotta floor tile

Marble floor tile

Slate floor tile

Ceramic floor tile

fiber directly in front of a fireplace where sparks may tumble out and burn it, or by a sink where water will splash and cause damage.

Hard flooring
Wood
There are various types of wood used for floors. The more expensive are the hardwoods such as oak, ash, walnut, Iroko, elm, and maple. The cheaper softwoods such as pine are often stained or decorated because they lack the rich color of hardwoods. Left in its natural state, wood flooring can be laid in herringbone patterns, in parquet-style designs, or as planks in a staggered configuration so that a pattern is formed by the wood.

Wood is a "living" material and therefore should be properly treated and dried before being laid. Central heating can cause the boards to dry out and shrink, whereas a spillage of water, such as a leak from a pipe, will make the boards swell. New wood floors should be left for at least 48 hours to acclimatize to a room's environment before being laid.

As an everyday surface, wood is comparatively easy to clean—you can simply brush it or wipe over the top with a damp cloth or mop. Depending on the finish of the wood, it may need to be polished with wax every month or so; if it is varnished, it may need to be stripped and recoated about every 10 years, depending on its location and the wear it takes.

A cheap alternative to wood is laminate flooring. The laminating process involves taking a photographic image of woodgrain, printing it onto paper, and then sandwiching it between chipboard and a plastic-coated surface to make a realistic-looking plank of flooring.

Stone
One of the advantages of stone is that it is virtually indestructible, making it an ideal choice for the kitchen. On the negative side, it is unforgiving to items accidentally dropped onto it. Also, stone can feel cold underfoot, although this can be easily remedied with underfloor heating elements that make it pleasant to walk on with

bare feet. Because of the cost of stone, it is advisable to have it laid by a professional.

Tiles
Tiles come in a huge variety of designs, many of which mimic stone and marble. Glazed ceramic floor tiles can be fitted by the competent home-improvement enthusiast and are less costly than other hard floor coverings. The tiles should be made specifically for floor use, because tiles destined for wall or work surfaces (see pages 56–7) will not be as thick or heavy and will, in time, crack and break if used underfoot. The shiny surface of ceramic tiles makes them very easy to clean but they are prone to breaking and chipping if a heavy object is dropped on them or if they are laid on anything other than a perfectly flat surface.

Industrial-style floors
Industrial-style floor coverings include hard materials such as concrete, stone, metal, and rubber. Concrete can be colored and polished to a sheen, when it

Natural sisal (front example has colored weft)

Mosaic-style vinyl

Ribbed wool carpets with a sisal weft

Wool twist carpet

Self-adhesive vinyl tile

Handsaw

will take on a highly decorative appearance and can therefore work well in homes.

Metal "treadplate" tiles have become increasingly popular in kitchens—they complement stainless-steel accessories and add to the professional appearance of a kitchen. Rubber flooring, which has long been associated with schools and hospitals, is now valued in the home for its warmth underfoot and nonslip qualities, making it an ideal choice for the bathroom.

Semihard floorings
Manmade floor coverings

These include linoleum, rubber, and vinyl tiles. They can be laid in many patterns, the most common being the black-and-white checkerboard design. Linoleum, vinyl, and padded vinyl floor coverings are also available in rolls and can be cut and laid like a carpet. Most are durable and low on maintenance but the surface may be harmed by a sharp or hot object. Linoleum was developed in the late 19th century but went out of fashion until recently—it is now definitely back in vogue. This type of flooring is regarded as being utilitarian, so it is most appropriate for bathrooms, kitchens, and hallways.

Cork

Cork, which is also returning to popularity, usually has a rubber backing and is treated with a surface sealant (especially if in tile form) to prevent it from becoming damaged by water or moisture.

Cork comes from the outer bark of the cork oak tree, which regrows so cork is a renewable resource. It is also a soft surface to walk on and it has good insulating properties.

Essential tools

When laying carpet, in addition to a craft knife for cutting the carpet, you will require a knee kicker to stretch the carpet as well as a blunt chisel and mallet to anchor it over the gripper rods.

Installation kits for tongue-and-groove wood and laminate flooring include plastic spacers, cork expansion strips, as well as a metal edging device used with a hammer to fit the plank nearest the wall. You will also need a handsaw to cut the final planks in a row to the correct size.

Use a large notched trowel to apply the correct depth of adhesive when laying a tiled floor. When working with thicker tiles, it is worth renting a professional tile cutter or angle grinder.

Paint, stain, or varnish can be applied to floors with paintbrushes or small rollers. When applying a clear finish, such as a varnish, it is worth investing in a good-quality brush specially for use on wood. Use a smaller artist's brush if you are painting a detailed pattern such as rows of thin lines.

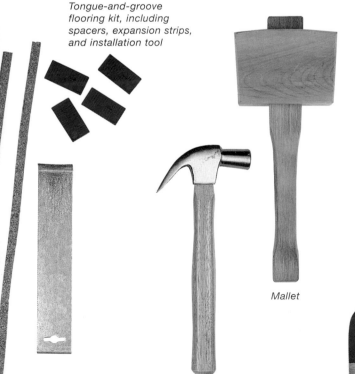

Tongue-and-groove flooring kit, including spacers, expansion strips, and installation tool

Notched trowel

Mallet

Angled brush (useful for drawing straight lines)

Hammer

Blunt chisel

Paintbrush

flooring techniques

Before installing a new floor or refurbishing an old one, you must first consider the length of time that the room will be out of use because this may affect the technique that you employ. You also need to remove all furniture and other movable items, making sure that the room is thoroughly cleared before beginning to lay anything. It is also a good idea to draw a floor plan on a piece of squared paper to allow you to calculate the quantities needed with accuracy.

Wood flooring

Wood flooring is a practical option for every room. Most older houses have floorboards throughout, which, if you are lucky, will be in good enough condition to restore. There are a number of different ways in which you can finish floorboards that have a build-up of years of old finishes. Sanding them back to bare wood is a labor-intensive job but it gives you the option of applying a natural finish or tinting with a translucent varnish in a variety of shades. Or if you do not want the disruption of sanding the floor, there are specialty floor paints available in a wide range of colors. They can be painted directly onto unstripped floorboards. This is a quick option but it is an opaque finish, so will not show the grain. On the positive side, it gives you the option of applying a decorative pattern or motif to the floor.

Preparation and repair of floorboards

Tools and materials

Hammer

Blunt chisel and pliers

Nail set

Nails

1 If the room is carpeted, roll up the carpet and remove it. Hessian-backed carpet will have been tacked in place with carpet tacks or gripper strips—work your way around the edges of the room with a hammer, blunt chisel, and a pair of pliers, pulling up the gripper strips or tacks that held the carpet in place.

2 Use the hammer and nail set to drive down any nails that are raised above the surface (this is very important if you are going to be using an electric sander because a raised nail can tear the sanding belt and damage the machine).

Drive down any nails that are raised above the surface.

3 Check for loose floorboards and secure them to the joists with nails.

Applying a painted finish over old floorboards

Tools and materials

Floor cleaner

Sanding block and coarse-grit sandpaper

Flexible wood putty and knife

Masking tape

Paintbrush or roller and extension pole and paint

1 Vacuum to remove dust, then clean the floor thoroughly with a commercial floor cleaner that will remove traces of old wax or polish. Allow to dry. Use a sanding block and coarse-grit sandpaper to remove any stubborn marks and areas of raised grain that might show through the paint. Use flexible wood putty to fill in any gouges or holes that will spoil the finish.

2 Mask off the baseboards with masking tape and begin to apply the paint, starting from the corner of the room farthest away from the door. You can use a large paintbrush, or if you prefer, a roller attached to an extension pole. Work quickly in the direction of the grain. Allow the paint to dry and recoat if necessary.

Use a roller to paint the floorboards in the direction of the woodgrain.

Electric sanders

Make sure that you rent sanders from a reputable company who will explain the controls and provide safety advice before you start. Most companies rent floor sanders and edging sanders as a package that you pay for by the day or the weekend—you will pay extra for the sanding disks and belts. It is essential to wear ear muffs, a dust mask, and goggles while operating the machines. Also, tape a plastic sheet over the door to the room in which you are working to stop the sawdust from spreading to other rooms.

Stripping and finishing floorboards

Large electric sanders can look difficult to use, but they make stripping floorboards a much less arduous task (see box, left).

Tools and materials

Electric floor sanders

Sandpaper—from coarse-grit through to fine-grit

Steel wool, cloth, and mineral spirits

Floor finish

Paintbrush

1 Fit the drum sander with coarse-grit sandpaper. Position it in the corner of the room so that you will be able to work your way across the room in diagonal strips. Holding the machine by the handle, tilt it back so that the sanding belt is off the floor. Switch on the machine and lower it so that the sanding belt makes contact with the floor. Begin pushing the machine forward immediately because if you leave it stationary in one place, it will sand a deep gouge in the floorboards. When you reach the end of the room, tilt the machine back and reposition it to sand the next strip. Work your way diagonally across the room. Change to medium-grit sandpaper and work your way back across the room at right angles to the first direction.

Use the drum sander in a diagonal direction across the floor.

2 Use the edging sander around the edges of the room, working your way through the grits of sandpaper as before. Finish awkward internal corners by hand with steel wool and mineral spirits, or with the pointed end of a shaped electric sander. Complete this task before finishing off with the drum sander (step 3) so that you will avoid walking across the finished boards unnecessarily.

Work around the edges of the room using the edging sander.

3 Finish off with fine-grit sandpaper fitted to the drum sander and work your way backward and forward along the floorboards in the direction of the grain for a really smooth finish. Allow the dust to settle, vacuum thoroughly, then wipe away any residue of sawdust with a cloth dampened with mineral spirits.

Finish the sanding by fitting the drum sander with fine-grit sandpaper.

4 Seal with the finish of your choice. There is a large number of different varieties of floor finish available. The most durable types are oil-based with a gloss finish. However, water-based finishes dry more quickly, making it easier to complete the job in a single weekend. Some finishes are completely clear, while others are tinted, stained, or dyed, which will subtly change the final color of the floorboards. Apply the floor finish with a large, good-quality paintbrush, working from the corner of the room toward the door. Allow the finish to dry completely and then reapply if necessary.

Apply your chosen floor finish with a good-quality paintbrush.

Tongue-and-groove wood and laminate flooring

Tongue-and-groove flooring is available in many different varieties. The most expensive is solid wood, which is both attractive and durable, and can be sanded and refinished if necessary. Most manufacturers recommend tongue-and-groove flooring for every room except the bathroom, where water could cause warping. Wood veneer varieties are mid-priced and have a surface of real wood on a composite base. Laminated designs vary enormously in price—the best-quality ones are virtually indistinguishable from real wood and they are also almost indestructible.

When laying laminate, some systems require the tongue-and-groove joints to be glued and allowed to dry overnight. The newest varieties available simply click together and can be walked on immediately.

Tools and materials

Laminate and underlayment

Handsaw or jigsaw

Plastic spacers and tool

Hammer

Metal S-shaped tool

Quadrant bead

Miter saw

Finish nails

1 Unpack the flooring and leave it in the room in which it is to be fitted for 24 hours—this allows it to acclimatize to the temperature. If possible, the baseboards should be removed. This will allow the expansion strip to be fitted underneath. If it is not possible to remove the baseboards, a quadrant bead will be needed to hide the expansion strip. Lay the manufacturer's recommended underlayment—this usually consists of a plastic dampproof layer followed by a cushioned foam layer.

Lay down the underlayment before you begin.

2 Cut the first board using a sharp handsaw or jigsaw, following the instructions on the packet. Place the cut end in the corner of the room with the cut end against the wall. Use the recommended wood glue, applied sparingly into the groove of the floorboards.

3 Continue adding planks of flooring following the pattern set out in the instructions. Use plastic spacers around the outside edge of the floor between the boards and the wall (or baseboard if it has remained in place). This will become an expansion gap. Use the plastic tool provided to join the planks by tapping gently with a hammer.

Join the planks together by tapping on the plastic tool with a hammer.

4 When you get to the end of a row of planks, hook the metal S-shaped tool over the edge of the last plank and gently hammer against the other end of the tool to fix the plank in place.

Use the S-shaped tool to fix the last piece of floor into place.

5 Repeat the whole process for the next row of planks and continue until the floor has been laid using the same method. Then remove the plastic spacers and push the cork expansion strips between the last plank and the wall (or baseboard).

Lay down the cork expansion strips between the last plank and the wall.

6 Replace the baseboard, or fit quadrant bead against the baseboard, using finish nails, to cover the expansion gap. Cut the quadrant with a miter saw to fit internal and external corners.

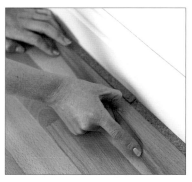

Fit quadrant bead between the flooring edge and baseboards.

Laying laminate flooring

Do not attempt to lay one of the more expensive tongue-and-groove floors yourself because you may actually invalidate the manufacturer's guarantee if you make a mistake. However, cheaper laminate varieties are relatively easy to lay yourself with a bit of planning (see steps, left).

Below: *Tongue-and-groove flooring creates a clean and contemporary look.*

Concrete floors

Concrete is gaining popularity as a flooring material, particularly in areas with an industrial-style look such as kitchens. On the negative side, it is fairly cold underfoot and unforgiving to items dropped on it. It can also stain easily if not sealed properly.

Concrete can look very attractive when polished to a sheen, provided it is in good condition. Using a self-leveling floor compound will sort out any uneven areas. For larger areas, it is advisable to call in the professionals, who will lay the floor and polish it. They can also supply more exotic concrete-based finishes such as terrazzo, which is a concrete and marble chip composition, polished to a high shine. Plain concrete floors provide a good base for a painted design. Some floor paints are specially formulated for painting onto concrete, although the colors tend to have an industrial feel.

Using a self-leveling floor compound

This simple product is great for use on existing concrete floors that have seen better days. Mix according to the manufacturer's instructions, then pour over the floor, leaving it to find its own level. Various decorative effects, such as flagstones, can be achieved by using a stick to make patterns in the compound as it begins to set.

Tools and materials

PVA solution and brush
Self-leveling floor compound
Mixing bucket
Stirring stick or drill attachment
Plastering trowel
Stick for flagstone effect (optional)
Paint plus paintbrush or roller and tray (optional)

1 Clean the floor, brushing away any loose areas of concrete. Paint a solution of 1 part PVA and 5 parts water over the floor.

Mix up a solution of PVA and water and paint it over the floor.

2 Mix up the floor compound, then carefully pour it over the floor, working from the far corner toward the door. Use a trowel to smooth the compound into every corner, then allow it to settle.

Pour the self-leveling compound on the floor, then smooth with a trowel.

3 To create a flagstone effect, use a stick to mark out the lines between stones.

Mark the stone "lines" with a stick to create a flagstone effect.

4 Alternately, if you want to paint the floor, wait until the compound has dried out thoroughly. First seal the surface with PVA solution or a multipurpose primer and allow to dry. Paint using special floor paint for concrete floors and apply with a broad brush or roller. Start in the far corner of the room and paint outward.

Use special concrete floor paint and apply with a roller or brush.

Tiled flooring

Before tiling a floor, you will need to ensure that the tiles have a completely flat, sound surface to adhere to. How you prepare the floor will depend on the finish that is currently in place.

Preparing floorboards for a tiled finish

Wood floorboards expand and contract in different temperatures and flex underfoot, which means that before laying ceramic or stone tiles on this type of floor you will need to lay a more rigid surface of sheets of plywood.

Tools and materials

Squared paper and pencil
Plywood
Jigsaw
Cordless drill/driver
Screws, hammer, and nails

1 Sketch the dimensions of your floor on squared paper to calculate the quantity of plywood you will need. It is sold in standard 8 x 4-ft. sheets, although many stores will cut it to your specification. Lay the sheets out over the floorboards, trimming with a jigsaw where necessary.

2 Start in the corner of the room, then screw the sheets of plywood in place every 6 in. until the whole floor is covered. Seal with a solution of 1 part PVA and 5 parts water before tiling.

Screw the floorboards in at 6-in. intervals with a screwdriver.

Laying ceramic tiles

These are thin glazed tiles that often mimic more expensive slate or stone tiles. Being thin, they are easier to cut and lay yourself than thicker tiles.

Tools and materials

Tiles

Wood battens and metal ruler

Adhesive and notched trowel

Plastic spacers

Level

Tile cutter

Grout

Cloth or sponge

1 Start by establishing the center point of your room (see box, right), then lay out a practice run of tiles, allowing approximately ⅛ in. for grout lines. This will allow you to establish what size you will need to cut the tiles that will fit around the edge of the room.

Calculate where the tiles will be positioned around the room.

2 Nail two straight wood battens to the floor at the point where the last row of whole tiles ends. Check that the angle between the two battens is exactly 90° before you begin tiling—this will ensure that the run is completely straight.

Nail wood battens in place where the last row of tiles will end.

3 Work in areas of approximately 1 sq. yd. so that the adhesive does not dry too quickly. Spread the adhesive evenly over the floor using a notched trowel to achieve good coverage.

Spread the tile adhesive over the surface of the floor.

4 Place the first tile at the point where the two battens meet, pressing it firmly into the adhesive. Use plastic spacers between tiles to ensure even spacing, and then continue laying all the whole tiles using the same method. Check the tiles are even with a level.

Put the first tile in place where the two battens meet and push down.

5 Calculate the sizes of the tiles to be cut by placing them over the last whole tile,

Finding the center point of a room

Draw two intersecting diagonal lines from each corner of the room. The point at which they meet is the center point. An alternative method is to use a steel ruler: find the center of the room by marking a line vertically and horizontally. The point where the lines meet is the center of the floor.

Above: *Before you begin laying floor tiles, make sure that your floor surface is perfectly flat so that you may achieve a smooth finish.*

butting another tile up to the baseboard and using it as a cutting guide. Allow an extra ⅛ in. space for the grout. Cut the tiles by gripping them in the tile cutter and using the cutting blade to score the glaze.

Score the glaze of the tile with the cutting blade.

6 Snap the tile cleanly in two by placing it in the relevant part of the tool.

Cut the tiles by snapping them cleanly in the mouth of the tool.

7 If the gap for the tiles is small, apply adhesive to the tiles instead of the floor. Allow to dry overnight.

Apply adhesive to the cut tiles before laying if the space is small.

8 Next apply the grout to the tiles, using the smooth edge of the notched trowel.

Apply the grout over the surface of the tiles using a notched trowel.

9 When the grout has hardened, clean off any residue with a cloth. Allow to dry, then polish.

Clean off any grout residue using a cloth and then polish.

Cutting around obstacles

Cutting tiles into regular shapes is fairly straightforward—once the glaze has been scored, they will break cleanly along the line. Cutting tiles into irregular shapes is much more difficult; most methods are fairly labor-intensive. It pays to plan your tiling carefully to avoid awkward cuts. Straight lines can be cut with an electric tile cutter, which works using a blade lubricated with water. These can be bought or rented from a tool rental stores. Irregular shapes, such as curves around pipes, can be cut with a tile saw. Or score the tile with a tile-cutting wheel, then use tile nippers to chip away the excess.

Using a profile gauge

This clever tool uses a series of plastic rods to transfer the shape of the obstacle onto the tile to ensure accurate cutting.

1 Align the profile gauge with the tile to be cut, then push the profile gauge against the obstacle. This will cause the rods to form a template of the obstacle on the tile. Use a pencil to draw carefully around the gauge.

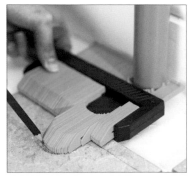

Use a profile gauge to measure the space around awkward obstacles.

2 Grip the tile carefully in a vise (padded with an old cloth), then use a tile saw to cut away the waste part of the tile carefully.

Laying slate and stone tiles

Slate and stone tiles are hard, natural materials that make excellent heavy-duty floor coverings. Although they are laid using virtually the same technique as ceramic floor tiles, they need to be bedded into a thick, cement-based adhesive. The irregular thickness of the tiles and their cost make laying these materials a job best left to experts. If you do choose to lay them yourself, seek advice from your supplier. Work slowly on a small area, checking the level of each tile carefully as you work. tiles will vary in thickness, which means you will have to vary the thickness of the cement bed. Stone and slate also require the use of special cutting tools, such as angle grinders, which shear through the extra tough material. They may also require sealing once laid to avoid surface staining.

Laying mosaic flooring

Before laying a mosaic floor, the surface should be prepared in the same way as for a standard tiled floor (see pages 68–9). Mosaic tiles come in a variety of different materials, including ceramic, glass, and stone. The individual tiles are called tesserae and are sold loose or stuck to a paper or mesh backing. For a large floor area, it is best to use the tesserae with a backing. Many are sold in blends of toning colors mixed randomly on a sheet.

If you wish to lay the tiles in a pattern, plan the design carefully first on a piece of squared paper. There are two methods of laying tesserae: the direct method where the tiles are laid directly in place in the adhesive, and the indirect method where tiles are stuck back-to-front on gummed brown paper and then pressed in place in the adhesive. For an expanse of tiles with a simple pattern, use sheets of single-colored tiles on a backing material and carefully pick off some of the tiles and replace them with other colors to build up a pattern.

Laying sheets of mosaic with a pattern

Tools and materials

Metal ruler

Floor tile adhesive

Notched trowel

Mosaic tiles

Newspaper and masking tape

Scissors or craft knife

Tile nippers

Sponge and scouring pad

Floor grout and spreader

Soft cloths

1 When using the direct method, plan your mosaic design before you start to lay the tiles.

Plan your design while the tesserae are still attached to the backing paper.

2 Prepare your floor as described above. Find the center point (see page 69), and working from there outward, spread the floor tile adhesive to cover about 1 sq. yd. at a time. Once the adhesive is evenly spread, use the notched side of the trowel to give the adhesive a surface pattern—this helps the tiles to stick easily into place. Lay the sheets of mosaic tiles, one at a time. Make sure that they are pushed well into the adhesive.

Lay the sheets of tiles one at a time and push firmly into the adhesive.

3 Work your way to the outer edges of the floor, using the same method until you are left with any areas that will need to be covered with cut sheets. Mask off the baseboards with newspaper and masking tape, then work your way

around the edges of the floor, applying the adhesive as described above. Cut any sheets that require trimming with a sharp pair of scissors or a craft knife and lay as described above.

4 Any tiles that require cutting should be stuck last of all. Use a pair of tile nippers and cut the tiles to size. If you work with the direction of the grooves (if using glass tesserae), you should find that the tiles snap cleanly. Shaping tiles to form irregular shapes with the nippers will take a bit more practice. Use them to nibble away at the tiles a bit at a time. Allow the adhesive to dry overnight.

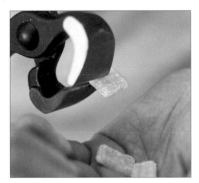
Any individual tiles that need cutting should be cut with tile nippers.

5 Use a sponge to wet the backing paper with warm water; allow to soak. Gently peel off the backing paper. Remove any stubborn areas of paper with a scouring pad.

Soak the backing paper with a sponge and then peel it away.

6 Mix up the floor grout following the manufacturer's instructions and apply with a grout spreader, making sure that you work it well between the tesserae. Allow to dry for about 20 minutes. Wipe off the excess grout with a soft cloth before it is completely dry. Use a clean cloth to polish the tesserae to a final shine.

Spread the floor grout over the tesserae with a grout spreader.

Vinyl floor coverings

Vinyl is an ideal floor covering for kitchens and bathrooms because it is resilient and easy to clean and comes in a multitude of different designs. Vinyl flooring is available in sheet or tile form. The sheet vinyl comes in a standard thickness or it can be "cushioned" with the addition of a foam underlayment. Make sure that the floor is properly prepared (see page 65) before laying the vinyl as described below. The vinyl should be left loosely rolled in the room for 48 hours before laying because this will increase its suppleness and ensure that it lies flat.

Laying sheet vinyl

Tools and materials

Measuring tape, paper, and pen

Vinyl flooring

Sharp craft knife

Vinyl flooring adhesive and notched trowel, or heavy-duty double-sided flooring tape

Scissors

Profile gauge (if there are obstacles in the room)

Metal straightedge

---

1 Measure the room and draw a rough plan on a piece of paper. This will allow you to plan any joints, if necessary. Cut the vinyl roughly to size, allowing about 1 in. all around and lay in position. Cut away squares of vinyl at each corner and make a series of "release" cuts; these will allow you to push the vinyl right into the baseboard. Trim away the excess with a sharp craft knife.

Trim away the excess vinyl at each corner.

2 To fit the vinyl against an uneven wall, use an scrap of wood and rest the pencil against it while you slide it along the length of the wall. Your pencil line will follow the contour of the wall—use this as a guide and trim the vinyl with a sharp craft knife or scissors.

Use a scrap of wood and pencil to mark against an uneven wall.

3 When you come across obstacles such as doorways, make release cuts on each side of the frame, or for more complicated shapes use a profile gauge, which is pushed into the molding and then used as a template for cutting. For simple, larger items like bathroom fixtures, simply make a series of release cuts around the object, then trim for a close fit.

When you reach an obstacle, make cuts in the vinyl, then trim to fit.

4 To make perfect joints in two lengths of vinyl, overlap them, making sure that if the vinyl is patterned there is a match between them. Use a craft knife and metal straightedge to cut through both thicknesses of vinyl at the same time.

Cut through the overlapped pieces of vinyl with a sharp craft knife.

5 Pull back the edges of the strips and stick down with double-sided flooring tape. Alternately, you could use vinyl adhesive applied with a notched trowel.

Laying vinyl, rubber, or cork floor tiles

Vinyl and cork floor tiles are laid using exactly the same method as has just been described. Some have a self-adhesive backing covered with paper, which is simply peeled off when you are ready to stick them down. Other tiles will have to be stuck in place with the manufacturer's recommended adhesive or double-sided flooring tape. Always make sure that you have a clean, level surface to work on, although soft floor tiles are more forgiving of slight irregularities in the surface than hard tiles.

Tools and materials

Metal ruler and pencil

Vinyl tiles

Adhesive and trowel (if required)

Scissors or sharp craft knife

Paper (if there are obstacles)

1 Find the mid-point of the room (see box, page 69). Lay out the tiles in a "dry run," working from the center point outward. If you are left with small, awkward cut tiles around the edges, adjust the start line, moving it farther away from the wall.

Use a metal ruler to figure out the center point of the room.

2 If you are using adhesive, work on 1 sq. yd. of floor at a time, allowing you time to position the tiles perfectly. If you are using self-adhesive tiles, simply peel away

the backing and position along the central line, making sure that each tile butts up closely to the next. Press down firmly with your hands to make sure that all areas of the tile have stuck to the floor surface below. Continue until all whole tiles have been laid.

Lay the first tile carefully along your center line.

3 You can achieve an accurate cut by positioning a whole tile on top of the last fitted tile, then adding another whole tile butting up to the baseboard. This will leave part of the tile below exposed. Draw along this line and cut with scissors or a sharp craft knife for a perfect fit. If fitting a tile around an external corner, simply move the tile into position over the last whole tile on the other side of the corner and repeat the process.

Use a tile butted up to the baseboard as a cutting guide.

4 When cutting a tile to fit around a large obstacle like a washbasin or toilet, cut a sheet of paper to the size of a tile and make a

series of parallel cuts to the depth of the obstacle. Push the paper up against the obstacle and fold back the cut strips at the points where the obstacle touches the floor. Use this as a template for cutting the tile. To get around smaller obstacles such as pipes, use a tape measure to gauge the position, then use a coin of a similar diameter to cut a perfect circle. Cut a slit from the edge of the tile to the circle and slot it into position.

Make a paper template to measure the size of a large obstacle.

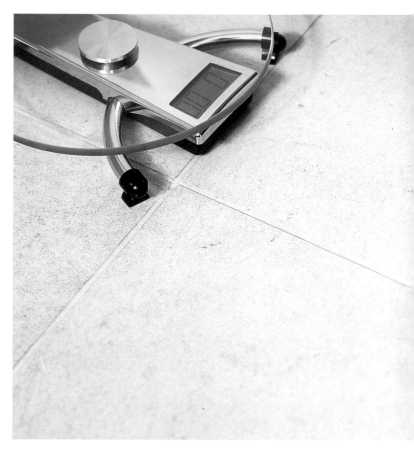

Above: *Stone tiles are particularly suitable for use in kitchens.*

Carpet

There is a huge variety of carpet designs available, but they are all either hessian- or foam-backed. Hessian-backed carpet is generally better quality and more expensive. It requires an underlayment that adds a cushioning layer, making it more comfortable to walk on. Using underlayment is important for a variety of reasons: it prevents dirt and dust working its way up from beneath the floor, it stops wear patterns developing along joints in the floorboards, and also adds a layer of soundproofing.

Foam-backed carpet is made with a foam rubber backing, which acts like an built-in underlayment. Before laying a foam-backed carpet, it is a good idea to cover the floor with a paper or fiber sheet—this will stop the foam rubber backing sticking to the floor and make it easier to remove when you wish to change the flooring.

Fitting carpet and underlayment

Tools and materials

Carpet

Underlayment

Pliers

Gripper strips

Hammer and nails

Craft knife

Staple gun

Blunt chisel and mallet

Knee kicker

Scissors

Hacksaw

Threshold strip

Screws and screwdriver

Straightedge

1 Give the room a thorough sweep and vacuum, then remove any old carpet tacks with pliers. If gripper strips were originally used and they are still in good condition, they can be reused. You should not reuse underlayment because it will begin to show the previous areas of wear through the new carpet. Nail gripper strips to the floor about ¼ in. from the baseboard all the way around the room.

Nail gripper strips securely in place around the room.

2 Roll out the strips of underlayment and cut them with a sharp craft knife so that they butt up to the gripper strip. Join the individual widths of underlayment with a staple gun to stop them from sliding around.

Use a staple gun to hold the underlayment in place.

3 Unroll the carpet and lay it loosely in place. Fix the machine-finished edge against one wall by pressing it into the teeth of the gripper strip. Smooth the carpet across to the opposite wall, then use the knee kicker to nudge it onto the gripper strips—do not secure it firmly until the carpet is evenly stretched.

Using the knee kicker, nudge the carpet onto the gripper strips.

4 Next, cut triangular "release" notches into each corner and continue around the room, stretching the carpet into the corners until you are completely happy that it is evenly tensioned throughout. Use the blunt chisel and mallet to push the carpet firmly into the angle between the floor and baseboard. Take care not to hurt your fingers when doing this. Trim with a sharp craft knife if necessary.

Use a blunt chisel and mallet to hammer the carpet into place.

5 In order to finish off the doorways, use a threshold strip suitable for the type of flooring that you are joining to (for example, a strip made for carpet to hard flooring). Cut it to fit the doorway using a hacksaw and screw into position on the floor. Cut the carpet to fit around the door frame, then using a straightedge, make a single cut across the doorway and tuck the carpet edge neatly under the threshold strip.

Using the blunt chisel, tuck the carpet under the threshold strip.

Loose-laying carpet on a straight stair run

Wall-to-wall carpeting of the stairs is a job best left to the professionals because it could be extremely dangerous for those using the stairs if it is not completed properly. As a compromise, if you have a straight run of stairs, you could loose-lay a strip of carpet with finished edges, and hold it in place with decorative stair rods. This method looks particularly attractive in period properties because it leaves an area of tread visible at each side. Stair rods are available in a number of finishes to suit your decor, including wood, brass-plated, and chrome-plated metal.

Tools and materials

Fabric tape measure or string

Carpet

Underlayment

Sharp craft knife

Carpet tacks

Hammer

Drill

Screwdriver

Screws

Stair rod clips

Stair rods in your chosen finish

1 Use a fabric tape measure or a piece of string to measure the length of carpet required, allowing around 1 ft. excess for turning under.

A piece of string can be used to measure the length required.

2 Cut pieces of underlayment slightly narrower than your carpet and attach it to the stair tread using carpet tacks.

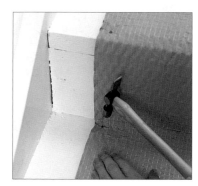

Use carpet tacks to attach the underlayment in place.

3 Start the carpet by tacking it to the back of the second tread— it is normal for the landing carpet to cover the first riser. Smooth it over the nosing and anchor in place by fixing the rod into the clips. Continue the same method down the stairs, turn the excess under at the bottom, and tack in place. To spread the wear, you

Tack the first section of carpet to the second tread.

can adjust the carpet by moving it up or down a tread on a yearly basis.

4 Use a drill and screwdriver to attach the stair rod clips just outside the width of the carpet.

Secure the carpet by screwing the stair rod clips into place.

Adjusting doors

When you have added extra layers to your flooring, you may find that doors in the rooms no longer fit easily over the surface. If this is the case, you will need to have the doors removed from their hinges and the necessary amount shaved off the base, otherwise the doors will stick and the constant dragging of the door over the carpet surface will cause marks and eventually wear it out.

Below: *wall-to-wall carpeting is best left to a professional.*

Windows and dressings

Windows are said to be the eyes of a room—they allow you to see out and let light in. Traditionally, windows were small because glass was costly and could only be made in small panes. Now, panes or panels have become larger, enabling whole walls to be replaced by a sheet of reinforced glass.

Assessing your windows

Before embarking on window dressing, assess the style, shape, and number of windows in the room. Think about how much sunlight your room receives. If it only has one or two small windows, your priority should be for a window dressing that does not restrict or hinder the small flow of natural light available. If you have many tall windows and the room is oriented so that it receives plenty of daylight, then you can afford to go for more complex dressings and valances that will, to some extent, inhibit the flow of light.

Window shapes and styles

The windows themselves may be of an interesting shape or style that makes them a feature of the room in their own right. To make the most of such a window, the dressings should be minimal. Use simple drapes or shades to accentuate the shape. Modern sash and casement windows without glazing bars or modern vinyl frames are rarely worth making a feature of, so the edges of these frames can be camouflaged by fabric.

Interesting windows and window features include French doors that open out onto a balcony or into a garden. These

Right: Modern window dressings are often quite simple. Here, shutters have been combined with plain no-sew drapes hung from a chrome curtain rod.

should be carefully dressed so that access is not hindered. Period sash windows with six, eight, or twelve panes of glass date from as far back as the 18th century, and even the single-paned lower sashes that came into popularity in the mid-19th century are worthy of drapes that highlight their graceful appearance.

If you have unusually shaped windows, such as round, oval, or arched, you may prefer not to dress them with drapes at all. Alternately, you can simply use an arrangement of flowers, a piece of sculpture, or a decorative object placed on the sill to fill the window space, so that it is like a painting within a frame.

where there is plenty of color and pattern. Try to achieve a balance between the strength of color, pattern, texture, and weight of fabric throughout the room.

The view is another consideration. If your view is less than desirable, you will want window dressings that obscure or camouflage the view without cutting back too much of the natural flow of light.

You may find it useful to build up layers of window dressings. To obscure the view and to provide privacy, a window shade or panel of sheer fabric is ideal. These will produce a light covering that does not hinder the daylight completely. Then, for decoration and a link with the main colors and styles of the room, you may add a more formal set of outer drapes.

Shades and voiles

Standard shades that work with a roller mechanism fit into the recess of the window, and when extended, cover the whole window. There are a number of more ornate shade designs. Deep, horizontally pleated Roman blinds are made with cords and rods attached on the reverse of the fabric so that when the cords

Bay windows are features that are often found in a living room or bedrooms. This style of window is generally made up of three or more individual frames set in a bow that curves outward in a graceful semicircular shape. This can be a difficult structure to dress. The traditional solution is to place a shaped rod or track along the upper edge of the window from which to hang three large drapes or a pair of drapes for each window. An alternative is separate panels of shades or shutters for each window.

Sloping attic windows or skylights pose a dressing problem but drapes can be held back against the sloping ceiling or wall with fine rods or corbels that are fixed to the wall. In the case of a large Velux window, a shade can be fitted to the top of the actual frame and fixed to a pair of clip retainers at the bottom. Or a solid panel can be made to fit inside the frame and clipped into place.

There are other types of windows where the practical aspect of hanging a window dressing is worth thinking about. For example, the best window dressing for a site above a kitchen sink or bathroom handbasin may be recessed or on the window itself. In this case, a shade may be better than a pair of drapes that will hang out over the edge of the windowsill and be in danger of getting splashed or stained by sink or basin activity. Or you may want to consider a simple acetate glass covering to avoid any kind of dressing.

Window dressings

When planning your window dressings, you should also consider the style of the whole room and the rest of the decoration. Ornate drapes will look out of place in a room where everything else is plain or minimal, and solid white or cream drapes may make the windows look bare and underdressed in a room

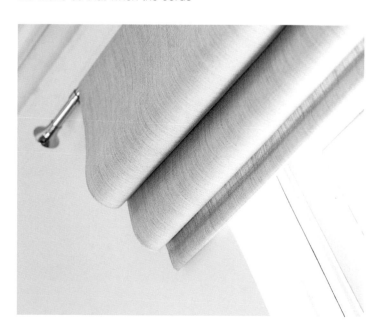

Right: *A decorative voile can soften the angular lines of a Venetian blind.*

Basic guidelines for drapes

If you are going to make drapes yourself or instruct someone to make them for you, you will need to understand the basic guidelines. If you have already decided on a material, the weight and type of the particular fabric may influence the style of heading you choose. You will also have to decide whether you want the drapes to be lined or not, and if they will be better hung on a track or a rod.

As a guideline, each drape should be one-and-a-half times the width of the window. You should also allow 3½ in. for the hems, top and bottom, and 1½ in. for side seams. With ornate headings that involve a lot of pleats or tucks, the amount of fabric required will be greater.

are pulled, the shades folds back neatly into concertina-like pleats. Ruched festoon-style shades make an even more ornate statement. Venetian blinds are also popular and can be used not only to screen windows but also as retractable room dividers. There are many materials to choose from when ordering Venetian blinds, including wood, metallic finishes, and vivid colors.

Although voiles are most commonly white or off-white, it can also be interesting to have colored or ombré-effect ones. Many contemporary window dressings feature voiles and shades that have cut decoration. This allows a glimpse of outside and means that interesting shadows and patterns are formed as the light passes through.

With simple shades, it is possible to give the window frame a little more dressing by adding a soft swathe or swag of fabric

draped around a curtain rod or simply pinned with small tacks to the upper edges of the window frame. In France, Belgium, and other parts of Europe, half-curtains are a popular way of restricting the view while still allowing light to shine through the upper levels of the window.

Shutters

Shutters are particularly popular in the United States, Australia, and southern Europe. In warmer climates, it is most common to have external shutters—these are used to reduce the access of sun and heat into the house and are also a security measure.

Internal shutters tend to be finer. In the classic style, they are generally paneled and fold back into recesses on either side of the window. Louvered shutters are also popular. These can be made to fit almost any window and divided into sections so that you can open them from side to side and up and down.

Drapes

By far the most common window dressing are traditional drapes. No-sew versions are currently fashionable because they are so easy to hang and change—they are simply secured in place by clipping them to hooks or eyelets. Ready-made drapes come in standard sizes and widths that fit the majority of commercially produced window frames.

Linings Lining drapes contributes to a more professional finish and give extra weight and density, which makes them hang well. There are several different types of lining—among them is the standard white or off-white cotton, which is perfect for lining lightweight cotton. Insulation linings are thicker, and suitable only for medium- to heavyweight drapes. Blackout drapes are useful for children's bedrooms and those who require total darkness to sleep.

There are also those who prefer colored linings rather than the traditional white or cream. A colored lining can be arranged so that it curls around over the inner side of the drape when pulled back.

Headings The traditional gathered heading produces neat, narrow pleats and is best suited to a window where a valance is going to be used so that the top of the drapes can be concealed.

Pleated headings come in a variety of styles—from pencil pleats, which are evenly spaced, to triple pleats in groups of three.

Simple, contemporary headings include the turnover top, where an extra 4 in. is stitched down to form a deep envelope or tube but leaving the ends open.

Tie-tops are also popular in modern homes. Pairs of equal-length ties are stitched to the top edge of the drapes and then tied to the curtain rod.

Tab headings are now popular in ready-made curtains, but are simple to make yourself. This type of heading can only be used with a straightforward rod support. To calculate the number of tabs you need, you should allow for one every 4 in. along the finished width of the drape. You will also need to place one at the beginning and end of the material.

Valances, tiebacks, and other dressings To complete a formal or traditional window dressing, it is customary to add valances. These can also help to reduce the height of a tall window as well as give a more decorative appearance to the drapes.

Valances can be made in the same material as the main drapes, in a contrasting fabric, or in a matching solid color selected from the pattern or color of the curtain. Valances are usually rigid—they can be mounted on a thin sheet of wood or made with a self-adhesive backing or stiffener. They are applied to the window with a box or bracket method that lifts the valance free of the bunched fabric

of the drapes when drawn back. The edges can be left plain or decorated with fringe or braid, or cut to form scalloped or crenellated edges. Soft valances are generally padded to give them body and to help them stand raised in front of the drapes.

Lambrequins are another option but work better with shades and small drapes. Lambrequins are fixed valances that follow the frame of the window. They sometimes extend down to the sill and are a useful way of adding something extra to a window where only a shade is practical. Lambrequins are made on a backing of thin wood or a self-adhesive, plastic-coated sheet that can be stuck directly onto the fabric.

Another type of window dressing involves arranging the generous pleats of the drapes themselves—this can be done with tiebacks and corbels. Tiebacks are used to scoop the edges of the drapes back and

create a curved frame around the window. The top edges of the drapes remain drawn together, edge to edge, or slightly parted.

Tiebacks are usually crescent-moon shapes and can be made of the same material as the drapes or in a color picked from the pattern. The fabric of the tieback is stiffened with an adhesive or grosgrain-style backing and a loop is sewn at each end. These loops, usually small metal circles, are then slipped over a hook that is secured to the wall behind the far edge of the drapes. Other types of tiebacks include twisted silk cord and tassels, braided rope or hessian, and needlepoint tapestry.

Corbels create the same effect as a tieback but are rigid arms that are fixed to the wall. A corbel can be as simple as a wooden knob or a more decorative design. The drape is scooped up and placed behind the corbel, which keeps it neatly in place.

Attaching lining and hanging drapes

Once you have selected your lining, you can attach it fixed or loose. Fixed lining is sewn inside the drapes and held in place by being stitched into the hems at the top, bottom, and sides of the drapes. A loose lining is separately hemmed all the way around and then just the top edge is joined to the drapes so that the lining hangs loose inside them rather than being part of them.

When calculating the length of the rod or track to be attached above the window, allow space at each end for the drapes to be pulled back beyond the edge of the window. Heavy fabrics or drapes that are lined will need more space because they are bulkier when pulled back.

Left: *This highly decorative carved wood valance would work well in a period setting.*

Far left: *Corbels complement fabrics that hang well when scooped over and around them, like this sheer fabric.*

window dressing techniques

Before you think about how to decorate your windows, take time to repair any damage, particularly if you have original period windows, which you will need to maintain in order to prolong their life. The window dressing style that you choose will depend on the effect that you wish to achieve and the degree of privacy that you require. Make sure that you opt for a dressing that works well with the decoration of the rest of your room.

Stripping and finishing windows

Windows need to be carefully maintained to keep them looking good. It is traditional to paint window frames and casings in the same paint color. White or off-white colors are most popular and give rooms a clean, simple look. You could opt for a more dramatic look and follow the example of earlier periods when woodwork was often painted a darker color than the walls. If you are going to put all the time and effort into fully stripping your windows, you may decide you like the look of the bare wood and opt for a clear, protective finish.

Wood windows

Wood windows are traditionally found in Georgian, Victorian, and Edwardian houses. The most common types of wood window are sash windows, which operate on a cord-and-pulley system contained within the frame, and casement windows, which are hinged. Sash windows need their cords replacing periodically to keep them running smoothly—this is a job best completed by a carpenter. All types of wood window are prone to rotting if they are not properly maintained.

Metal-framed windows

These types of window are most commonly found in houses built in the 1920s through to the 1950s. Metal frames are susceptible to rust, which will attack areas of exposed metal if the painted surface is damaged. Before repainting, any patches of rust should be removed with a rust inhibitor/remover. A chemical stripper in gel or paste form is the best way of removing a build-up of paint. Do not attempt to use a heat gun on a metal window frame because the metal will conduct the heat from the gun and shatter the glass. It is important to use a metal primer that will ward off rust under the paintwork.

Vinyl windows

These windows are most commonly found in new homes or when double-glazed units are installed in older houses. They are made from tough plastic, usually in white or "wood" effect, and need very little maintenance. However, they can ruin the look of period houses so think about this before installing them. Vinyl frames can also discolor with time and begin to look shabby— special paint is available for this. Vinyl windows can be prone to mildew, so make sure that you clean the frames regularly with mild detergent.

Stripping with chemical stripper

If you plan to leave your windows with a translucent finish, it is best to strip them using a method that will not harm the surface of the wood. Opt for a chemical stripper in a gel or a paste form. Bear in mind that this method is labor-intensive and may require several applications of stripper before you finish off with steel wool and fine-grit sandpaper.

Tools and materials

Heavy-duty rubber gloves

Putty knife

Chemical stripper

Shaped paint scraper

Fine-grade steel wool

1 Wearing rubber gloves, use a putty knife to apply a thick layer of the stripper onto the window frame. Leave it in place for the manufacturer's recommended time.

Using a putty knife, apply a generous coat of chemical stripper.

2 Carefully remove a small area of stripper with the paint scraper to check if the paint has been removed. Reapply if necessary. Remove any stubborn areas of paint with fine-grade steel wool dipped in liquid stripper, or with a metal cabinet scraper.

Remove the stripper from the surface using a shaped paint scraper.

Stripping with a heat gun

Heat guns are another effective way of stripping wood frames. However, care must be taken not to singe the wood by directing the flame at one area for too long. When working on the glazing beads, it is essential to use a special metal attachment that deflects heat away from the glass.

Tools and materials

Glass shield

Heat gun

Shaped paint scraper

Fine-grit flexible sandpaper

Cloth and mineral spirits

1 Fit the glass shield to the heat gun and hold it up to the window frame at a 45° angle so that paint does not drip back into the heat gun.

Hold the gun at a 45° angle to stop the paint from dripping back on it.

2 When the paintwork starts to blister and bubble, remove with a paint scraper, or the integral scraper if your heat gun has one. Continue until all the paintwork is removed. Any remaining slivers of paint can be removed with a sharp cabinet scraper. Pull the scraper down across the grain, holding it at a 30–45° angle. Sand with fine-grit sandpaper, then wipe with a cloth dipped in mineral spirits before refinishing the windows as desired.

Remove the stripper from the surface using a shaped paint scraper.

Stripping with an electric sander

Sanding is a good option if you want to "key" a previously painted surface ready for a new coat of paint. There is a wide range of electric sanders available. Some come with shaped attachments to fit different profiles of molding. Sanding back to bare wood with an electric sander will remove most of the surface patina of the wood. Hand-sanding is a gentler method, although not recommended if you have a heavy paint build-up.

Tools and materials

Electric multisander with shaped attachments

Sandpaper in assorted grits from coarse to extra fine

1 Sand any flat surfaces with the main sander attachment, starting with the coarsest sandpaper to remove a build-up of paint. Work your way through the grits of paper, finishing with extra fine.

2 Fit the sander attachment to suit your window's molding and work your way through the grits of sandpaper.

Fit the sander attachment and then sand the molding.

Finishing windows

If you are painting windows, choose a fine day so that you can leave them open while they dry. Always begin with the parts that will meet the frame so that they dry first. Any accidental drips of paint that end up on the glass can be removed when dry with the blade of a craft knife. Use a good-quality paintbrush with bristles that come to a point—this will help you reach awkward corners.

Tools and materials

Window guard or low-tack masking tape

Small paintbrush

Gloss or satinwood paint

1 Mask the windows with low-tack masking tape, allowing a fraction of an inch of glass to remain visible. When painting, you should paint over this area of glass because it will help to form an airtight seal between the glass and the window frame. Make sure that you pull the masking tape away before the paint dries completely or you will pull off the paint.

Tape around the window edge before painting the frame.

2 Alternately, you could use a plastic window guard that you simply hold up against the frame while you paint it.

Hold a window guard up against the frame and then paint the frame.

Decorative techniques for windows

The most common ways of dressing windows are with drapes or shades. In order to buy them to fit correctly, you will have to take accurate measurements of your windows. It is also important to choose the correct fittings for your type and shape of window.

Measuring for and hanging window shades

Some windows are recessed, which means they are set back into the wall and have a sill or ledge. This recess is often called the "reveal." With this type of window, it is usual to fit a shade within the reveal, which makes accurate measuring crucial. Other window frames are level with the wall, meaning that shades are fitted onto the frame or on the surrounding wall. In this case, accurate measuring is not as crucial. Shades are often sold with brackets that give you the option of top-fixing, side-fixing, or face-fixing. Shades over 3 ft. wide may have a central support bracket as well as end brackets. Top-fixing means drilling into the reveal above the window, side-fixing means drilling into the side of the reveal, and face-fixing is fixing directly to the frame or to the wall. Ready-made shades include those with roller mechanisms, Venetian blinds, and Roman blinds. Roller-style shades can be cut to size but most others cannot. If your window is not a standard size, you can order a shade for a perfect fit.

Tools and materials

Tape measure

Shade and brackets

Pencil

Screws

Drill and suitable bit

Plastic screw anchors

Level

1 Measure the window within the reveal and note down the dimensions. Buy a shade to fit or cut one to size. Hold the brackets in place and mark screw positions with a pencil, making sure they are level. Fit a suitable-sized masonry bit and drill holes, insert

Screw the brackets into the surface of the frame using a masonry drill bit.

plastic screw anchors, and screw the brackets in place.

2 Slot the shade into position, and if outside the reveal, check it is level.

Slot the shade into position within the brackets.

Measuring for and hanging drapes

There are drapes available to suit most interior styles, from elaborate swags to simple tab-topped panels. Voile or cheesecloth drapes let light through while maintaining privacy, and drapes in heavier materials such as velvets and damasks block out light and act as efficient draft excluders. More expensive drapes tend to be lined, which improves the way they hang. The most sumptuous curtains are "interlined," meaning that they have a thick, fleece-like material sandwiched between the lining and the fabric to give them extra fullness. As the area above the window can often be difficult to drill, it is a good idea to fit a wood batten to which any window treatment can be attached.

Drapes can be various lengths—just above the windowsill, just below the sill, or floor length. It is a good idea to buy or make drapes slightly too long to allow for any shrinkage during washing. When measuring a window for drapes, begin the measurement at the curtain rod or track from which they will eventually hang.

Curtain rods

Curtain rods are available in wood or metal and in a multitude of finishes. They are often used in conjunction with curtain rings that fit onto the rod. The hooks on the heading at the top of the drapes are then suspended from a small metal loop at the bottom of the ring. Curtain rods are held on brackets that are attached to the wall or a wood batten about 6 in. above the window. Special rods with flexible or angled sections are available to fit angular bay windows. Generally, drapes hung from curtain rods are simply drawn by hand, although some more expensive tracks are "corded"—opened and closed with a cord system.

Attaching a curtain rod with concealed brackets

Tools and materials

Tape measure

Level

Curtain rod

Fixing plates and brackets

Drill and suitable bit

Screws and plastic screw anchors

Screwdriver

Curtain rings

1 Use a tape measure and level to mark the positions of the brackets in pencil. The brackets should be at equidistant from the corners of the window. Rods over

Use a screwdriver to attach the plates securely in place.

6½ ft. long should also have a central support bracket. Use a masonry bit to drill the holes, then insert plastic screw anchors. Screw fixing plates in position.

2 Slot the bracket over the fixing plate, then tighten the screw that anchors it in place.

Push the bracket in place over the fixing plate.

3 Fit the pole in position with the curtain rings in place. Remember to leave a ring on the bracket side of the rod to hold the drapes in position. Tighten the small screw on the underside of the bracket that holds the rod in position.

Secure the bracket and curtain rod with a screw.

Curtain tracks

Curtain tracks are an alternative to rods and are available in plastic or heavy-duty metal. Tracks are suitable for awkward round bay windows. Curtain tracks have hooks that are looped through the heading tape on the drapes and slide along the tracks. Corded tracks that work on a pulley

system are available. Most tracks simply slot onto brackets screwed into the wall or onto a batten.

Tools and materials

Tape measure, level, and pencil

Drill and suitable bit

Brackets

Screws and plastic screw anchors

Screwdriver

Hacksaw

Curtain track

Curtain hooks

1 Use a tape measure, level, and pencil to mark the position of the brackets at equal intervals. Drill, plug, and screw into place.

Screw the wall brackets to the wall at equal intervals.

2 If necessary, use a hacksaw to cut the track to the correct length, then fix the end stop in place by tightening the small screw.

After cutting the track to length, fix the end stop in place.

3 Finally, slot the track into place on the brackets, following manufacturer's instructions.

Measuring drape lengths

Decide on the length of the drapes: either to the floor, windowsill, or above a radiator. (It is a good idea to buy or make drapes slightly too long to allow for any shrinkage during washing.)

For sill- and radiator-length drapes, measure from the track or ring mark to ¼ in. above the sill or heater and add a hem allowance. For floor length drapes, measure to ½ in. above the ground, to allow for carpet clearance, and add a hem allowance. For floor-length drapes that have a generous overflow and spread over the carpet or floor, measure to the floor and add 2–4 in. plus the hem allowance.

4 To hang the drapes, simply hook the metal or plastic curtain hook over the sliding runners.

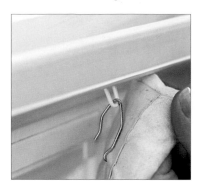

Slot the curtain hooks onto the integral sliding runners.

Attaching tension wire

This is a recent invention that gives lightweight drapes a modern look. Steel wire is stretched on a tension system between walls or on brackets. The drapes are held on small rings with pincer-style clips that grip the fabric and slide along the wire.

Tools and materials

Tension wire kit with wall brackets and cover pieces

Wire cutters

Drill and suitable bit

Screwdriver

Screws and plastic screw anchors

Curtain rings and pincer clips

1 Cut the tension wire to length, thread the wire through the cover pieces, and use the tool provided to attach the end pieces.

Once you have cut the tension wire to length, attach the end pieces.

2 Drill, plug, and screw the two wall brackets in place on opposite walls.

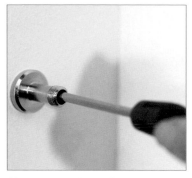

Use a screwdriver to fix the wall brackets in place on opposite walls.

3 Screw the cover piece in place over one wall bracket. Feed the curtain rings onto the wire and then fix the other end to the opposite wall. (If you are using tab-top curtains, thread them onto the wire first.) Pull the wire tight.

Fix the torpedo-shaped cover pieces over the top of the wall brackets.

4 Use the pincer clips attached to the rings to secure your panel of fabric in place.

Attach the fabric to the rings using the pincer clips.

Alternative window treatments

Drapes and shades are not the only methods that you can use to screen or dress your windows—the only limit is your imagination. New, exciting materials to treat glass are available that allow you to create your own etched or stained-glass effects. If you prefer something more substantial, shutters are a good solution and give your windows additional security.

Shutters

Although most traditional shutters are made from wood, they can also be made from a variety of other materials, including plexiglass, particle board, and metal.

Tools and materials

Tape measure

Shutters

Screwdriver

Hinges

Awl

Level

1 Measure your window carefully and order the correct size shutters—the supplier will advise on the best way of attaching them to your window. Screw in hinges at equidistant positions from the top and the bottom of the shutters.

Fix hinges halfway between the top and bottom of the shutter.

2 Use an awl to make pilot holes, then screw the hinges in place at the top and bottom of the window.

Screw the hinges to the side of the window.

3 Fit battens to the sides of the windows if required so that the shutters do not damage the wall when opened. Check with a level to ensure that they are straight.

Frosted window panel

Frosted windows can give bathrooms a more contemporary look than old-fashioned textured glass. Using spray-on frosting gives a temporary finish that will withstand cleaning but can be removed with a sharp blade if you feel like a change. If you want a more permanent type of frosting, you can commission a personalized sandblasted design from a glass supplier or get a sign-writing company to make a design on frosted plastic film.

Temporary frosted finish

Tools and materials
Glass cleaner
Cloth
Glass etch spray

Clean the window thoroughly with glass cleaner to remove grease and grime. Spray the glass etch evenly all over the window. Use two thin coats rather than one heavy coat to avoid runs.

Spray glass etch onto the window, ensuring an even coverage.

Semipermanent frosted finish

Tools and materials
Frosted plastic film
Straightedge
Sharp craft knife
Cloth
Squeegee

1 Cut the frosted film to size with a straightedge and craft knife. Dampen the window.

Use a damp cloth to wet the entire surface of the window.

2 Peel off a corner of the backing and position the frosted film in position in one corner of the window. Gently peel away the remainder of the backing.

3 Use a good-quality squeegee to smooth the film gently into place—the water will act as a lubricant. Use the squeegee to force all air bubbles away to the sides of the film, leaving it smooth and wrinkle-free and taking care not to damage it.

Use a squeegee to remove air bubbles from beneath the film.

Below: Shutters are not only an attractive window dressing, they can also increase security.

Fires and fireplaces

Fireplaces were once the sole source of heat in a room. Now they are mainly decorative because central or underfloor heating provide warmth. There are ornate period fireplaces as well as modern versions using gas flames and ceramic shapes to create the effect of a real fire.

Below: The jamb (the upright part of a fireplace) can be engraved to match other architectural features in the room, such as a chair rail or coving.

Below right: An open fire makes a dramatic feature in a contemporary "hole-in-the-wall" fireplace.

Types of fireplaces

Although there have been many innovations in the world of heating, with hot-air and central heating and the revival of underfloor heating, there is something special about the glow of an open fire that still holds universal appeal. The flicker and appearance of the flames may still look to us as they did to prehistoric people, but there have been many developments in how the fire is fueled and laid. Coal and wood are traditional fuels, whereas in most cities gas and electricity now supply the power. The modern "fake" fire is often chosen over the traditional variety because it provides all the color, glow, flicker, and warmth without the soot, ashes, and effort of having to light the fire and refuel it.

Early log fires consisted of chunks of wood laid on an earthen hearth, but sometimes the wood was raised up from the floor by resting it on andirons. This allowed the air to circulate through the wood. Later, andirons were replaced with a basket and then a grate. The latter comes with a façade that forms a panel inside the surround. Fire baskets are now placed on a noncombustible base made of marble, stone, or granite.

Structure of a fireplace

Fireplaces usually come in two main sections: the surround and the jambs. The surround is made from stone such as limestone and marble or wood such as pine. The jambs are the two upright sides of the fireplace, which often have foot blocks at the base. The jambs line up on either side of the opening to support the shelf that runs across the top.

The details found on large fireplaces include a mantel, a fire front, and the grate (the cast-iron

Left: *This elaborate carved fireplace is a focal point of this dining room.*

Below: *When choosing a fireplace, make sure that it will suit the decor of the rest of your room. This impressive example would look good in a large period-style room, but might look out of place in a small, minimalist setting.*

part), which holds the coal or wood. The hearth is the area inset into the floorboards and is often made of stone, marble, or tiles that protect the flooring from falling coals. In bedrooms you usually find smaller fireplaces, cast in one piece from molten iron and called "registers."

In recent years, the fireplace has been reinvented and a basic "hole-in-the-wall" look is becoming popular.

Fireplace style

Fireplaces vary widely in style, from the roughly hewn wood beam with a brick or stone interior in a rustic home or farmhouse to ornately carved marble in a period house. Surrounds can be simple with little detailing or highly ornate with swags, cameos, mythical scenes, recesses, foliage, and urns carved into the jambs and shelf. The most important thing when buying a fireplace is to choose a style, size, and shape that sits comfortably within the

room in which it is to be positioned. If the room is small, then opt for a neat, simple design that will be a focal point but not overwhelm the space. If the room is large with period features, then try to match the decoration of the fire surround to the other features in the room and choose a material that is also in keeping.

The classic style of fireplace with jambs, columns, and pilasters is still popular and found in many homes today. The salvaged originals command high prices and even modern reproductions are far from cheap. Marble fire surrounds are among the most expensive, but a cheaper pine or more inexpensive carved wood surround can be painted to look like marble. Pine can also be stained and waxed in order to give it the appearance of a richer wood such as mahogany.

Some modern fires use geometric ceramic shapes called "geologs" that sit in a stainless-steel or black geometric grate.

Gas flames flicker around the "geologs," which come in matte black, orange, blue, green, and yellow. Or you can choose to have flames emerging from a hearth of pebbles.

Restoring or replacing your old fireplace

Putting a new fireplace into your home has its own set of complications, whereas reviving one that has been boxed in or painted over by a previous owner provides a different agenda. If an old fireplace has been boxed in, you may be lucky and find that it is in good condition and needs nothing more than a thorough clean. However, if it has been painted over, it will require some work to restore it.

First of all, you need to establish what sort of material the fireplace is made from. In an area near the wall on the base of the footblock, take a sharp knife and scratch away the upper layers until you come to the original surface.

Once you have established what it is made from, you should be able to find a commercial paint stripper or peeler that will remove the layers of paint (see pages 90–1 for more details on how to do this).

Modern gas fires can be run using main or bottled gas and will have automatic ignition, a flame failure device, and an oxygen depletion sensor.

Looking after your fire

With real coal and log fires, the chimneys should be regularly swept by a professional who works to an authorized code of practice—otherwise soot will build up and may lead to a chimney fire. Smoky fires can be caused by the material you burn, such as damp logs, or perhaps through poor ventilation. Another reason can be the incorrect ratio of distances between the hearth, the chimney opening, and the chimney top. This latter problem can only be remedied by a professional, who may raise the hearth, add extra height to the chimney, or put a baffle or shield on the front of the hearth.

Dressing your fireplace

There are a number of dressings and accessories associated with the fireplace, including the fender. This is a metal frame that prevents coals that spill out of the fire from falling onto the carpet. In Victorian times, the small border fender grew into a surround with leather padded ends that doubled as a stool. Andirons may no longer be required for their original purpose of supporting burning logs off the earth floor, but they can be a decorative feature and may now be used to prop up a fire poker, tongs, and shovel.

Even when the fireplace is not being used, you can employ the mantelshelf as a focal point and decorate it accordingly. In the summer months, the "black hole" can be camouflaged with a screen, decorative tray, or panel. Or place a wicker basket of logs in front or an arrangement of branches or wild grasses. You could also make a decorative feature of the space by placing church candles or a display of fossils and pebbles in it, or in an unused grate, by storing books or magazines in it.

Left: *Marble is a particularly attractive material to use for fireplaces.*

Fireplace techniques

Restoring an existing fireplace or installing a new one will require the services of a professional if you want it to function as a fire. However, there is nothing to prevent you from preparing a reclaimed fireplace ready for its installation. Make sure that the grate you have chosen will fit your chimney breast. If there is no breast, then you could always construct a simple surround yourself that will be used for show purposes only.

Restoring fireplaces

Original fireplaces that have been overpainted for many years lose the sharpness of their details. If you have a chimney breast that is missing a fireplace, then it is often cheaper to buy an unrestored one from an architectural salvage company rather than installing a reproduction. In either situation, it is well worth spending the time and effort to strip the surround and restore it carefully in a sympathetic manner.

Before starting the restoration, identify the material from which the fire surround is made. The most common materials are wood, cast iron, marble, stone, and brick while in houses built in the 1920s and 1930s decorative fireplaces were stepped tiled designs, often holding electric fires. Each material needs to be treated differently during restoration. Wood surrounds can be stripped using chemical paint stripper in a gel or paste form. Stripping with a heat gun is less advisable because of the danger of singeing. Cast iron can be stripped using a heat gun but beware of scraping the surface, which is prone to scratching—the best option is to use a paste stripper, which peels off gently.

Marble, stone, and brick are porous materials that are therefore prone to staining, so check the recommendations of any chemical stripper before you use it on your fireplace.

Wood surrounds

Tools and materials

Liquid or gel chemical paint stripper
Heavy-duty rubber gloves
Paint scraper
Fine-grade steel wool
Cloth and mineral spirits
Wax polish and soft cloth, or primer, waterproof sandpaper, and paint

1 Apply the paint stripper according to manufacturer's instructions. Use a paint scraper to push the stripper into any crevices. Leave for the recommended time, at which point the paint will bubble.

Use a paint scraper to push the stripper into the crevices.

2 Remove the paint carefully with the paint scraper and reapply stripper if necessary. Remove any stubborn traces of paint using liquid stripper dipped in fine-grade steel wool. Neutralize the wood surface by wiping with a cloth moistened with mineral spirits.

Use the paint scraper to take off the stripper and paint layers.

3 If you want to achieve a natural finish, sand the surface lightly with fine-grit sandpaper and then simply apply a neutral wax polish with fine-grade steel wool. Allow this to dry, then polish with a soft cloth.

Apply a neutral wax polish, and once this is dry, polish with a soft cloth.

4 If you prefer a painted instead of a wood finish, apply a quick-drying primer/basecoat and gently sand with waterproof sandpaper. Finish with a paint of your choice. Apply two coats and sand with waterproof sandpaper between coats.

Cast-iron registers and grates

Tools and materials

Liquid or gel chemical
paint stripper

Old paintbrush

Heavy-duty rubber gloves

Paint scraper

Fine-grade steel wool

Stiff wire brush

Rust-inhibiting solution

Grate polish

Soft cloths

1 Apply the paint stripper thickly,
following manufacturer's
instructions and using an old
paintbrush to work it well into
any crevices.

*Apply the paint stripper to your
fireplace using an old paintbrush.*

2 Wait for the recommended
time to elapse. When the paint
begins to blister and bubble,
remove the stripper and old paint
carefully with a paint scraper,
taking care not to gouge or
scratch the surface.

*Use a paint scraper to take off the
layers of stripper and paint.*

3 Reapply where necessary—
remove any stubborn paint
residue with fine-grade steel
wool dipped in liquid stripper.

*If there are some stubborn areas,
use steel wool and liquid stripper.*

4 Before refinishing the fireplace,
remove any rust by brushing away
away any flaky rust and corrosion
with a stiff wire brush.

*Remove any rust and corrosion
with a wire brush.*

5 Paint on a rust-inhibiting
solution that also inhibits new rust
from forming. Leave for the
recommended time, then clean
with fine-grade steel wool.

*Use the old paintbrush to apply a
rust-inhibiting solution.*

6 To retain a cast-iron finish,
apply black grate polish with
a brush or cloth.

*Apply black grate polish with a
soft cloth.*

7 When the polish is completely
dry, use a clean, soft cloth to buff
to a graphite sheen.

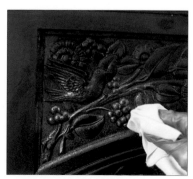

*When the polish is dry, polish to a
graphite sheen with a soft cloth.*

Above: *A cast-iron
fireplace restored to
its former beauty is a
magnificent addition
to any room.*

Painted finish

For a painted finish on
a cast-iron grate, first apply
a rust-inhibiting basecoat/
primer that is formulated for
ferrous metals and allow
to dry. Apply two coats of
your chosen paint color.

Changing fireplaces

If you wish to restore a working fireplace to a chimney breast that has been boarded up or is inactive, then it is important to get professional advice. You will need to have the flue checked for obstacles and make sure that the fireproof lining is intact. A chimney that has been unused for several years will almost certainly need to be swept. A simple test to see if a chimney is "drawing" properly (removing smoke) is to hold a lit spill in the opening—the flame should be noticeably drawn upward. If the flame sputters or dies completely, it clearly indicates a lack of oxygen, often caused by blockages farther up the chimney.

Once your chimney and flue are in working order, you can then consider the type of fireplace you wish to install. A gas fire is a popular choice for many people. Many cities also have a smoke ban, meaning the only coal that can be burned on an open fire is an expensive smokeless variety. However, real fires are appealing if you live in an area without a smoke ban— nothing can beat its evocative smell and sound.

Period fireplaces are not to everyone's taste—heavily tiled, dark marble, and overly ornate fireplaces can dominate a room and make it difficult to create a contemporary look. However, many people consider removing a period fireplace as sacrilege, and before taking this drastic step, you should consider carefully how it could affect the value of your home. Period features are a highly sought-after selling point, and although it may not appeal to you, your period fireplace could be appreciated by the next owners. If you find a fireplace too overpowering to live with, consider less drastic ways of disguising it.

Painting over a tiled fireplace

Victorian and Edwardian fireplaces often have tiled "slips" set into a cast-iron insert. If the colors of these tiles are not to your taste, they can be painted over in a more neutral shade. 1920s- and 1930s-style fireplaces, which are often tiled in murky colors, can be painted in the same way to make them less obtrusive.

Tools and materials

Tile cleaner/detergent and cloth

Tile primer

Special tile paint or gloss or satinwood paint

Two small foam rollers and trays

Low-tack masking tape

Waterproof sandpaper

1 Clean the tiles thoroughly to remove any traces of dirt or grease. Mask off the tiles that are to be painted.

2 Apply the tile primer sparingly to avoid drips using a foam roller. Allow to dry. If the pattern or color has not been covered, apply a second coat.

3 Sand lightly with waterproof sandpaper. Apply the top coat using a foam roller and allow to dry. Sand again lightly before applying a second coat.

Making a simple particle-board surround

This plain surround will not dominate a room but provides a focal point to display a few carefully chosen items. It can be used to dress up a bare chimney breast where there is no working fireplace, or be made to fit over an existing fireplace that you do not like. This type of surround is purely decorative and should not be used in conjunction with a working fire.

Tools and materials

Paper, pencil, and straightedge

Sheets of ¾-in. thick particle board

Several lengths of square, planed wood

Electric jigsaw and clamps

Electric screwdriver with countersink bit

Screws with countersink heads

Mirror plates

Plastic screw anchors

Masonry drill bit

Wood putty

Primer and paint

Paintbrush or roller and tray

1 Sketch out a plan for your fireplace, taking into account any existing fireplace you wish to cover. The dimensions will vary according to the width of your chimney breast. If there is no existing fireplace, the new version should sit comfortably in the available space, allowing about 1 ft. of space on each side. Draw out the components of the new fireplace on the sheets of particle board. You will need a front piece, two side pieces, three inside pieces, and a top piece cut from ¾-in. thick particle board. Use a straightedge clamped to the particle board to make accurate cuts. Alternately, ask your local wood supplier to cut the pieces for you. Cut lengths of wood to frame the opening and outside of the fireplace.

Glue the frames to the fireplace and clamp in place.

2 Apply wood glue and clamp the wood frames to the outside and inside of the front piece of the fireplace.

3 Drill pilot holes and use a countersink bit to screw the pieces together. Screw the outside and inside panels in place in the same way.

Screw the panels in place using a screwdriver.

4 Fill all the screwholes with wood putty, allow to dry, then sand until smooth.

Fill all the screw holes that you have made with wood putty.

5 Prime and then paint in a color of your choice using a paintbrush or roller. Allow it to dry completely. Place the new fireplace on a hearth that has been cut from a piece of thick particle board, then attach the fireplace surround to the wall using mirror plates screwed to the inside of the fireplace. Once the fireplace is securely fixed in place on the wall, touch up any areas that need additional paint.

Prime and paint the fireplace in a color of your choice.

Installing a salvaged fireplace

When shopping for a salvaged fireplace, take the dimensions of the existing hole with you so that you can be sure the new fireplace will fit. Try to choose a style appropriate to the age of house that you live in if you want it to look original. Consult period-style books for advice on what to look for (if you have neighbors living in houses built at the same time who have original fireplaces, take photographs for reference). If you want the fireplace to be a working one, consult a builder or gas fitter before purchasing a fireplace. Make sure that a salvaged fireplace is complete—it can be difficult finding items such as grates to fit your particular fireplace if they are missing when you buy it. Decide on a material for the hearth, which should be sympathetic to your chosen surround. If you are choosing a wood surround, your supplier should be able to recommend a cast-iron insert to fit.

Tools and materials

Brick or blunt chisel and mallet
Mortar
Electric drill with masonry bit
Plastic screw anchors and screws
Screwdriver
One-coat plaster
Plasterer's trowel
Level
Wood batten
Sandpaper
Latex paint and paintbrush

1 Remove the existing hearth material. If it is concrete, chip it out with a brick chisel and mallet, but if tiled, use a blunt chisel to lever them up. Mix up a dryish mortar and apply it to the hearth, using a piece of wood notched to the thickness of the new hearth material as a depth gauge.

2 Lay the new hearth material in place and tap down firmly with a rubber mallet, using a level for accuracy. Allow the mortar to harden. Mark the position of the new fireplace in the center of the chimney breast. Note the height of the fixing plates and use a brick chisel to remove some plaster from around this area. Make a hole with a masonry bit, fit a plastic screw anchor, and screw in place.

3 Use a plasterer's trowel to apply a one-coat plaster mix over the plates; allow it to harden slightly before leveling off with a dampened trowel. Sand and then paint.

Below: You can paint your fireplace or retain the original stone finish.

Architectural features

Many architectural features started life as purely practical fixtures—a casing around a window helped to hold it in place and reduce drafts, picture rails were used to hang pictures and protect the soft plaster walls, while chair rails would prevent furniture from chipping or cracking paintwork.

Ancient influences

It is said that the level of the chair and picture rails, as well as the cornice and baseboard, echoes the various levels and elements of a classic Greek or Roman column. This reference to classic style shows how many of the traditional elements of interior design are based on ancient logic, form, and scale.

Decorative molding

Molding has always played a fundamental role in the quality period house. On a practical level, it was usually applied to conceal the joint between the wall and ceiling, and on a decorative level it added relief and embellishment to plain areas.

There are various types of molding that are generally applied in three main areas. First, the coving or cornice that is positioned over the joint between the walls and ceiling. Second, the baseboard that runs between the wall and floor. Third, the casing that is found between the door surround and the wall.

As well as its practical purposes, molding was also used to add to the grandeur and status of a room. This can be clearly seen in the panelwork and ceilings in grand period homes and important civic buildings.

Baseboards

Although decorative molding is rarely found in modern homes, baseboards have survived the test of time because they are still practical. They not only provide a neat joint between wall and floor, but also protect the plaster and paintwork from knocks from feet and furniture. They can also be used to hide wires or even a small safe.

Above right: Well-positioned lighting may be used to highlight ornate molding.

Restoring or adding molding

To restore existing ornate plasterwork, it is best to employ the services of a professional. For smaller cracks and touching up, you may be able to do it yourself with a thick mix of spackle. If your molding suffers from years of overpainting, take the time to strip it back.

If you have a room without any molding features, then you can add simple detailing with coving.

Coving is a straightforward plaster curve that arcs between the wall and ceiling—simple and cheap versions of these are easily glued in place and then painted over. Ceiling roses and cornicing at the upper levels of a room are not subjected to close scrutiny, so cheap imitation products can work well. Fine wood bead can also be used to create paneling on doors and walls.

Chair and picture rails

In some classic or period-style homes, you will find that walls are divided and decorated with chair and picture rails. Originating in the 18th and 19th centuries, these rails had a practical purpose, too. The chair rail, which is roughly at hip height, protected the fragile wall finish of the time (which was made from horse hair, lath, and plaster) from being damaged by people or furniture banging or bumping against it.

These days, chair rails are often employed for purely cosmetic or decorative purposes—to divide a large expanse of wall or to create a two-tone or bi-colored scheme for a hall or staircase, for example. You can also create interest by using different textured wallpaper above and below the rail. A chair rail can easily be applied to a wall using both glue and screws.

The picture rail was also a functional feature in such homes, providing a hanging point for pictures. Today, pictures are hung from deep brass clamps that clip over the thickness of the rail, which is now often metal. Modern picture rails tend to stand above the level of the wall rather than being an integral part of it.

Staircases

In many period houses, the main staircase was often a show piece, with decorative carved wood or iron balusters (the vertical supports for the handrail).

In modern homes, the staircase is not just a means of getting from one level to another, it is a way of making the most of available light. Light from a skylight above can filter down through many levels if the staircase is of an open construction. As such, high-tension steel wire, like yacht rigging, and reinforced glass paneling is popular for the sides of staircases.

Restoration and decoration

If you are restoring or repairing an existing staircase, you may need to replace some of the balusters or change them completely. Wood is the most common and cheapest material used for these supports and it can be fashioned either into simple, four-sided pillars or more ornately carved and turned spindles. When it comes to decorating, the wood can be left plain, painted, or stained.

Iron is also a common feature of period houses—staircases used to be edged with ornate balustrades. Iron balustrades can be found at architectural salvage yards or new ones can be specially commissioned. The last baluster on a flight of stairs is usually a thicker post that is often decorated with a knob or carving.

Left: *Using different colors above and below a picture or chair rail will help you to break up a large expanse of wall.*

Below: *Staircases need not just be a practical element in the home—be bold and make a feature of them.*

Laying stair carpets

When decorating a staircase, safety must be foremost in your mind. Whichever floor covering you choose, it should be laid so that there is no overhang or surplus on the edge of the step. This is the surface that is most prone to wear because it receives the brunt of the weight and frequent rubbing from the soles of shoes. A loose carpet may cause someone to slip.

Architectural feature techniques

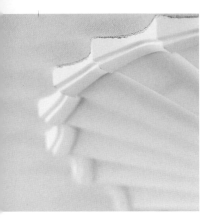

Many people are put off by the prospect of adding architectural features to a room because they think that this may entail major structural work. In fact, the opposite is true—it is relatively easy to install molding and wall paneling. Make sure that you opt for an architectural feature that is in keeping with your style of house. For example, while traditional wall paneling may look stunning in a period house, it may look out of place in a contemporary-style interior.

Decorative molding

Most decorative molding is installed using the same methods. In period houses, molding was simply nailed into wooden plugs that were fixed into the masonry. Recent advances in adhesives mean that nails can be replaced with adhesive applied with a caulk gun. Alternately, you can countersink small screws into the molding and then fill with wood putty for an invisible finish. The most important device to master is using a miter box, which allows you to cut perfect internal and external corners.

Putting up a chair rail

Tools and materials

Tape measure

Miter box

Handsaw

Caulk gun and adhesive

Nails and hammer

Drill with countersink wood and masonry bits (optional)

Screws with countersink heads and plastic screw anchors (optional)

Chalk line

Pencil

Wood molding

Pliers

Spackle

1 Measure the length required and cut the molding using a miter box and saw to achieve an internal or external corner.

Use a miter box and saw to cut the corners.

2 Use a level and tape measure to mark a horizontal line along the wall to indicate the position of the bottom of the molding. Chair rails are traditionally positioned about a third of the way up from the floor. Gently hammer small nails along the length of the line. For a more secure attachment, drill in place in the same was as baseboards (see opposite page) as well as using adhesive.

Tap a line of nails along the line marking the bottom of the molding.

3 Apply the adhesive with a caulk gun along the entire length of the wood molding.

Use a caulk gun to apply adhesive to the molding.

4 Press the wood molding firmly into position against the wall. The nails will support it and hold it firmly in place while it dries. Leave the molding until the adhesive is completely dry.

5 When the adhesive is dry, remove the nails from below the molding carefully using either a pair of pliers or the end of a claw hammer.

Remove the nails supporting the molding when the adhesive is dry.

6 Fill the holes that are left by the nails with quick-drying, ready-mixed spackle.

Putting up baseboards

Tools and materials

Tape measure

Mitre box and handsaw

Drill with countersink wood and masonry bits

Nails, screws, and plastic screw anchors

Caulk gun and adhesive

Wood putty

1 Measure and cut the boards as above. Predrill holes near the ends and the center of the boards.

Drill holes near the ends and center of the baseboards.

2 Use a nail to mark the corresponding positions on the wall.

With a nail, mark the corresponding positions on the wall.

3 Drill holes with a masonry bit and insert plastic screw anchors. Glue in the same way as a chair rail, but also screw firmly in place. Fill the screw holes with wood putty and sand before painting or staining with color.

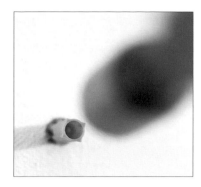

Insert a plastic screw anchor before screwing the baseboard in position.

Wall paneling

Wall paneling is a common period feature in older houses. It reached the height of popularity in Georgian times, when the main reception rooms of a house were often paneled up to chair-rail height. By Victorian times, paneling had become rarer, and when it did appear, it was made of softwood and then painted to mimic more expensive hardwoods.

Putting up tongue-and-groove paneling

This common wall paneling is composed of thin planks of wood that slot together with the tongue of one plank fitting into the groove of the next. It is an excellent way of covering up a less-than-perfect wall surface and is commonly used to update kitchens and bathrooms because it can be treated with a water-repellent varnish. It can be painted to suit any color scheme or given a clear finish that allows the grain to show through. There are various types of tongue-and-groove paneling—some incorporate a rounded bead between each plank. Most types of tongue-and-groove paneling can be attached vertically or horizontally, and it can be used on ceilings as well as walls.

It is worth buying good-quality tongue-and-groove paneling

because the cheaper, thinner varieties tend to warp and bow. It can be attached using a variety of methods, including "invisible" nailing into the tongue of the boards. Some varieties have special clips that hold each board in place. For quick results, you can also use adhesive to stick the boards directly onto the wall. Vertical tongue-and-groove paneling is usually finished off with a baseboard at the base and a molding on top.

Tools and materials

Level

Wood battens

Jigsaw

Tongue-and-groove paneling

Wood screws

Plastic screw anchors

Nail set

Long finish nails or panel adhesive

Hammer

Neutral-colored wood putty

Molding

1 Decide on the height of your tongue-and-groove paneling— it is available precut to chair-rail height—and cut it to size if necessary. Use a level to mark two lines on the wall, one toward the top and the other toward the bottom of where the paneling will attached. Cut lengths of wood battens to size, then drill, plug, and screw them in place along the marked lines.

Screw the battens to the wall, using a level to check they are straight.

2 If your room has external corners, use one as your starting point so that any cut boards will be hidden in the corner of the room. Start with the groove of the board lined up with the external corner. Use the hammer to knock the finish nails in place and a nail set to make sure that the heads of the nails are inserted below the surface of the wood. Fill over the top of the nails with a neutral-colored wood putty.

Use a nail set to push the head of the nails below the surface.

3 Continue along the wall and when you reach the corner, cut the tongue off the final board to ensure a good fit. To turn the corner, butt the groove of the next board against the previous board and nail in place.

4 To turn an external corner, cut the tongue of the first board and butt it up to the groove of the previous board to form a neat corner. Cover the corner with a piece of right-angled molding.

Use a right-angled molding to cover external corners.

5 When the cladding is complete cap with lengths of hockey stick or right-angled moulding mitred at the corners and held in place with panel adhesive or panel pins.

To finish the paneling, apply lengths of molding to the top.

Plaster molding

This term encompasses all the different types of decorative details in the home that are made from plaster and plaster composites, including coving, cornice, ceiling roses, corbels, pediments, and niches. They are commonly found in period houses. If you have damaged molding, it is possible to have it copied by specialty companies who will make a mold from a cast of the existing molding and reproduce it. This can be a costly process, but there is a wide range of standard mass-produced reproductions available.

Putting up plaster coving

This will help to soften the gap between wall and ceiling. There are lightweight varieties available made from a number of different materials. It is advisable to choose the most authentic-looking design for the style of your house—an ornate period-style coving will look out of place in a contemporary interior. If you do not feel confident about mitering corners, some manufacturers make internal and external corner pieces that fit snugly over the gap.

Tools and materials

Paint scraper

Straightedge

Level

Adhesive

Plaster coving

Putty knife

Small finish nails

Caulk

Caulk gun

1 Remove any loose or flaky areas of plaster or paint and use a straightedge and level to mark the position of the coving on the wall and ceiling to provide you with guidelines.

2 Mix up the adhesive following manufacturer's instructions and apply it onto the back of the coving using a putty knife.

3 Press the coving firmly into position on the wall and gently tap small nails above and below it to support it while the adhesive dries.

4 Remove the nails and fill the resulting holes. Use excess adhesive or flexible caulk applied with a caulk gun to fill any gaps between the coving and the wall/ceiling.

Putting up a ceiling rose

Ceiling roses were traditionally positioned above the pendant lights in period houses. When putting up or replacing a ceiling rose, it is important to identify the position of the joists to make a firm attachment. You can do this by lifting up the floorboards in the room above, or by using an awl to pierce the ceiling until you find one. There are also various electronic tools available that locate the presence of metal in walls or ceilings that may help you in this task. Make sure that if there is a working light in the position where you want to fit the ceiling rose that you turn off the main electricity supply and disconnect the light before you start drilling in the area. Seek the help of a qualified electrician if you are unsure of what you are doing.

Tools and materials

Ceiling rose
Soft pencil
Drill with countersink drill bits
Adhesive
Screws with countersink heads
Screwdriver
All-purpose white spackle

1 Hold the ceiling rose in position and draw around it using a soft pencil.

Hold the rose in place on the ceiling and draw around the shape.

2 Drill holes to accommodate the wiring for the light (if required) and also drill a hole through a flat area on each side of the rose.

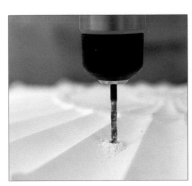

Drill a hole through a flat area on each side of the ceiling rose.

3 Mix the adhesive following the manufacturer's instructions and then press the rose firmly into position on the ceiling.

Mix up the adhesive and spread it onto the back of the rose.

4 Use two long countersink screws to support the rose. Screw them directly into the joist. Cover the screw with white spackle.

Use countersink screws to attach the rose securely in place.

Left: An elegant cornice such as this can add the finishing touch to your wall.

Living
rooms

Planning your living room

A living room is a relaxing space where family and friends meet but it is also a public room where the interior decoration should make a statement. As such, planning is essential—for example, furniture should be arranged in sociable groups but without obstacles blocking any pathways through the room.

Planning your space

Unless you are fortunate enough to have a den or private space where you alone can closet yourself away, the main focus for daytime relaxation in the home tends to be the living room. But the living room is a hybrid space, often a public venue where, at certain times, guests and friends are entertained. It is also a family room where group, as well as individual, rest and leisure time is spent.

Because the living room is a shared space, it is usually the focus of communal family gatherings and a place where a number of activities take place at the same time. Children may play games or watch television while adults read or listen to music.

As well as being adaptable for day-to-day family life, the living room should also be able to cope with the changes that are brought about between

Below: It important that the main pathway through the living space is free of clutter and obstacles so that a person entering can reach their destination easily.

being a night and daytime venue as well as a summer and winter location.

During the day, the room should be a bright and enjoyable place to be, lit by natural light. In the evening, with drapes or shades closed, the emphasis is on a more cozy and secure environment. During this time, different levels of lighting that are focused on the various recreational tasks and activities that take place in the room are important.

In the summer, the room should be appealing because it is cool and fresh, and in the winter, it should be a comforting place into which you can retreat, leaving the cold and dark outside.

As such, the planning and furnishing of the space needs to be thought out carefully so that the room can cope with these various requirements and levels of wear and tear.

History of the living room

In centuries gone by, the furniture in the living room was arranged around the walls. This, the main entertaining room, was a formal place for people to gather and talk, so the center of the room was left empty to enable people to walk around or stand still and converse.

Later, in Georgian and Victorian times, the living room was a drawing room or salon in the homes of the wealthy and the middle classes. This room was used only for special entertaining or for adult family gatherings. The drawing room, or more properly withdrawing room, was the place that the ladies withdrew to as the men smoked cigars and drank port after a meal. In more humble homes, this room was known as the parlor, although it still had the formal, rather straightlaced approach to relaxation time.

Above: *This traditional room has chairs and sofas arranged near a natural light source.*

Left: *You can make the most of period features in your living room, such as this elaborate fireplace, and draw attention to them by arranging seating nearby.*

Creating play areas

It is useful for children to have their own play space. In an ideal allocation of rooms, the play area should be separate from the bedroom so that the sleep area is not associated with play or entertainment at all.

If children can have their own play area, this will give them freedom to make noise and play without restrictions. It will also leave the main living area for mostly adult use. In turn, this allows the living space to be clearer and the decoration more oriented toward relaxation.

However, you can create a play area within a living room by using a screen or mobile divider to partition off an appropriate space.

In grand houses the drawing room was often on the second floor, and in some modern homes this layout has been adopted in order to make the most of a view or to raise the room above street level and car noise.

Instead of the nursery, play room, morning room, study, and parlor being separate spaces and in different parts of the house, some or all of these functions are now housed in the living room. A lot more is expected of the contemporary space, and in turn, the general decorative style has become more simple and streamlined. Beneath the layout, however, storage and planning has become more complex.

An effective layout

Current interior design thinking advocates making rooms within rooms, and this can work well in a large living area. Furniture and rugs can be used to delineate different areas. For example, if there is a fireplace, that will probably be the focal point of the room around which people gather. The fireplace area can be defined by a large rug on which a semicircular arrangement of sofas or armchairs are placed around a central coffee table. The U shape may have to be broken to allow access, but its outline marks the sociable area where people will sit.

Arranging seating

Make an effort to avoid long or continuous lines of seats—this is visually uninviting but also makes it difficult for a group of people to communicate. Arrange chairs and sofas so that they form a unit, enabling people to talk to those opposite them or at an angle to them. Also, avoid placing small tables between every chair or setting a chair in a space on its own because this creates a barrier between those sitting in the main seats and a feeling of isolation for those on their own. The backs of the chairs and sofas form a visual barrier, making "walls" that enclose the space in front.

Elsewhere in the room, perhaps by a window or French doors, there could be a chaise longue or recliner that is specifically placed on its own, denoting another "room" reserved for private reading or contemplation. In a different area there could be a television and bean bags or a small two-seater sofa for children to sit on and play.

By dividing the room into sections, you can accommodate various requirements. The only problem that will occur is in volume control when all three divisions of the room need to be used at the same time—this is when headphones can be useful.

Another configuration that works well is the extendible seating unit. This can be L-shaped with a short side in front of the window (so that it does not block out too much light) or near a wall, and the long back of the seats placed across the open room. The open end of the sofa, without an arm, makes it accessible and open to those arriving in the room. This configuration does not create such an enclosed space as the U shape, but the long back of the sofa or the backs of a similar

arrangement of chairs still provides a delineation between one part of the room and another. The corner of the L also creates a small, intimate space where people can sit side by side to talk.

Another option is the parallel line configuration. This lines up a matching pair of sofas or a sofa and two armchairs on either side of a fireplace or central room feature. This provides two equally sized and spaced seating areas that connect face to face.

Heavier pieces of furniture such as sofas and armchairs can be supplemented by lighter, easier-to-maneuver chairs that can be kept against a wall or in an arrangement by a table or light and brought into the main space when guests arrive. In a small apartment or living area, these chairs could be foldaway. Chairs without arms look less bulky.

If your setting is contemporary or you want a feature chair, then opt for the work of a classic, modern designer such as Arne Jacobsen's series 7 chair.

Adjustable and adaptable furniture is important in a living room. There may be times when you need to clear the center of the room for a party or social function. Some chairs and smaller sofas can be moved more easily if put on castors or wheels, which enable them to be pushed without much effort. The wheels or castors may need to be placed in cups—solid plastic dishes that fit under the wheels—to protect a deep-pile carpet or valuable rug.

Positioning tables

Smaller pieces of furniture, such as tables, should serve as useful accessories rather than clutter the limited space or become obstacles to easy movement.

Opposite far left: *This U-shaped configuration of built-in seating maximizes a small space and forms an intimate salon away from the main living room.*

Opposite left: *A raised area in a bay window creates a private sitting place with a 180° view.*

Above: *The sofas in this room are arranged in an inviting manner so that people can talk to each other easily while relaxing in a comfortable seat.*

buy a table that incorporates laminated or reinforced glass, which are both tough and resilient and can withstand most knocks and bumps.

Another style of table that is useful in a living room is a console table, which has a narrow format. Traditional styles are supported by brackets fixed to the wall, while modern console tables are usually freestanding.

Subconsciously, many people prefer to sit with their backs to a wall and to have a clear view of anyone entering the room, but in a circular or group arrangement of chairs and sofas this is not usually practical. To create a barrier between the back of a sofa and an open space behind, a console table can be placed so that it butts up to the back of the seat. This creates a screen or small wall-like feature that makes the sitter feel less vulnerable and the room less open. The console table is also an area where small displays of photographs or ornaments can be displayed, but the number of artifacts should be limited to stop if from becoming cluttered and a hazard for people walking past.

Above: *This period-style room has a large ottoman for books and a small console table against one wall for ornaments.*

Right: *This coffee table is positioned within easy reach of the daybed, so that the person seated there can reach it without getting up.*

Opposite: *In a split-level space like this, it is important to have schemes that work together because you can see both areas at the same time. Here, the spot-decorated pillows act as a link between the upper and lower levels.*

The positioning of side tables is particularly important. To encourage and promote relaxation, a table should be within easy reach of the person in an armchair or on a sofa. For example, a good reading light should be at hand on a table in order to avoid eye strain. There should also be space where a drink can be placed or where a book, newspaper, pen, or pencil can be laid. To meet these requirements, you may need a series of small tables, which are more formally known as occasional tables. Or you could use a nest of tables—tables of graduated sizes that fit one on top of another. When selecting or buying this type of table, ensure that it is at the right height for the chair. In a family room, the tables should also be robust with good, solid legs to make them resilient to the occasional knock or bump.

Glass-topped coffee tables are extremely popular because the material is attractive to look at and can make a pleasant feature in a room. However, it may be dangerous so make sure that you

Above: *A radiator cover can be used as a display surface instead of a side table.*

Below: *The layout is arranged so that there is room to move between the tables and chairs.*

It is worth thinking carefully about where you place your tables, and how many of them you use. If you have a long wall with a doorway in the center, or a fireplace with space on each side, then you can position a table on either side of the feature and use it to support a pair of table lamps or a pair of artifacts such as marble columns or large glass vases. The pleasing nature of matching items appeals to our sense of symmetry and proportion, which alludes to classical style.

Traffic paths

One of the most important factors in arranging a busy area such as a living room is to figure out the traffic paths. People will need access from one side of the room to another as well as to bookcases, television, and other elements within the space. Your priority should be to avoid arranging the main seating area so that it has a traffic path through it because this will be disruptive for those sitting there and awkward for those passing through.

Try to map out the areas where a clear pathway is necessary and arrange the placement of the furniture to accommodate this. If the room is small, then there may be only one main thoroughfare, but in a large room there may be several routes. The journey around a room should be simple and easy to execute, not an assault course of low stools, haphazardly arranged side and coffee tables, and baskets of newspapers, magazines, or logs for the fire. Try to place small objects adjacent to the large one they are meant to be used with. For example, slot a footstool

under a seat or coffee table so that it is out of the way when it is not in use. A log basket should be set right beside the fireplace. Baskets of magazines and newspapers should be regularly edited so that only a few relevant issues are kept.

Focal points

In a living room a focal point, such as a fire or a particular painting, can be attractive as well as reassuring. There should be at least one object that draws the eye and on which the mind can focus. This helps in the calming procedure and the process of unwinding, as well as providing a center of attraction for the space.

If the fireplace is the focal point of the room, the area around it should be well-planned. The space directly in front of the fire may be a hearth or stone block

Left: *The fireplace is the focal point in this room and the side table and pictures have been arranged symmetrically on either side to bring the eye back to the center point.*

Above: *This small, modern niche fireplace breaks up an expanse of wall, and although there is no traditional fire surround, a single painting hung above the fire alludes to a more conventional setting.*

that protects the floor from sparks. To either side you could build seats under which you could have cupboards. These seats would allow the sitter to use the wall as a back support and should have a padded seat on the base to make it comfortable. Throw pillows or a covered pad suspended from hooks or a rod attached to the wall would also work well. In a contemporary setting this could be a low, wide wood shelf that doubles as an occasional sitting area as well as a place for display.

In a traditional style of sitting or living room, there are often deep recesses on each side of the chimney breast. These areas are commonly filled with bookcases or cupboards at the lower levels and with shelves above. In a classic setting, the top shelf may be finished off with a decorative feature such as a pediment or broken pediment. This is a triangular- or pyramid-shaped feature originally used to crown the top point or level of an important Grecian or Roman building. The arrangement of shelving can vary in width to accommodate differing heights of books and artifacts but the shelves should be equally spaced on either side of the chimney breast so that they form a continuous line. Having them staggered or at irregular distances will upset the harmony and balance of the layout.

If the fireplace is opposite a window, an appropriately framed mirror can be a useful feature to reflect and increase the effect of the daylight. Alternately, the space opposite a fireplace could be used to display a painting or print. As this wall space is usually substantial in size, the picture could be large. Although elsewhere in the room groups of pictures may be arranged to create a feature, the area above the fireplace is generally reserved for one single, impressive image.

Incorporating sounds and scents

Scents and sounds can be used, like color, to create the perfect atmosphere. Scents are very personal— some people love a room richly scented with perfumed candles and the aromas of sandalwood and musk incense, while others opt for the fresh smells of pine, lemon, lime, and orange peel.

Sounds can be therapeutic and relaxing, too. The soft tinkle of a water feature outside a window or the gentle movement of wind in the branches of trees serve as a reminder of nature and open spaces. A favorite piece of music played at a gentle volume can be all that is required after a busy day of ringing phones and traffic noises.

When framing an overmantel mirror or picture, take inspiration for the frame from the fire surround itself. If the surround is simple with geometric or linear detail, then the frame of the picture should complement that. On the other hand, if the fire surround is ornate (such as carved with swags and cherubs), then the picture frame you choose can also afford to be a lot more decorative.

If your living room does not have a fireplace, there are other ways to create a focal point. First, the arrangement of furniture will draw the eye to a certain point in the room. For example, if the majority of chairs and sofas are arranged around a coffee table, then that will become a focus. A piece of sculpture or art that is well-framed and highlighted by a picture or light will also draw the eye.

A room that has no focus will feel unsettling, but if you want to opt for a minimalist style of decoration, then use color to create interest. In a room that is all-white or decorated in neutral colors, a bowl of bright red flowers on a table or a group of vivid blue pillows on the end of a sofa will catch the attention of the person entering the room.

It is best to keep the focal point at standing eye level. If you use a mat or rug, too much attention will be drawn to the floor. Or a brightly colored central lightshade will cause people to look up rather than at your feature.

Communal living areas

The living area of a home may also be linked to another room. It is increasingly common in contemporary homes for a living area to incorporate the dining and/or kitchen space, too. The barriers and walls that once divided these different rooms are being knocked down to provide large, through spaces. These large, all-in-one living areas need to be linked by decoration because it looks odd if the kitchen is a cool, minimal contemporary scheme while the sitting area is decorated with ornate Victorian drapes and rich colors. The key is to find a base color that works in all areas and then use accessories to vary the tempo and mood in each space.

The simplest way is to choose a neutral base scheme—for example, a beige or pale gray for floors and wall throughout, with white woodwork and detailing.

Using color

To create a truly relaxing environment, you need to think about color. Depending on the size of the room, your character, and your likes and dislikes, you may find that rich, warm colors help to create a calm atmosphere. Deep reds or dark blues can be enveloping and give a sense of security, but conversely these colors may also make some people feel boxed in and uneasy, especially in a small space. Those who prefer lighter colors may find a mousy, mid-brown, or a muted shade of green much more comforting and relaxing.

You may, however, choose to paint your living room white. There are actually many shades of white available today that have a hint of another tone—for example, stone-white is slightly muted with gray, and sand white has a soft, brown tinge. These off-whites prevent the walls from becoming too stark and clinical, while still providing a minimalist background.

At-a-glance color guide

Traditional colors that suit sitting rooms are red, against which gilt-framed pictures and mirrors work well; blue, which is attractive with silver accessories; and bottle green, which is often associated with Victorian studies and private gentleman's clubs.

Mid-shades such as yellow and magnolia are classic and help to bring a subtle form of light and color to a room while still providing a presence in the background.

Contemporary sitting rooms often have white or off-white walls.

floorboards

with stenciled fall leaves

Use this simple idea to create the illusion of colorful fall leaves that have been blown in by the wind. You will need to start off with new or unfinished floorboards that can be whitewashed. Then simply gather fallen leaves and flatten them for a few days inside a heavy book before using them as templates.

Materials

Pressed leaves of various shapes and sizes

Piece of glass

Acetate sheet

Wood putty

Woodwash in white, terra-cotta, amber, and driftwood gray—buy ready-made or use a diluted latex

Spray adhesive

Satin-finish floor varnish

Tools

China marker pencil

Stencil cutter

Putty knife

Fine-grit sandpaper with sanding block or an electric sander

Large brush

Stencil brushes

Fine paintbrush

Positioning the leaves

1 Space the flattened leaves out and place a piece of glass over the top of them.

Tracing the leaves

2 Place the acetate sheet over the leaves, then use a china marker pencil to draw around each of them.

3 When the stencil cutter has heated up, use it to trace along the pencil lines. Then carefully remove the waste pieces of acetate and throw them away.

Smoothing the floor surface

4 Fill any holes or dents in the floorboards with wood putty and sand until smooth.

Applying the woodwash

5 Apply white woodwash in the direction of the woodgrain over the floorboards.

Fixing the stencil to the floor

6 Use spray adhesive to stick the stencils to the floor.

Coloring in the leaves

7 Dab the colored woodwash with a dry stencil brush and apply, working away from the edges of the stencils.

8 Use pale gray woodwash to paint shadows. Allow to dry, then varnish.

Space out your chosen leaves in a row so that you can place a piece of glass over them.

Put a sheet of acetate over the top and draw around the leaves with a china marker pencil.

Once you have filled any holes or dents with wood putty, sand the surface until smooth.

Using a large brush, apply white woodwash over the whole surface of the floor.

For a realistic effect, paint shadows on the leaves, making sure they fall in one direction.

creating

your own wall art

Finding the perfect piece of artwork to complement your interior can be difficult, so why not create your own? You do not have to be a talented artist; just choose colors that inspire you and work well together. You can buy ready-made canvases but it is much more economical to stretch your own canvas before you begin to decorate it. And don't be afraid to experiment with color and texture. You can create impact by hanging several similar-sized canvases side by size, or create one giant canvas that will give dramatic impact to your room.

Materials

4 lengths of 1½ x 1 in. wood

Scraps of masonite

Finish nails

Fine-gauge artist's canvas

Gesso primer

Selection of latex or artist's acrylic colors

Low-tack masking tape

Texturizing medium

Coarse sand

Gilt transfer leaf

Tools

Miter saw

Jigsaw

Hammer

Scissors

Staple gun

Spray gun and water

Paintbrushes

Palette knife

Establishing frame dimensions

1 Decide on the dimensions of your frame and then cut the four pieces of wood to length with a miter saw to ensure tight-fitting miter joints.

Making the frame

2 Cut the masonite into triangular pieces using a

jigsaw, then butt the corners of the frame together and place the pieces of triangular masonite over the top of the joints. Use finish nails to secure the masonite in position.

Stapling the canvas

3 Cut a piece of canvas that is large enough to fit over the

whole frame. Then secure the canvas on the reverse of the frame using a staple gun (see picture bottom left, page 116). You should work systematically around the frame, pulling the canvas tight to ensure that it is evenly stretched. You should also make sure that the corners of the canvas are neatly folded under.

Use a miter saw to cut the four pieces of wood, making sure the joints are tight.

Position the triangular pieces of masonite over the wood joints and nail in place.

Preparing the canvas

4 Spray the canvas with a fine mist of water to make the cotton fibers shrink slightly. This will improve the overall tension of the canvas. Once dry, prime it with two coats of gesso primer and then allow this to dry for approximately one hour.

5 Paint the entire canvas, including the edges, with a basecoat. This will be the dominant color. Allow to dry.

Applying color

6 To add a block or stripe of texture, mask off an area with low-tack tape. Then mix your second chosen paint color with texturizing medium and apply this to the canvas with a flat palette knife. Before the medium has set, pull away the tape so that you avoid pulling away dried paint.

Adding texture

7 When the second color is dry, mask off different areas of the canvas. Choose another paint color and mix coarse sand into it. Apply this to the masked-off areas and allow to touch-dry.

8 Add the finishing touches with gilt highlights. To do this, press squares of gilt transfer leaf onto areas of paint while they are still tacky. Smooth the squares down with your fingers, then peel off the backing paper.

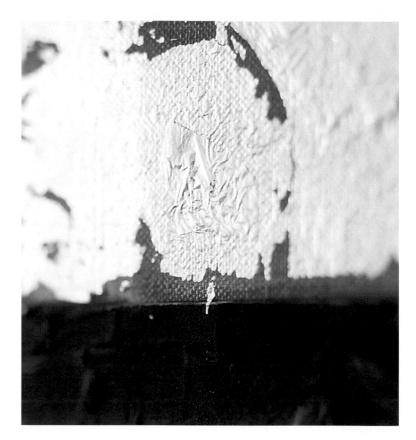

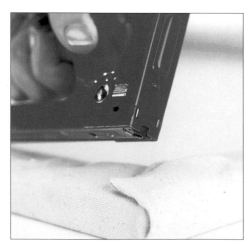

Staple the canvas into place on the back of the frame using a staple gun.

Paint the whole surface of the canvas with gesso primer and allow it to dry.

Choose your dominant color and cover the whole canvas with it.

Alternative

A single, large-scale painting can look just as effective as a group of smaller paintings. Creating a canvas of simple stripes in colors that complement your interior is an ideal way of using up leftover paint.

A quick alternative to stretching your own canvas is to use a piece of lightweight particle board instead. This can be fixed to the wall using screws or mirror plates.

Lightly sand and then seal the particle board with a basecoat of multipurpose primer or a slightly diluted coat of latex paint before you begin. Choose the color that you wish to dominate the painting and apply it with a brush or small roller to the particle-board surface. Allow it to dry. Decide where you would like to position your stripes, then draw them in lightly with a soft pencil using a square. Mark out the stripes using low-tack masking tape, then apply the different colors. Finally, you should pull off the masking tape before the paint dries completely.

Mix your second color with texturizing medium and apply it using a flat palette knife.

Mask off various areas of the canvas and apply paint mixed with coarse sand.

Use gilt transfer leaf as a highlight over the design and then peel off the backing paper.

decorative

screen with colored panels

This practical screen has many uses in the living room. It is both light and easy to move and the semitranslucent panels make it suitable for positioning in front of a window if you require extra privacy during the day but do not want to lose any light. It is also excellent as a room divider, so it can be used to screen off a dining or home office area. The screen is constructed using simple butt joints and the frame is colored with a natural beech woodstain, but you may prefer to paint or stain it in a darker shade. Feel free to experiment.

Materials

12 lengths of planed
16 ft. x 2 in. x 2 in.
softwood

Wood glue

Wood screws

Wood putty

Square bead to form
the rebates

Finish nails

Mineral spirits

Beech varnish

8 sheets of polypropylene
in various colors

9 flush hinges

Tools

Paper and pencil

Handsaw or electric jigsaw

Square

C clamp

Drill

Screwdriver

Palette knife

Hammer

Medium- and fine-grit
sandpaper with
sanding block

Cloth

Paintbrush

Sharp craft knife

Staple gun

Planning the screen

1 Start by drawing a plan of your screen. To calculate the spacing of the horizontal battens, multiply the thickness of the wood by six. Subtract the resulting number away from the height of vertical uprights. Now divide this number by five to find out the internal height of each square. (If you are using the suggested wood, this measurement should be 1 ft.) Use a sharp handsaw or electric jigsaw to cut out each of the 16 horizontal battens. The vertical lengths should also be 1 ft. long. Cut these out in the same way.

2 Mark the final positions of the horizontal battens on the vertical lengths of wood using a square.

Fixing the joints

3 Clamp the joints together using a C clamp, then drill a pilot hole in the center of each

Calculate the lengths of each batten and then, using a handsaw, cut them to size.

With a pencil, mark the positions of the horizontal battens on the vertical lengths.

Know your materials

Polypropylene is a type of plastic sheet, thin enough to cut with scissors or a craft knife but stiff enough for use in this screen project. It comes in a variety of translucent and opaque colors and textures. Because light filters through it, it is also suitable for making modern lamp shades, window hangings, and mobiles. It is readily available from all good art-supply stores

joint using a small wood bit. Make sure you use a countersink bit to ensure that the screw head sits beneath the surface of the wood. This is important because you do not want the screw heads to be visible on the finished screen. Spread a thin layer of wood glue over the joint, then make sure the screw is firmly in place. Continue this process at each joint until all the panels are complete.

4 Fill the countersunk screw holes with a neutral-colored putty. Allow the putty to dry (following manufacturer's instructions), then sand the surface smooth.

Fixing the rabbet battens

5 Cut the rabbet battens to the required lengths. (You will need eight pieces per screen square.) Use a hammer and finish nails to secure the battens in place, slightly inset, around each square in order to form a rabbet on the front of each panel. (Blunt each nail by tapping the point with the hammer because this will help to prevent splits in the wood from occurring.) The second set of rabbets will be fitted later to hold the polypropylene in place.

Varnishing the screen

6 Sand the whole surface of the panel frames thoroughly using medium- then fine-grit sandpaper wrapped around a sanding block. Once you have finished, remove any remaining sawdust with a cloth that has been dampened in mineral spirits. Next, apply beech varnish to the panel frames using a 1-in. paintbrush. Allow the varnish to dry and then lightly sand over the areas as before. You should now apply a second coat of the varnish in exactly the same way.

Stapling the sheets

7 Carefully cut the sheets of polypropylene so that they will fit neatly over each square. Use a sharp craft knife to do this. Then secure the sheets in place against the rabbet using a staple gun. For a neat finish, you should now secure the second set of rabbets on the back of the screen using the hammer as before.

Assembling the panels

8 Fix each screen panel together to create the large screen. This should be done using three flush hinges screwed at equidistant points along the length of each panel. Hold the hinges in place and mark the positions of the screw holes. Drill holes and screw the hinges firmly in place.

Use a C clamp on the joints and then drill a pilot hole and screw the joints together.

Fill the countersunk screw holes with a neutral-colored putty and allow it to dry.

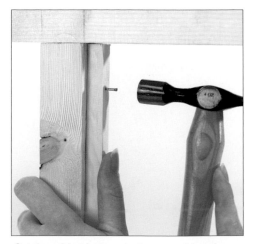

Cut the rabbet battens to the correct lengths and then hammer them into place.

Alternative

Decorative screens can make ideal display panels for photographs—you can make a simple display screen using particle board.

Get your wood supplier to cut an 8 x 4-ft. sheet of ½-in. thick particle board lengthwise into three equal pieces. Mark out the five photograph apertures, and the feet at the bottom of each panel using a pencil and square. Drill a pilot hole in the inside corner of each square, then use a jigsaw with a sharp blade to cut out the apertures and around the feet. Sand lightly, then apply several coats of black eggshell paint with a small paintbrush or mini-roller and allow to dry. Get a hardware store or glass supplier to cut sheets of clear plexiglass or safety glass about 1 in. larger than each of the apertures. Enlarge all your photographs so that they are the same size as the glass or plexiglass. Cut stiff cardboard to fit onto the back of each and use metal mirror corner plates to fix the glass, photograph, and cardboard in place on the back of the screen.

Sand the panel frames, apply two coats of beech varnish, and allow to dry.

Cut the polypropylene sheets to size and then staple them to the rabbet battens.

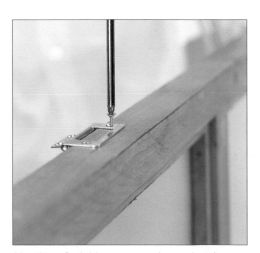

Use three flush hinges on each panel and screw them into place to complete the screen.

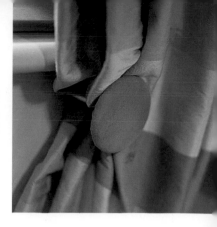

Furnishings and textiles

Furnishings and textiles are like the makeup, shoes, and belt that go with a dress—they are the finishing touches that create individual style and appearance. Furniture should be selected for comfort, quality, and shape, while textiles can introduce fashionable or seasonal colors and patterns.

Choosing your furniture

The type of furniture you choose for your living area should be conducive to relaxation. When trying to imagine a place for unwinding, the first thing that comes to mind is a huge, squashy, enveloping sofa, but this type of seat can be uncomfortable and detrimental to your relaxation.

Finding the right sofa

You should take your time and try out plenty of sofas before buying one. You may want to rush out and buy the inviting-looking squashy sofa mentioned before, but there is often no proper lumbar support on this type of seating, unless of course you lie flat on it and arrange pillows to provide specific underpinning to the right areas of your body. If the seat is too deep, then you will perch on the edge, sit back and tuck your legs underneath you to provide an anchoring point, or dangle your legs unsupported in the air. If two people sit beside each other on an overlarge sofa, they tend to lean toward each other or end up slumped up against an arm at one end, which means that their spines will be curved and unsupported as a result.

A smaller two-seater sofa with a seat that is just deep enough to accommodate you comfortably in the sitting position is a better choice. It may not look as inviting as an oversized three-seater, but it can be more comfortable and ultimately more relaxing, too.

Armchairs and footstools

Similar criteria also apply to a single armchair. Big, deep, cozy chairs may look the best, but in fact a neat, upholstered, and well-proportioned chair will be better for you in the long term as it gives you good support.

The ideal sitting position for relaxation should allow the feet to rest lightly on the floor, with an angle of slightly more than 90° between the hips and the lumbar region of the spine. The back of the chair should support the whole length of the spine as well as the base of the head. If the seat is too low, you will feel the need to cross your legs, which is bad for blood circulation.

Upholstered furniture with arms not only makes you feel more enclosed and secure in the seat but also helps you get in and out

Below: Choose a sofa carefully—it must not be too big or it will overpower the room, but at the same time it should not be too small or it will look lost or insignificant in a large space. The most important thing, however, is to choose one that has proper lumbar support for the spine.

of a chair. For older people, a chair with a high frame and raised arms that meet the elbow will make it easier to get in and out of.

"Putting your feet up" has long been an expression used in conjunction with having a rest, and there is a lot of truth in it. For those who spend a lot of time standing at work or around the house, or people with leg problems such as varicose veins, putting their feet up while sitting is beneficial. An ottoman or footstool at the same height as the edge of the seat of the chair is ideal because your legs will be straight out in front of you. If you have a circulatory problem in your legs, it can be beneficial to raise the height of your extended legs above your hip level for some time to help blood flow. There is a

number of chairs designed with retractable footrests that slot neatly into the base of the chair when not in use, but are easily raised by means of a lever at the side of the chair when wanted.

Electrical considerations

Television, video, and DVD equipment are almost always located in living rooms today. The positioning of such equipment is very important, not only for aesthetic reasons but also for your health. First, try to avoid glare on the screen, which can cause eyestrain and headaches. Also, reduce the effect of the radiation given off by the screen by sitting well back from it. Radiation diminishes by the square of the distance away from the source, and a minimum of

6 ft. is suggested. The level of light when watching television should also be regulated. The intensity of light in the room should be similar to that emitted from the screen. It can be detrimental to your vision to watch television in a dark room (see pages 134–5).

Another electrical consideration is the management of wires and cables in living rooms. There will be cables for table lamps, lampstands, television, music, and other electrical items that all require access to an electrical outlet and a clear route to their base. Never overload an outlet, especially with adapters—by all means use an adapter to extend the use of a single outlet to two plugs, but do not put one adapter into another because you may not

Above: A sofa with high arms is easier to get in and out of. Pillows on sofas can be used not only to provide color but also support.

Above: Fun fabrics, such as this Dalmatian print, are ideal for accessories where they can be used in moderation.

Right: A simple bucket chair offers good support and has a raised shape.

Below: Raw-silk pillows have an interesting slub texture and a soft sheen.

Below right: By mixing shapes, you will bring a change of emphasis.

only overload the circuit and cause the power to trip the fuse, but you may also, inadvertently, cause an electrical short circuit that could start a fire.

If running electrical wire, such as a cable for a lamp, under a rug or carpet, make sure that the cable is properly insulated and that it does not run directly under a wheel, castor, or any other sharp or heavy object that may cut or damage the wiring or its casing.

Textiles

Textiles and textures play a vital part in encouraging relaxation. However, the practical element of wear and tear must also be kept in mind.

Upholstery

Soft and sensual fabrics such as silk, velvet, and wool can be comforting, especially in the fall and winter when it is icy and dark

outside. However, these fabrics are very delicate and therefore are best used for accessories where they will not become worn.

An increasingly popular material for upholstery and even floors and wall panels in living areas is leather. Leather can be used to

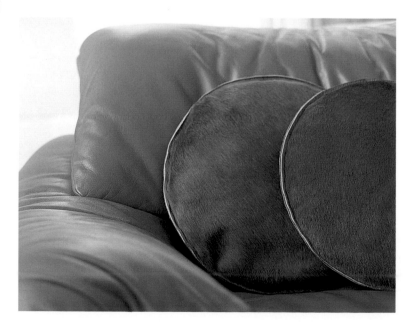

cover traditional as well as more contemporary furniture. This material is great for upholstery because it is soft but durable.

If you choose to upholster your furniture in pale shades, make sure that the fabric has a stain-retardant or repellent finish. Light colors can form a good neutral background to a room but will easily become stained and marked. These protective finishes create an invisible coating on the fabric, preventing spillages from soaking into the weave or texture of the fabric and making it easy to wipe them clean.

Another option is to have loose or removable covers. These are fitted to the shape of the chair or sofa but can be removed by unzipping or untying. Depending on the fabric, loose covers can be machine-washed or dry-cleaned. The main thing to be wary of with loose covers is to check that they are prewashed or shrink-tested. There is nothing worse than trying to refit a loose cover after it has been washed and discovering that it has shrunk. Dry-cleaning is usually the safest option. Manufacturers make many textiles suitable for upholstery in heavier weight such as woolen weaves,

Left: *The bold shapes and colors on the furniture and accessories act together as an effective contrast to the basic minimalist look of this room.*

Below: *This simple turned corbel allows a light voile curtain to be drawn back from the edges of the window and arranged in a soft drape.*

jacquard, and damask self-patterned designs as well as textured cotton or canvas. When looking in a fabric store, ask to be directed to the fabrics that are specifically designated for this type of use.

Floor coverings

These days living room floors are most often carpeted or covered in a hard surface such as wood. A luxurious, wool or wool-mix pile carpet is still among the most popular of finishes but is best used in a room that is not subjected to heavy use because the pile will eventually wear. Heavy traffic areas can be protected by a rug or runner or by rearranging the furniture from time to time to expose different parts.

If you use a hard flooring such as wood, tiles, or stone, you may want to soften its appearance by adding a decorative flatweave mat or rug, such as a kelim or dhurrie. (Remember to attach a nonslip backing onto the rug.)

Another popular way of covering a large wooden floor is with a substantial square or rectangle of carpet. This will cover the majority of the floor but leave a rim of wood exposed around the edge of the room.

Drapes and pillows

The fabric used on drapes does not need to be as durable as that used for upholstery. However, lightweight fabrics usually need to be interlined and lined, and even heavier ones hang and drape more easily if they have a light backing or cotton lining.

Throw pillows can be round, square, rolled, or even triangular. They are decorative, fun elements that can be made from scraps of material that link them in to the other furnishing fabrics in the room. Alternately, they can be made in dramatic, contrasting colors and patterns.

felt rug and floor pillow

Felt is an increasingly popular furnishing material. It has many advantages because it is naturally ecofriendly (made from boiled wool scraps), warm, and does not fray when cut. Felt is not often considered as a flooring material but ¼-in. thick industrial felt is an ideal choice—it is warm, durable, and soft underfoot. This patchwork-style rug is stitched together using a traditional blanket stitch. It is important to use a nonslip underlayment if the rug is to be used on wooden or laminate flooring. For a coordinated look, add a comfortable floor pillow made using the same method.

Materials

¼-in. thick felt in three colors (6½ x 6½ ft. of each color is sufficient for the rug but make sure you also have enough to cover your pillow if required)

Black tapestry wool

Nonslip backing strips (optional)

Pillow form

Hook-and-eye fastenings

Tools

Soft pencil

Metal ruler or square

Sharp scissors

Tailor's chalk

Hole punch

Darning needle

Making the squares

1 Mark out three squares on each of the different-colored felts using a pencil. Use a metal ruler or square to make sure they are identical sizes—this one is 1½ ft.

2 Cut out each of the felt squares carefully using a pair of sharp scissors.

3 Mark the position of the stitching holes at ½ in. intervals along all of the sides of each piece of felt using a soft pencil or tailor's chalk (see picture bottom left, page 128). Check that the holes will line up.

4 Use a hole punch set on its smallest hole setting to cut out the holes you have marked on each piece of felt (see picture bottom middle, page 128). (The felt is too thick to be pierced with a darning needle.)

Stitching the squares together

5 Thread a darning needle with a double thickness of black tapestry wool. Sew the squares together using a simple overstitch, making sure that they butt

Measure each felt square using a pencil and square to make sure they are all the same size.

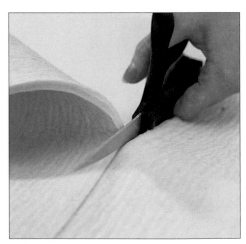

Using sharp scissors, carefully cut out each of the felt squares.

Know your materials

Because of the thickness of the felt used in this project, it is essential to punch holes in the material before sewing. Here, the squares of felt are joined with a simple overstitch that, when pulled tight, butts the two pieces of felt together. This is simply formed by passing the needle from one piece of felt and into the other (see picture bottom right). Traditional blanket stitch has been used to bind the edges and give them a neat, finished appearance. This is formed by passing the needle through the fabric, then under the loose thread (see picture bottom left, page 129).

together closely. Alternate the colors of the squares in order to build up the required checkerboard pattern over the surface of the rug.

6 When all the squares have been joined together, use blanket stitch to finish off the outside edges of the rug. Make sure that you join the wool with a neat knot on the underside of the rug or it will eventually work its way undone. You should then position self-adhesive, nonslip backing strips onto the back of the rug if it is going to be placed on a hard surface because it would be difficult to walk on without slipping otherwise.

Making the floor pillow

7 Use the same technique to make the coordinating, large floor pillow. It is very simple to do this: first, cover a large pillow form with two squares of felt and then join them together securely using the blanket stitch once again. You should then make a slit down the center of

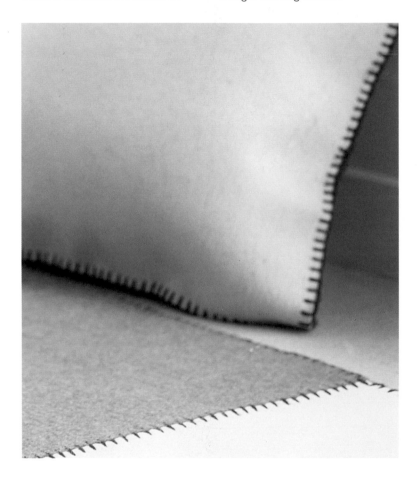

one side of the pillow using a sharp pair of scissors.

8 On either side of the slit, sew on hook-and-eye fastenings using a darning needle.

With a soft pencil, mark out the position of the holes on each piece of felt.

Use a hole punch set on its smallest setting to cut out the holes.

Use black tapestry wool to overstitch each of the squares together.

Alternative

If your preferred style is more opulent than the simple, understated look of felt, adapt the design to use luxurious fabric with beautiful glass bead trims. Affordable beaded trims are now available in notions stores and work well alongside rich velvets and silks.

To make an opulent patchwork throw, cut out six equally sized velvet squares with a ½-in. seam allowance all the way around. Press them, pin them together, then machine stitching them. Cut a piece of silk or satin backing fabric and a lightweight lining fabric to the same dimensions as the velvet top section. Sandwich the layers right side facing inward. Place the bead trim between the layers, lining up the flat edge of the trim with the raw fabric edges. Carefully pin it in place so that when it is turned right side out only the beads are visible. Machine stitch all the layers together almost all the way around, leaving enough of an opening to turn the throw the right side out. Hand stitch this closed using slip stitch.

Finish off the outer edges of the rug using blanket stitch all the way around.

Once you have made the basic pillow, use scissors to cut down the middle of one square.

On either side of the opening, sew on hook-and-eye fastenings.

Display and storage

Different sizes and types of objects should be treated in various ways to suit their purpose. It is best to store useful, but not necessarily attractive, items out of sight or in an orderly way, while interesting and decorative pieces should be grouped attractively and given prominence.

Storage choices

In a living space storage is important because it helps to keep order and to make movement around the room easy. Bookcases, freestanding or built-in, are the most usual way to contain books, CDs, videos, and general household artifacts. Open shelving gives the easiest access, but is also the most dustprone arrangement. Shelves contained in cupboards, whether glass- or wood-fronted, will keep the contents within cleaner for longer.

The secret to success in clutter management is to edit the amount of things you possess to a controllable number, selecting those that you really need or want and then allotting them to a specific space or area. Throw or give the rest away.

Simple shelving systems

Modern storage is usually practical as well as aesthetically pleasing. Even shelves can be of interest in their own right.

Purpose-built and contemporary shelving often appears to hang magically in the air, although it is in fact attached to the wall by concealed brackets. The most basic, ready-made shelving systems have open, usually prefixed, shelves and are made of a cheap wood such as pine that can be painted or stained for a more decorative finish. Adjustable shelving with support brackets that slot into regularly spaced niches in the uprights are also available.

As well as shelving systems, you can buy single shelves with individual supports such as gallow brackets. These are triangular wooden supports that are screwed into both the wall and the base of the shelf with a cross support between the two right-angled legs. Another single shelf option is the fixed steel shelf bracket that consists of two metal legs at a right angle to each other. These strong metal brackets are screwed into the wall and the base of the shelf.

Alcove supports are lengths of wood, preferably with a sculpted or finished front end, that are screwed into the wall with a glass

Right: This wall-mounted CD storage is very striking but also displays the CDs in such a way that they are easy to identify, remove, and return.

Left: *A row of small cubic storage spaces makes use of what otherwise would have been an empty space.*

Above: *The upper surface of storage units can be used to display favorite ornaments.*

or wood shelf resting on top. Finally, you can make the support invisible by using a wood or laminated shelf that is grooved or drilled along the back surface. This hollow section slips over dowels or fixed supports into the wall.

Special shelving

As well as single or purpose-built shelves, there are also more special modular and flexible systems that can be bought from good furniture and office storage suppliers. Many have fine metal frames with adjustable brackets and shelves but will come with additional features such as angled display shelves so that a flat object such as a book or plate can be supported but easily seen on a shelf that is raised at the back. Other options such as cabinet and roll-front enclosures are also available. This type of system is usually attached to the wall by brackets and screws so it is secure.

When planning a set of fixed shelves, calculate the distance between them carefully because once they are in place they are there for good. For example, if a mid-height shelf is to support a television or music system, measure the depth and height of the piece of equipment and allot the appropriate amount of space. Also, look at your collection of books and artifacts and see if they fall into height categories so that you can allocate two narrow shelves for small paperback books and one taller shelf for hardback, glossy art books.

Another popular modular system comes in cubes. These wooden cubes can be empty, with one shelf, two shelves, three drawers, or a door. You select the number of cubes

Decorative shelving

Shelves need not be dull—they can be beautiful architectural features. They can be cut and arranged to form a shape, such as a pyramid, or be "sculptures" in their own right.

Shelves can be painted the same color as the wall so that they almost disappear, or painted in a vibrant contrasting color so that they become a definite feature. Polished or varnished wood can also be used, and the wood can be chosen to highlight or emphasize the wood elsewhere in the room.

You can also embellish shelves with a fringe, panel, or cutout attached to the front edge of the shelf. Another option is a beaten metal strip, such as copper.

Right: *The different-colored interiors of this storage system, and the objects within, form several small "pictures" or points of interest. The concealed internal lighting also highlights objects such as the glass balls and the pyramid.*

Concealing or decorating radiators

Radiators are rarely elegant or attractive, so they are best disguised. Radiators are often placed under windows, and if the window is long and elegant and the radiator small and painted the same color as the wall, the window will be the eyecatching feature and the radiator hardly noticeable. At night, drapes may also be drawn over the radiator.

On the other hand, if the radiator is in a prominent position, you may want to cover it up or disguise it. Do this by boxing in the top and sides using particle board or wood. The front should not be completely obscured, so that heat can still flow, so choose an open mesh panel.

you need to fill your area and then pick the arrangement of storage you want, thereby tailor-making your own system. This style of unit is usually connected across the back so that the units are interlocked and will form a single freestanding block, but for safety, especially if you have an uneven or irregular floor surface, you may also want to secure them to a wall.

Displaying objects

Some of the shelves in your room will probably house small objects and photographs, arranged in a set-piece display. These items should be carefully chosen because they are going to be in such a prominent position.

When arranging items you should also think about height and depth—try to avoid having everything at the same level

because this can be monotonous. A group can be placed so that a taller item is at the back, with a mid-height and small item in front. This sort of display could include a plate propped up against the wall with a bottle in front and a little dish or bowl in the foreground. Above all, you should try to avoid clutter—do not let your shelves become places where general household mail,

matchboxes, and unframed photographs build up or they will detract from the display items and make the area look messy.

Storage systems can also make wonderful room dividers. A set of freestanding shelves can provide a screen between one part of a room and another without permanently blocking it off.

Open shelves will also allow light to pass through them from one side of a room to another, maintaining an open and airy feel. Conversely, a shelving system with a solid back will provide a dense screen that will make a space feel more enclosed and much more private. Bear in mind, however, that unless the shelving unit reaches right up to the ceiling, sounds from each area will still carry.

Practical considerations

When deciding on the type of storage for your room, try to identify what belongs where. In the case of a living room, this will depend of the amount of space available and the allocation of tasks to the room (see Planning your space, pages 102–3). If it is a multipurpose room, you will need practical elements such as bookcases or shelves and cupboards but you may also be able to introduce decorative storage, for example an antique wood trunk, a decorative chest of drawers, or a console table with drawers. Consider what your shelves will be supporting— lightweight objects only need light shelves, but heavier things need robust shelving that is securely attached to the wall.

Try to keep things that you use frequently at hand; other items that are only used occasionally can be stored in a less accessible area or even in another room or the attic. For example, place video and DVD storage next to the television and CDs near the CD player. If the living area is a place for plants and displays but also a space for children to play in, it can be worth providing some high-level shelves or storage so that fragile or breakable objects are placed out of the reach of small hands.

Think about subdividing storage to fit objects into a container of an appropriate size. For example, if you are putting a number of small things into a drawer, consider subdividing the space so that you have several small compartments, each containing one or two things that are easily accessible rather than a jumble of objects.

Finally, beware of providing too much storage because any resulting empty gaps in your room will probably have an ominous ability to become full, and not necessarily with useful or beautiful objects either.

Left: The niches in this decorative display unit are painted in bright colors to create a feature of them.

Below: These deep boxes slot neatly under the coffee table but keep magazines and books close at hand.

TV cabinets

For those who find the presence of a large television screen ugly or distracting, there are purpose-built cabinets and tables that will conceal it when it is not in use. Behind the doors there is usually a sliding shelf on which the television rests and beneath are shelves for storing videos and DVDs.

Another option is a deep box such as an old-fashioned traveling trunk. This unobtrusive rectangular box can house a concealed elevator that is operated by remote control.

Or you could use a console or side table with a lower shelf. Place your television on the shelf and conceal it with a cloth that hangs to floor level.

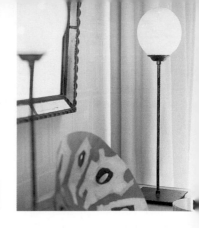

lighting your living room

The lighting in the living room should be variable and flexible so that during the daytime task or reading lights can be focused for close work, while at night decorative and ambient lighting may be used to create a relaxing mood and atmosphere.

Types of lighting

Background or ambient lighting is a substitute for natural light, providing a general level of visibility. On its own, this type of lighting is fairly uninspiring.

Task or work lighting has specifically directed beams that provide a localized light in a prescribed area where an activity such as reading takes place.

Accent lighting is a creative light used to highlight color, texture, or objects. It can range from a fine pinhole beam to a broad spotlight.

Decorative lighting covers anything that is attractive but not necessarily useful as a main source of light, such as candlelight.

Effective lighting

The real skill of lighting design is to have a good balance so that the light can be adjusted to suit every action or event that takes place under its beams. The color and finish on walls, floors, and furniture will also have an effect on the lighting you need in a room. For example, in a room with white walls and few pictures or additional wall decoration, plain light carpets, and natural or neutral upholstery, a lot of light will be reflected, so fewer and less high-strength lights will be required. However, if a room has dark walls, a heavy rich carpet, and heavily upholstered furniture, more lights will be needed because each of these dark-colored items will absorb a certain amount of the natural light.

Matte finishes tend to absorb light whereas shiny ones reflect it. Therefore, fabrics such as suede, felt, and tufted coverings will reduce the effectiveness of electric lighting whereas silk, lacquer work, and chrome will give a limited but useful amount of light amplification.

Planning your lighting

You need a central or main light that illuminates the room when you first enter it. In a traditional setting, this is usually a pendant light. In modern homes, however, this is often replaced with a number of recessed ceiling spotlights or wall lights.

In a living room, a general scheme usually includes three or four levels of lighting. The first is general ambient light, which is provided by the pendant and other elements such as wall lights. These can also be wired to a dimmer switch so that the level or brightness can be lowered to alter the atmosphere of the room.

In order to choose the other levels of lighting, you first need to identify specific areas of use in the room. Task lighting may be required if there is a table or a desk in the room, or close to the CD player and television so that you can see the controls.

Right: Instead of having one small wall light that might get lost in the center of a vast wall, this group of three forms a sculptural feature.

It will also be needed near chairs and sofas where newspapers and books are read or knitting or sewing occurs.

You may also want to include accent lighting to highlight a certain feature or collection in the room, such as a picture, glass, or a particular plant. These accent lights can vary from a specific wall-mounted picture light to a recessed, ceiling spotlight that has its beam directed onto the chosen object.

The adjustable spotlight gives a broad spread of light to the immediate area but draws the eye to its focus. A strip light or picture light runs along the width of a picture and casts an even light from top to bottom, thereby illuminating the whole of the picture but not the space around it. Another option is a special framing light with adjustable shutters that train the beam of light exactly onto the picture.

Architectural features, such as decorative arches or pillars, can also be "painted" with light. Halogen spotlights or eyeball downlighters are useful to pick out this type of feature and can be particularly effective if the ambient lighting is dimmed to a level lower than the spot.

Using light as a disguise

Although light is usually seen as a way of illuminating things and making them easily visible, it can also be used to disguise areas, and surprisingly enough, to make a room seem more spacious.

By placing larger pieces of furniture away from the walls and locating a couple of tungsten uplighters behind them, the light will reflect off the walls and make the place look larger. You can also focus light away from an area that you do not want to be seen, leaving it in shadow and making it retreat into the background.

Above: *By opening up the roof and installing laminated glass panels, the amount of natural light in this room has more than doubled.*

Left: *Classic white plaster uplighters can be painted to blend in with the color of the wall. Candles provide additional decorative lighting.*

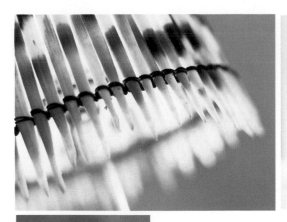
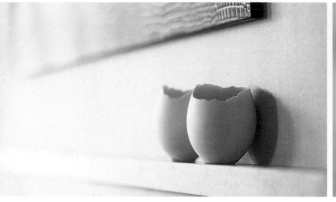

Living room accessories

Accessories are the finishing touches that bring personality and individuality to a room. In a living room, these small items help to create a complete interior and should be selected for their individual merit as well as their contribution to the overall effect. The choice of accessories will be influenced by your chosen color and theme, but there may also be architectural limitations to consider—for example, small windows and a deep windowsill may point you in the direction of shades rather than drapes; a large expanse of wall may call for decorative, wall-mounted lights; and a dark or richly colored room will require more light than a pale-colored, sunny room. Even practical aspects such as radiators, door handles, and light switches should be considered because these will all contribute to the general appearance of the room. Radiators, for example, need not be ugly or dominant. There are many discreet low-level radiators to choose from, and if you already have a large featureless style, it can boxed in and disguised.

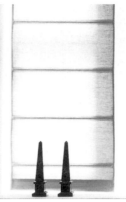

CLOCKWISE FROM TOP LEFT:

An ornate lampshade made from porcupine quills creates an unusual pattern and coloring when the electric light passes through it.

A mantelshelf is often a place where cards, letters, and general paperwork accumulates—try to keep it clear and choose just a few, special pieces for arrangement and display. The mantel and fireplace are usually the focal point of a living room and therefore the first place that someone entering the room will look.

In a room with a low ceiling, a neat, close-fitting lightshade like this will provide light but not restrict head room.

This magazine storage is made from leather. Although unusual, it still provides ample space to keep magazines and other papers tidy.

If you have small windows, a well-tailored set of shades will be more space-effective than large, pleated drapes.

The lighting in this living room has been carefully planned to focus on this magnificent statue.

Door and cupboard handles should not be overlooked because the sum of these small details is significant.

Dimmer switches can be used to lower the lighting and instantly change the mood of the room. It is a good idea to cover all light switches with a protective shield that can be wiped clean easily.

Textured fabric can add a luxurious finishing touch to your living area.

Bookshelves are a neat storage solution but can also become an attractive feature in a living room.

Pieces of artwork should be displayed to look their best. Here, the grain of the wood shelf supporting this bowl accentuates its shape and texture.

Photographs that have been mounted and framed in a similar way can be arranged together on a wall.

This twisting glass lampbase is topped with a plain but pleated shade that does not distract from the intrinsic beauty of the base.

A whimsical plain and colored glass chandelier adds an opulent decorative touch.

Bedrooms

Planning your bedroom

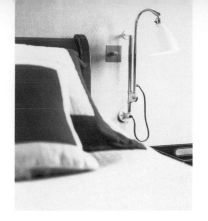

We spend a third of our lives in bed and so the bedroom is an important part of the house and should be a space where you feel comfortable and can retreat to after a busy day. Above all, it needs to be warm, inviting, relaxing, and quiet.

Below: Wood paneling such as this will provide a certain amount of sound insulation for your bedroom.

Below right: As well as creating a tranquil scheme for your room, ensure that it is located in a quiet part of the house.

Opposite: The leather-paneled wall acts as a screen for the bathroom and doubles as an attractive headboard.

Planning your space

The quality and quantity of sleep that you get has a profound effect on the way that you function both physically and mentally. During periods of deep sleep, the body restores and heals itself. Sleep also affects the body's ability to process and store carbohydrates as well as regulate hormone levels. And during the day the spine is compressed by gravity but at night it is given the chance to recover. So it is important that the room where you rest at night is designed to encourage good sleep.

The bed is one of the most important pieces of furniture in the home and so the general advice given is to spend as much as you can afford on a good-quality bed (see Choosing the right bed, pages 148–50). And don't think that a bed is for life—you should replace it every 8–10 years.

Finding the right location

Almost more important than the amount of sleep you have is the quality of it, so ensure that you are not disturbed unnecessarily. If you have a choice, locate your bedroom at the back or on the quietest side of the building, away from traffic noise.

If you are in a block of apartments, check what rooms are above and below you. Also, investigate what happens on the first floor of your building—you may have moved away from traffic noise at the front only to have repositioned yourself above the kitchens of a restaurant or the doors of a nightclub where activity carries on until well into the night, or begins at daybreak.

To ensure a quiet space, you may need to install double glazing, double doors, or other forms of soundproofing.

Above: *If the best position for your bed is close to the door, a screen can provide a useful shield for creating privacy.*

Above right: *This clever sliding wall panel has been covered in fabric to link with the rest of the room. It can be pulled across to conceal the storage when access is not needed.*

Safety tips

Those who follow environmental researches believe that synthetic materials, such as nylon carpet, encourage static electricity, which can be potentially harmful, especially in a bedroom.

It is also best to keep electrical appliances to a minimum because of radiation or electromagnetic fields, and to avoid running electrical cables under the bed. Therefore, make sure that the cable for bedside lights runs along the baseboards or edge of the wall to the bedside table.

Double glazing will muffle exterior noise, while double doors reduce noise by creating a small barrier between you and the outer elements. Sound insulation underfoot can also be improved with good underlayment beneath a carpet or with insulation boards or cork tiles.

An effective bedroom layout

More often than not, it is the shape and configuration of the space that dictates how the bedroom is laid out, and particularly where the bed can be set. If you have a window in the room, it is pleasant to have it at the foot or side of the bed so that you can look out at the sky or view beyond, but avoid sleeping with your head directly under a window because you may be subjected to drafts while you are asleep, which can cause stiffness in the neck and shoulders.

The door to the room will also influence where the bed is. Try to allow adequate space for the door to open and for the person entering the room to have a clear space in which to turn around

without walking straight into the bed. Some people prefer to place their bed behind a door so that it is hidden or shielded from view. This is because a bed is the most personal and intimate piece of furniture in the home, and one that some people prefer to keep as private as possible.

The position of cupboard or closet doors will also have to be considered, and if the closet is built-in, then the location of the bed will have to be fitted around it. There should be enough space for the closet door or doors to open and give adequate access to the contents without having constantly to move other pieces of furniture.

Creating the right environment

Once you have decided on the layout of the room, there are other important considerations, such as good ventilation and maintaining the right temperature. There is a tendency to make the bedroom too warm because people feel that this is a place where they are naked or only lightly clothed, but

an overheated bedroom may cause the sleeper to dehydrate. The ideal temperature for a bedroom is 55–60°F, though it should be slightly warmer for children and older people.

A humidifier helps keep a little moisture in the air, especially during the height of the summer. You do not need an expensive humidifying machine, just a good-sized, shallow bowl of water with a reasonable surface area. Wash the bowl and replace the water every day so it does not become stagnant. Although it is best to sleep in a well-ventilated room, do be careful to avoid drafts.

It is also beneficial to air the bedroom each day by opening the window and door to get a flow or circulation going. If you live in the city or close to the road, leave a washable cotton sheer or voile curtain over the window while it is open to help reduce the amount of smog and grime that will inevitably come in through the window. Bedding should be turned back each morning so that the bed can be well-ventilated.

Bedroom flooring

Floor coverings in a bedroom are important because they help dampen noise and also because they usually come in contact with bare skin. Wool carpets are the softest and warmest underfoot, but if you suffer from allergies or are dust-sensitive, a carpet can be a place that harbors fine particles and produces fluff.

Wood floors are relatively warm on bare skin but need to be well-sealed to prevent splinters. Wood is also easy to clean. To soften the area around the bed, you can use rug or mat made from cotton or other washable fiber. Stone is not usually a good bedroom floor covering because it is hard, and unless underheated, also cold.

Above: *Warm colors can be enveloping and soothing when used in a bedroom.*

Left: *In this attic bedroom, mirrored panels on the cupboards reflect light and create the illusion of depth.*

Positioning pictures and mirrors

If a mirror is to be used for applying makeup and for checking clothing, it should be positioned so that it benefits from a source of natural light.

Some people find it disturbing to have a mirror directly opposite or over the foot of the bed because it reflects their image, and the play of shadows makes them think someone else is in the room. But in a small space, a large mirror can help to reflect light from a window and make the room seem larger.

Right: *This basement bedroom is painted a bright, warm, vibrant color because there is little access to natural light.*

Below right: *This young girl's bedroom has soft decorative touches, such as the painted closet, and is not overtly childish, making it a comfortable and enjoyable room for an adolescent, too.*

Color and style

The bedroom is often the room where people indulge in decorating fantasies, opting for a favorite color or theme, something with richly colored Victorian overtones or a Zen-like, cool space.

If a husband and wife, partners, or young children share a bedroom, then it may also be a place where a compromise has to be reached regarding color and style so that it is neither overpoweringly feminine nor too masculine. Many people prefer to keep the decoration of the bedroom simple so that it is easy to clean and maintain. Swags and frills tend to collect dust and a plethora of knickknacks and decorations just adds to the burden of cleaning.

Left: *This skylight is not overlooked so there is no need to add a shade or screen unless you prefer total darkness in your bedroom. The use of a mirror also reflects the natural light and makes this compact top-floor room feel more spacious. The neutral colors give it a relaxed feel.*

Clear space is also more therapeutic and relaxing than a cluttered room. A bedroom should be comfortable and an enjoyable place to be, but not a area full of unwanted collections of clothes, shoes, and books. Well-placed and plentiful storage is extremely necessary in a bedroom (see Display and storage, pages 164–7).

Using color

Good colors for bedrooms are those from the neutral and pastel range of the spectrum. Warm, soft yellow, watery blue, or pale green are all worth considering.

Yellow is a sunny color that is cheerful and heartening on winter mornings. Choose your tone of yellow carefully—one with a paler, white base can be more comfortable than one with a red/orange emphasis, which might make you feel overheated. Some sludgy yellows with green overtones also look slightly grubby in low electric lighting, which is not an inspiring or appealing sight in a bedroom.

Some people find blue cool, but it is the color of natural elements (water and the sky) and it is said

At-a-glance color guide

Light pastel colors are good for bedrooms because they are relaxing and calming. Yellow is a warm color at night but sunny and bright in the morning. Blue can be cool and refreshing but may need elements of pink or lavender to prevent it from making a room seem cold.

Green is a color associated with renewal and rebirth and it can be invigorating and refreshing to wake up to in the morning. Red is a bold color that is rarely used in quantity in a bedroom because it can make a small room feel very claustrophobic and overheated.

Opposite: This child's bedroom has been carefully planned to fulfill changing needs. The fabric around the bed can be pulled across while the room is used as a play area during the day. And as the child gets older a quiet study area will be needed. The desk will provide that, but for now, it is a display area for the child's doll house.

Below: This young girl's bedroom is warm and comforting with soft peach-colored walls with a delicate print, which is repeated in the drapes at the small window above.

Below right: Timeless pieces, such as this brass bed, look good in a traditional setting. The cool blue used in the room has been warmed up by the brass accessories.

to be a color that can aid relaxation. Cool blues can be warmed by a touch of red, taking them to the lavender side of the color wheel, or with the addition of accessories and bed throws that are decorated with patterns that include various warmer shades.

Green is said to be a color of rejuvenation and growth, and the right shades can be bright and fresh. But be wary of teaming it with its contrast color of red in a bedroom because these colors are diametrically opposed and in certain strengths and shades can appear to "fight" or clash, which is neither calming nor relaxing. Soft almond or pale mint green can be used successfully with wood furniture because green and brown have a natural earthy affinity. These colors together can be used to create an extremely pleasant and tranquil bedroom.

Potent, strong colors may be used to create a bedroom with impact. You can create an

interesting scheme using one wall of strong color or pattern and then decorate the rest of the room in a soft, solid color. The wall that is often chosen to make a feature of is the one behind the bed's headboard. This is because the color creates an impact on entering the room and highlights the bed, which is the main feature and purpose of the space.

The other advantage of putting strong color or pattern behind the headboard is that you do not see it when you are in the bed, unless you deliberately turn your head around. In this way, the color and fun are there, but when you are lying on the bed or are in it, unwinding or going to sleep, your eyes focus on the soft, plain color that has been used on the other walls.

Using fabrics to create mood

Light and decorative fabrics such as toile de Jouy can be attractive in a bedroom. These prints are generally in red, blue, or gray on a white or off-white background. They depict cameo scenes and views—many are inspired by 18th-century pastoral paintings, but modern interpretations can also be found.

When using fabrics in a bedroom, try to keep the words "fresh and simple" in mind. If you are keen to have a multifloral material or dense pattern, restrict it to the drapes and perhaps a bed cover, or maybe a single chair or pillow, but avoid teaming it with a floral or busy wallpaper. If you cover every surface with a dense pattern, the room will appear small, overcrowded, and stifling.

Secondary uses

In an ideal world the bedroom would be a single, dedicated sleeping space, but in reality, and particularly in metropolitan living, the bedroom may need to double up and be used as an exercise facility, dressing room, and clothes storage area, or even a place to study or work in. It would also be great if every child could have a large playroom and garden den, but modern homes rarely provide this luxury. Instead, space often has to be found within their bedrooms.

Whether in an adult or children's bedroom, making the secondary function fit in around the main one will require careful planning. For example, in one-room or studio apartments, it may be worth considering a foldaway bed that pivots back against the wall. This sort of flip-up bed is generally housed in a purpose-built cupboard so that when it is not in use its presence in the room is unnoticed. Other options are foldaway sofa beds and futons.

Another solution that works well in tall, high-ceilinged rooms, and provides a dedicated bedroom space, is the sleeping platform. This is a purpose-built mezzanine level that needs only to be the width of the bed plus a few feet around it. This can be installed against an end wall, leaving the floor space underneath free for use as an office or living area. With sleeping platforms it is important to have enough head room above to make it comfortable. To save even more space on the lower level, a sleeping platform may be cantilevered or supported on brackets, therefore negating the need for pillars. This sort of structure should be devised by an engineer or architect.

In children's rooms, space can be invented by the installation of a platform bed with a play area

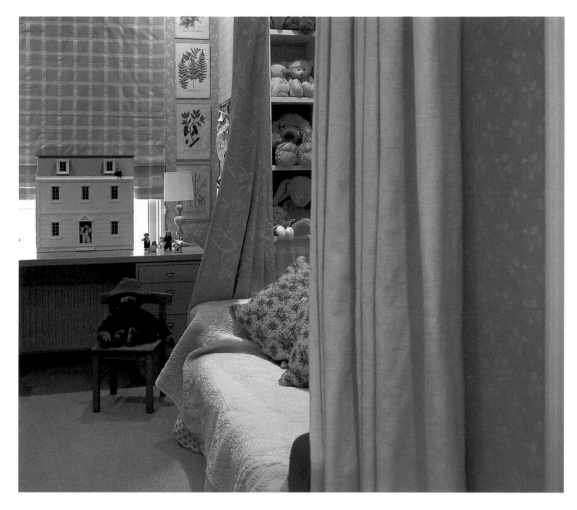

underneath it. Of course, this is only suitable for older children who will be able to climb up and down a ladder. By raising the height of the bed to the level of the upper bunk of a bunk bed, a desk or den area can be created underneath. The newly reclaimed floor area can house a desk or work station with a chair. To save more space, the desk could be built-in against a wall and a set of shelves constructed to one side, for storing books, crayons, and other items (see Display and storage, pages 164–7).

Elsewhere in this underbed zone there could be a curtain so that the lower area can be screened off from the rest of the room. A couple of floor pillows could be introduced because these take up less space than rigid chairs and can be easily

stacked one on top of another when not in use. Whether the space is used for play or study, your child will love having such a unique room.

Another option is to raise the floor level by building a row of deep steps up to a bed platform. This does not need to be as high off the ground as the other option, because the room underneath will be used for general storage rather than a built-in desk.

By raising the bed to about 3 ft. off the floor, you will gain copious amounts of storage space underneath. The access to the bed is by two or three long, but shallow, steps. These steps can be softened with pillows and used for sitting when not needed. The space under the steps, accessed by doors in the side, will provide valuable storage.

Containing a work area

A specially devised cabinet or cupboard is one way of containing your work area. This type of cupboard is deep and opens in half—one side contains shelves for storing files and paperwork and the other forms a desk with a computer. When it is not in use, one half folds over the other to conceal the contents.

A deep wall cupboard can also be kitted out in the same way with a desk shelf or platform on a slide or pivot base so that it can be pulled out on a runner. The shelf may be folded back and closed up out of sight in the cupboard door when work time is over.

Furnishings and textiles

The golden rule for a relaxing and calming bedroom is to keep the furnishings and decoration simple. The cleaner and more accessible the space, the more enjoyable it will be to live in. Natural, soft, and absorbent fabrics are ideal.

Choosing the right bed

The major piece of furniture in a bedroom is, of course, the bed. On average, we spend a third of our lives in bed so it is vital that you try out plenty and then buy the one that is right for you.

Below: *This traditional-style bed is raised off the floor, which ensures all-round air circulation.*

There are those who strongly advocate a firm mattress for a good night's sleep but that may not be the best type for you, especially if you already suffer from aches and pains.

What you really need is a bed that offers the right support for your spine while allowing the hips and shoulders to lie comfortably in their natural curvature. Your spine should form a shallow "S" shape when you lie flat, and a straight horizontal line when you lie on your side. Use a pillow, neither too thick nor too thin, that supports the nape of the neck correctly and aligns the head.

It is also advisable to raise the bed or mattress off the floor to enable adequate air circulation around the whole bed. Also ,sleeping on the floor puts you closer to dust and fluff and can make it more difficult to get in and out of bed.

The standard bed available today comes in three main parts: the mattress, the base, and the head- and footboards.

Mattresses

On the surface most mattresses look the same, but there are several different interior constructions on offer. Foam mattresses are made from different layers and densities of material that "give" when a body lies on the surface. This type of mattress is best suited to a slatted base.

The most popular type of mattress on the market today is the pocket-sprung. A good bed will have a high number of tightly packed springs, as many as 1,500 in a double bed, that offer great individual support. Pocket-sprung beds do not have completely flat surfaces—there is a slight undulation—so the bed molds itself to the body shape.

Futons, originally Japanese mattresses used for sleeping on the floor or low wooden platforms, are another bed option. The traditional futon is unsprung and offers a firm place of rest. It is a space-saving option because it can be rolled up after a night's sleep and stored in a box or cupboard.

Base options

The base of a bed is usually slatted or a divan. Some old-fashioned beds have a frame with springs, but these are rarely found in modern stores.

The divan base is the most popular type. It is a box-shaped construction with a slightly padded top. It is generally upholstered in the same fabric as the mattress and has with castors for mobility. Some even come with deep drawers, which is

Left: *The walls of this Scandinavian-style bedroom have been covered, above chair-rail height, with a fresh blue-and-white gingham material, which creates a soft and cozy environment.*

Below left: *The bedcover and pillows here are quilted. Fabric can be quilted by sewing along the lines or motifs of a printed pattern—this insulates the piece, making it warmer.*

useful for storing spare bedding. A divan base generally comes without a head- or footboard but these can be bought separately and added as necessary.

Slatted bases have flexible slats made from laminated wood and supported on a frame. These offer a certain amount of "give," and in some systems the tension can be adjusted for firmer/softer support. A slatted base is recommended for foam mattresses.

When buying a mattress and base, make sure that you try the two together before purchasing to ensure that they are compatible.

Bed frames and boards

The most traditional bed dressing is the four poster. This dates back to the time when drapes were

Adjustable beds

A fairly recent introduction to the mass market is the adjustable bed. Adjustable beds usually operate electrically, and in the case of a double-width bed, there are two single mattresses and bases so that individual arrangements can be made for each sleeper. The adjustable bed allows you to raise the head, foot, or both ends at the same time. By raising the head it can be more comfortable for reading or drinking tea, and raising the feet slightly may help people with digestive or circulatory problems.

149

Above: *A pillow echoes the trim and fabric used for the comforter.*

Above right: *Neutral furnishings, such as this lamp, work well next to simple, understated bedlinen.*

Below: *This tone-on-tone scheme is lifted by a variety of textures from waffle to slub linen.*

Looking after your mattress

Mattresses should be replaced every 10 years because they will have deteriorated as much as 75 percent. Many mattresses need to be turned over regularly to spread the wear and tear and give springs a change to rebalance.

A mattress protector is also important. This can be a simple muslin or cotton cover that is pulled on over the mattress's own ticking cover and can easily be removed for regular washing. There are also special dust mite protective covers that people with eczema and asthma find particularly helpful.

hung around the bed so that they could be drawn to keep the cold at bay. Now, in the days of central heating, the drapes have a purely decorative purpose. The traditional four poster has turned wooden posts and a frame over the top. The back panel is sometimes hung with a thick or tapestry-style material between the two posts at the headboard. Then a canopy is placed over the top and drapes are hung around the side.

This ornate and heavy dressing has, in recent years, been refined and simplified into a simple, plain wood frame over which a single length of cotton voile is

draped. In country-style bedrooms, gingham and printed fabrics may be used on the voile.

The simplest dressing option is the covered headboard that can be attached, with long screws and washers, directly into the divan base. When choosing a headboard, whether it is fabric-covered, wood, or metal, find a style that is best suited to your overall decorative scheme. If your room is to be simple and Zen-like, a natural cherry wood, paneled, or rail-topped headboard or a waxed pine surround would be in keeping with the overall mood. On the other hand, if you are opting for a scheme that is more decorative and colorful, then a padded headboard covered in a bright fabric with contrasting cording is a good option.

There is also the contemporary padded pillow or long hanging with tab- or tie-tops—these are hung from a rod fixed to the wall so that there is a buffer between your head and the wall (see Removable headboard hangings, pages 152–5).

Tall people often prefer to have a bed without a footboard so that they are not restricted by it, but for many traditional styles of bed surrounds, such as those wrought from iron, wood, and copper, matching head- and footboards are part of the overall effect.

Although there are many old bedsteads to be found in antique stores, they tend to come in smaller sizes and may require custom-made mattresses and bases. There are, however, many modern copies of these traditional designs. These brand-new versions are made in contemporary bed sizes and will most likely be coated or treated to make them rust-resistant, and in the case of brass bed frames, tarnish-resistant.

Traditional materials are also used to create modern steel and iron bedsteads. These can be simple, following traditional wood designs, or they can be more ornate with Art Nouveau-style fronds and tendrils. Many can be custom-made to your own specific design by a metalworker.

Bedlinen

Dressing the bed is also an extremely important decorative element. There is such a wide choice of bedlinens that it is often difficult to choose what you want. Changing your bedlinen can also be a simple but very effective way of marking seasonal differences in a room, keeping deep colors for winter and white or lighter colors for summer. There are many reversible comforter covers and pillow sets available today that are designed specifically to help create this very type of mood change.

Although colored and patterned bedlinen has been popular since the 1960s the classic white, crisp, cotton bedlinen has been a perennial favorite and suits every scheme and style, from simple to ornate. White bedlinen does not have to be boringly plain—the small details are what make it special. For example, cording, eyelet lace trim, a self-pattern, or monogram will all lift the appearance of a white linen-covered bed.

A range of pillows can make a bed attractive and contribute to the overall decoration of the room. There are many different shapes and sizes—some pillows are large and square, others long and rectangular. The old-fashioned bolster is a long, cylindrical pillow that was traditionally placed across the top edge of the bed to provide an angled support for a second pillow. Try experimenting with variously shaped pillows to find an arrangement that suits your bed.

You can also use different-colored pillowcases to emphasize the decorative scheme in a room. For example, you could use a dark shade on large, square pillows in the background and a paler cover for the rectangular pillow in the foreground.

Drapes and shades

Drapes and shades are a great way of pulling the overall color scheme in the bedroom together. When choosing the color, look at the fabrics that have been used elsewhere in the room, such as the bedlinen or pillows, and try to find a tone that will complement them.

Make sure that the style of drapes you choose fits with your decorative scheme. Light, sheer voile drapes work well in a contemporary bedroom, while heavy, rich-colored drapes, complete with swags, create an opulent ambience that would complement a traditional period-style scheme.

Below: It is important that the fabrics that you choose for your drapes and bedlinen are complementary. Here, simple white pillows work well with the neutral drapes that have a colorful trim.

Below left: White bedlinen is not boring. The details, such as eyelet lace or a raised pattern, make it special.

removable

headboard hangings

Muslin hangings work well in a modern interior and also provide useful storage space for bedtime reading matter. The hangings shown here form a fabric headboard at one end of a four-poster frame. Basic sewing skills are needed to make the storage pockets. Thick bamboo is inserted in channels at the bottom of the hangings to weight them down, while mother-of-pearl buttons provide a decorative touch and secure the hangings in place. Adding embroidered monograms gives a personal touch to a utilitarian bed.

Materials

39 ft. length of natural, undyed deckchair canvas

Cotton sewing thread to match

Gray silk stranded embroidery floss

9 large mother-of-pearl buttons

5 ft. length of 2-in. diameter bamboo

Tools

Sewing machine (or needle and thread for hand sewing)

Calligraphy book

Photocopier or computer, scanner, and printer

Tracing paper

Soft pencil

Embroidery hoop

Needle

Tailor's pencil

Square

Dressmaker's pins

Tape measure

Craft knife

Preparing the fabric

1 Cut three lengths of deckchair canvas to fit the space between the top of the bed frame and the mattress. Allow half a length extra on one piece for storage pickets plus a 1 in. hem allowance at each end. Press and hem. Fold two of the lengths of fabric in half and position these over the top of the bed frame. Choose some initials from a calligraphy book and enlarge them on a photocopier, or size and print them using a computer. Trace the initials onto a piece of tracing paper to form a monogram pattern.

Sewing the monograms

2 Transfer the monograms of your choice onto the hangings using a soft pencil. Secure an embroidery hoop in place over the monograms and use satin stitch to form the letters. Choose a color that complements your bedroom scheme.

Transfer the monogram onto the fabric using tracing paper and a soft pencil.

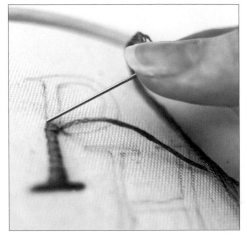

Use satin stitch to form the letters of the monogram pattern.

Know your materials

Canvas is a strong, utilitarian material that is available in a number of different weights, which makes it suitable for many different uses. Deckchair canvas has prefinished edges and is available in widths suitable for re-covering deckchairs. It can be found in various striped colors as well as the natural color used here. Its main advantage in this project is its strength because it can easily support the weight of books and magazines. It is readily found in large fabric stores and at scenic (theatrical) suppliers.

Making the pockets

3 Take the third piece of fabric and fold the front section of fabric forward to form a loop, and pin in place. With tailor's chalk and a square, mark out two channels using a folded magazine as a guide. Pin in place, then sew.

4 Use a couple of paperback books or magazines to measure the required depth for the top pockets. Pin the fabric in place, then sew using a medium-length straight stitch.

Hanging the fabric panels

5 Drape the fabric loosely over the bed frame, making sure that all three pieces are level. Mark four equidistant points across the top of the fabric, 1½ in. down from the top. Measure the buttons and mark the positions of the buttonholes with tailor's chalk.

6 Machine sew the buttonholes. If you prefer to hand sew them, make the buttonholes slightly smaller than your chosen buttons. As a finishing touch, neaten the edges with a buttonhole stitch.

7 Pin both ends of the buttonholes and slit with a sharp craft knife.

8 Stitch the buttons on the insides of the hangings and slot the bamboo into place.

Use a magazine to measure the size of the looped pocket and then pin in place.

Make sure that you leave enough room to store books in the bottom pocket.

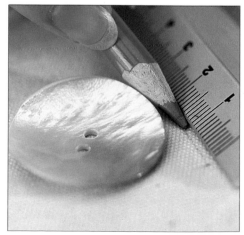

Measure the position of the buttonholes and mark with a tailor's pencil.

Alternative

Canvas is also an ideal material from which to make strong hanging storage because it can be folded up when not in use. The shelves are made from thick cardboard covered in canvas. These are stitched to each side panel, giving a concertina effect. It is essential to measure the depth of your hanging space before you begin, and to consider the dimensions of the items you wish to store.

Cut two equally sized side panels, then press and hem with a sewing machine. Decide on the number of shelves you require—do not forget the top and bottom pieces. Cut these all from thick cardboard using a craft knife and square. Cut pieces of canvas to cover each and machine stitch in place. Mark the position of each shelf in tailor's chalk on the inside of each side panel, then stitch in place. Stitch two flaps to the top panel and stitch strong Velcro onto them so that they can be secured around a clothes rod. Machine stitch the top and bottom panels in place.

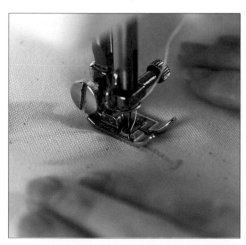

It is easiest to use a sewing machine to make the buttonholes.

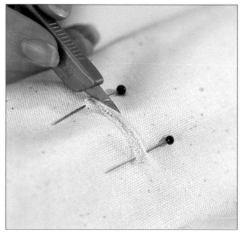

Cut open the buttonholes, using pins to mark the edges as a guide.

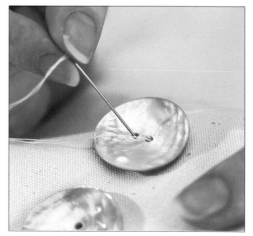

Stitch the buttons securely in place before hanging the panels on the bedframe.

whitewashed cork
headboard with
decorative niches

This simple, minimalist headboard is designed to look as if it is a built-in piece of furniture. The dimensions are dictated by the size of the sheets of plywood, which come in 8 x 4 ft. sheets, making it perfect for use behind a futon bed. The cork covering is an ideal surface for pinning up mementos while the shallow niches hold bedtime essentials like alarm clocks. The open sides of the headboard are ideal for storing magazines. Due to its height and weight, it requires careful handling and should be firmly secured to the wall using mirror plates.

Materials

2 x 2 in. planed wood cut to the following lengths: 4 lengths of 8 ft. and 5 lengths of 3 ft. 10 in.

Wood glue

Wood screws

2 sheets of ¼-in. thick plywood

Cork tile adhesive

Cork tiles

White woodwash

Quick-grip adhesive

Water-based satin varnish

Tools

Pencil

Square

Handsaw

Chisel

C clamp

Electric drill

Jigsaw

Metal ruler

Craft knife

Sandpaper

Miter saw

Making the framework

1 Begin by marking up the halving joints on the 2 x 2 in. wood in order to make the framework. To form the center, use one length of 8-ft. long wood. Use a pencil and square to mark the positions of five equally spaced horizontals (remember to take the thickness of the wood into consideration when doing this). Use a handsaw to make two parallel cuts halfway through the thickness of the wood. Then use a sharp chisel to remove the waste wood, leaving a U-shaped notch. Do the same to three of the 3 ft. 10 in. lengths, laying them across the center vertical and marking the corresponding notch on them.

2 With all the halving joints cut, spread a layer of wood glue in the notches and then slot them together. Grip each joint in turn in a C clamp, drill a hole, and then

Using a chisel, remove the wood so that you end up with a U-shaped notch.

Apply a layer of glue into each notch and then slot the halving joints together.

Know your materials

Miter cutters and saws are useful tools that enable you to cut a perfect 45° angle, which is essential for neat frame-making joints. If you do not want to buy one, they can be rented from all good tool rental stores. Alternately, you could use a more primitive miter box, which consists of a U-shaped trough made from wood or plastic with precut 45° slots. Your wood can be placed in the trough and then the slots used to guide a handsaw through to cut the required angle.

screw in place, making sure that the heads of the screws are countersunk below the surface. Secure the surrounding battens in place using simple butt joints.

3 Lay the framework onto each sheet of plywood in turn and mark the positions of the battens on it using a pencil. Clamp the marked side of the plywood onto the front of the frame and drill through the thickness of the plywood into the wood frame using a wood bit. Use countersink screws to attach.

Marking out the niches

4 Mark the positions of the cutout square niches on the remaining piece of plywood using a pencil and square. Make sure that each niche will sit just above a wood batten, which will provide the shelf.

5 Cut out the niches from the plywood sheet using a jigsaw. Attach the sheet to the front of the frame, screwing it into the battens with countersink screws.

Applying the cork tiles

6 Spread adhesive over the front piece of plywood and lay the tiles. Cut where necessary with a metal ruler and craft knife.

7 Lightly sand the cork tiles, then paint with a couple of coats of white woodwash.

8 Finish off the edges of the niches and the headboard by cutting an L-shaped trim with a miter saw. Attach this with quick-grip adhesive and hold in place with a C clamp until set. Varnish with a water-based satin varnish.

Drill through the plywood into the wood frame and hold in place using screws.

Mark the positions of the niches on the remaining piece of plywood.

Using a jigsaw, cut out the niche squares from the plywood sheet.

Alternative

If you prefer a softer, tailored look, why not create a padded headboard instead? Keep the dimensions tall and square to ensure a contemporary look. Upholstering a headboard in soft suede or leather is the ultimate in luxury and it will last for years, but for a budget version try imitation suede or moleskin in a subtle color.

Decide on the dimensions you want your headboard to be. Get your wood supplier to cut two pieces of ½-in. thick particle board, then sand the edges lightly. Get two firm pieces of thick foam cut to the same size as the particle board, then stick them in place using strong adhesive. Cut two pieces of fabric large enough to cover the foam-covered boards. Use a staple gun at the back to anchor the fabric cover in place, pulling it tightly over the foam as you do this. Staple opposite sides at the same time so that you achieve a good, even covering. Attach the boards to the wall just above the mattress using mirror plates.

Glue down the cork tiles over the whole surface of the front piece of plywood.

Lightly sand and then paint over the cork tiles using two layers of white woodwash.

Hold the L-shaped trimming around the niches and headboard in place using a C clamp.

framed

linen window shades with decorative panels

These panel shades are a great tailored alternative to fussy, frilly window treatments. Natural linen is sheer enough to let plenty of light in while still maintaining privacy. Here, a woven linen ribbon cross motif is fixed in place with a no-sew fusible web. Fixed on a light wood framework, the shades can be made to fit any size of window and can be mounted on the window in a variety of ways. A sliding mechanism has been used here, but if you have a window that is level with the wall, simply attach the panels with hinges to the frame and add a hook-and-eye fastening.

Materials

½ x ½ in. planed wood

Wood glue

Finish nails

White latex paint

Natural linen or similar-weight material

Linen or "linen-look" ribbon in two different widths and colors

Dressmaker's pins

Fusible web

Fabric glue

Tools

Tape measure

Miter saw

Hammer

C clamp

Paintbrush

Scissors

Iron

Staple gun

Hinges or sliding door kit

Making the frame

1 Calculate the size of frames you will need to make by measuring your window accurately. Next, cut the ½ x ½ in. wood to make the frames using a miter saw. Apply wood glue to the mitered pieces, then fix them in place using finish nails and a hammer. Clamp them using a C clamp until the glue is firmly set. Repeat the process in all four corners of each frame, allowing them to set overnight.

2 Paint over the surface of the frames with a coat of white latex paint.

Preparing the panels

3 Cut panels of linen that will be large enough to stretch around the frames. Next, cut the lengths of your widest ribbon and arrange them so that you form a cross on each panel. Add narrower ribbon over the top to form a border. Use dressmaker's

Glue the miters together using wood glue and then secure them with finish nails.

When the frames have been constructed, paint over them with white latex paint.

Know your materials

Fusible web consists of a thin material and backing paper in sheet or tape form that has been impregnated with fabric glue. It is used in sewing and dressmaking as a quick way of hemming a garment or applying an appliqué patch without actually sewing. It comes in a variety of different widths and strengths suitable for joining different weights of material. The glue is activated by pressing the fabric with a warm iron. Then the backing paper is peeled away. The two layers of fabric are then sandwiched together and pressed again with a warm iron to fuse them.

pins to hold all the ribbon in place while you turn it over.

4 Iron on lengths of fusible web to the back of the ribbon, following the manufacturer's instructions.

5 Spread the linen panels on a large, flat surface that has been protected with a heatproof cloth and iron the ribbon trim in place. The fusible web will cause it to stick to the linen.

6 Stretch the linen panels tight over each frame, folding the raw edges under. Staple these in place, making sure the fabric is pulled tight in each direction.

7 Use a nonstaining fabric glue to fix the ribbon trim around the edges of both frames, hiding the staples for a neat finish. (We

also added an optional border of ribbon to frame the panels.)

Attaching the panels

8 Attach your linen panels in the most suitable way. If you want the panels to swing open,

screw hinges to the sides of the panels and attach to the window frame. For panels that slide to the side, use a sliding door kit that consists of a channel fixed to the wall or ceiling. Then attach wheels or runners to each panel.

Make a cross pattern with the two sizes of ribbon and pin them together.

Turn all the ribbon over and iron fusible web onto the backs.

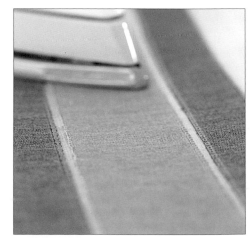

Put the ribbon back on the linen and iron it into its final position.

Alternative

If you do not have space for linen panels, or prefer a simpler window treatment, make a pull-up shade. These are less structured than Roman blinds; rather than forming stiff folds, they are gently gathered. They look particularly effective when made of a soft, natural fabric and hung unlined so that the light can filter through them.

Measure and cut a piece of fabric approximately 4 in. larger all around than the dimensions of your window. Turn over the edges, press, and hem with a sewing machine. Machine stitch a channel at the top of the fabric and insert a wood batten the same width as the shade—hand stitch to enclose it at each end. Stitch three vertical rows of small brass rings at regular intervals (of about 1 ft.) along the back of the shade. Attach three brass screw eyes along the back of the batten. Feed a length of cord through the screw eyes, then along the rings. When pulled, this will raise and lower the shade. Attach the batten with "L" brackets to a second batten fixed just above the window.

Staple the linen onto the frame using a staple gun. Make sure the material is pulled tight.

Hide any staples by gluing on ribbon trim around the edges.

Attach the panels to your window using an appropriate method. One way is to use hinges.

Display and storage

The more efficiently your closet is arranged, the easier it will be for you to see what is there and to select your clothes. Bundles of sweaters stuffed at the back of a shelf and shoes hidden under the bed slow down the process of dressing and make it a difficult rather than pleasurable task.

Storage furniture

Effective storage in your bedroom is essential to keep it tidy and inviting. When planning your bedroom, consider what storage option would be most suitable to meet your requirements.

Closets and cupboards

Division of closet space is important—keep one section for long coats and dresses but subdivide the rest of your hanging space into two levels to double the capacity. Shirts and skirts can go in one half and jackets and half-folded trousers in the other.

Closets come in a variety of styles and shapes. The most common these days is the built-in closet or prefabricated built-in closet, which stretches across one wall or is built into niches on either side of a chimney breast. Nowadays, the freestanding armoires that are available are usually either the traditional heavy wood style or the more modern particle-board variety.

If space in the bedroom is limited, you could use a simple metal rod fixed to the wall or on its own supports, with a fabric curtain to cover the clothes and prevent dust from gathering on them. Sliding doors also work well on closets in a small room where there may not be enough room to open hinged doors fully.

On the other hand, if space is not a problem, divide off a section of your bedroom and create a walk-in closet. You can install directional, recessed spotlights into the ceiling so that the light is good and everything is visible.

In a child's bedroom, the divides between hanging and shelving can be smaller because children's clothes need less space. A recess could be fitted with a deep drawer at the base for shoes and boots, a couple

Below: Built-in closets can be tailored to fit in and around even the most awkward spaces. The interiors can also be arranged to provide hanging and storage to suit your clothes and accessories.

Below right: This wall of closets was built around a fireplace. The shelves above the fireplace are less deep, but are still perfect for smaller items such as folded T-shirts or knitwear.

Left: *A walk-in wardrobe combines hanging and storage space with a dressing room.*

Below: *By subdividing a drawer with a storage tray you can keep small items such as socks and tights neat so that they are easy to find.*

of narrow shelves for small sweaters, T-shirts, and shirts, and then a hanging space incorporated above. If you use curtains instead of doors to cover this space, choose a bright, fun fabric to reflect the child's interests.

Chests of drawers

The other main area of storage in a bedroom is usually a chest of drawers. Drawers can benefit from being subdivided so that things are kept in separate niches instead of in a jumble. Small items such as socks and pantyhose can easily be rolled up into a ball and slotted into individual sections of a drawer divider.

When planning your shelf storage, think carefully. Some people opt for fewer big, deep shelves, but in fact they would be better with more narrow shelves because you tend to end up with two piles of clothes with a deep shelf. This means that the ones at the back are difficult to access without removing everything in front. Narrow shelves allow the clothes to be positioned in easily accessible stacks.

Bedside tables

A bedside table or tables are also practical. These can be freestanding units or in some cases are an integral part of a headboard. As the bedroom is a place for relaxing, books, a radio, and a CD player may be placed on these tables, along with a telephone and bedside light. Then there are all the things that may be needed—a box of tissues, alarm clock, a glass of water.

This essential night equipment can build up until it eventually overflows onto the floor or under

Above: *These units are ideal for storing folded shirts.*

Below right: *This wall-mounted bedside table takes up a minimal amount of space but provides neat storage for essentials.*

the bed. Therefore you should try to make sure that your bedside table is commodious enough to house all the things that you need. Look for something with shelves or a cupboard underneath so that there is plenty of storage for different-sized objects.

To ease the pressure on the limited space of a bedside table, you could use a wall light instead of a table lamp— something with an adjustable head or arm so that the light can be positioned for reading. If you have a fabric cover for your headboard (see pages 152–5), you could also sew pockets at the edge to hold small, light, useful objects such as tissues and a pocket alarm clock.

Additional storage items

If your room is spacious, you may like to add a wooden trunk or chaise longue at the end of the bed. The trunk provides more storage but is also a useful place to lay clothes and sit on.

An easy or occasional chair, whether it is a small armchair or a more genteel style such as a slipper chair, can also be an asset in bedroom. As well as being attractive to look at, it is useful.

Storage solutions

Another consideration in bedroom storage is the diversity of size of things that are kept there. Items range from earrings to overcoats and from flimsy lingerie to boots and shoes. Each requires special containers to suit its size and shape.

Shoes and boots

Boots and shoes take up space and are awkward to store unless placed in a specially designed container. You can buy or make hanging shoe pockets. These have a banner-shaped backing with rows of deep pockets sewn on the front. Each pocket is long and deep enough to hold a pair of shoes.

Another alternative is a shoe rack or drawer that can be stored in the lower part of the closet. Shoe racks come in two main styles. One is a metal version that has upright loops onto which the shoes are slotted so that the toe of the shoe points upward and the heel down. The second style is made of wood and a simple, narrow, two-shelf construction onto which the shoes are lined in

Scented liners

Both closets and drawers can benefit from the introduction of scented liners. In closets, especially where men's clothes are stored, the woody, slightly musky aroma of blocks of cedar can be most attractive. These can also be slotted among shoes and boxes at the base of the closet.

Liners are decorative paper sheets, impregnated with scent, that are placed at the base of a drawer to release their scent gradually and keep clothes resting on top of them lightly perfumed. Some people also put bars of good-quality soap in drawers to perfume the contents.

However, you may prefer to use a mirror in the bedroom that is adjacent to a window in order to benefit from the daylight.

Decorative storage

Large boxes that may be used for storing blankets and thick sweaters can be made to look more attractive and more an integral part of the room's scheme if you cover them so that they coordinate. If you are wallpapering the room, you could simply use excess paper to cover the boxes. Otherwise simple and inexpensive lining paper is a plain alternative.

For a more ornate finish you could staple or glue on remnants of material, such as pieces of leftover fabric from drapes or upholstery. For a really simple finish, you could paint the boxes the same color as the walls, or cover them with a couple of layers of gloss paint to make them look like a lacquered container.

Above: *Perfume bottles are attractive items to display and look good on glass shelves.*

Left: *These are specifically designed shoe drawers in a bedroom cupboard.*

Below: *This cupboard has narrow shelves where shoes are stored in neat rows.*

pairs. Another option is to store your shoes in bags or shoe boxes—label these on the outside for easy identification.

Boots are usually best stored with boot trees. Another option is to hang them from coat hangers with clips at the end. The weight of the base of the boot helps to pull the boot straight.

Jewelry and ties

Jewelry is generally small and delicate so it needs to be stored extremely carefully to avoid any damage. Long chains or necklaces may be best arranged in curls or circles in a deep box or hanging from a coat hanger. Earrings should be stored in pairs. You can buy boxes that are subdivided into small compartments and these are ideal. Otherwise, visit a jewelry store where you can buy specific earring boxes.

Ties and belts can be hung on small brackets or racks fixed to the inside of a closet door, once again keeping them in groups and subdividing them into colors so that they are easy to select and remove.

Cosmetics and toiletries

As well as clothes storage, there will be a certain amount of space needed for cosmetics, hairbrushes, hairdryer, and other toiletries. A collection of little bottles and pots may be best stored on a tray or in a small box that is kept in a cupboard or on a dressing table. The tray or box will enable them to be easily lifted out together.

A few decorative bottles and attractive pieces can be left on show, but remember that perfume is adversely affected by exposure to direct sunlight. Therefore, even though the bottle may look pretty on your dressing table, its contents will deteriorate if it is left out in the bright sunlight for too long.

If you have an en-suite bathroom, a certain amount of cosmetics and toiletries can be stored and used in there.

lighting your bedroom

Lighting in a bedroom should be on two levels—a general central light or wall lights that illuminate the whole room, and small bedside lights that can be used for reading. Remember to position the main light switch beside the bed so that you can switch off all the lights without having to get out of bed.

Planning your lighting

The lighting that you use in a bedroom can play a fundamental part in creating a relaxing atmosphere. For general points about lighting design, see Effective lighting on page 134.

Bedroom lighting needs to work on two levels. First, you need to have an efficient ambient lighting system. This light needs to be powerful enough for you to see clearly when selecting clothes or

Below: A decorative sheer-fabric shade softens and diffuses the light.

Right: An adjustable task lamp, attached to a headboard, provides a light to read by.

applying makeup. Second, the bedroom is the room where you wind down and read before you go to sleep, so good use of task and decorative lighting is vital.

Ambient lighting

In most bedrooms ambient lighting is provided by a pendant or by a series of recessed lights in the wall or ceiling. The decoration of these central lights can be as ornate or as simple as you wish. Chandeliers and pretty decorative

shades work well within a traditional scheme, while recessed ceiling lights complement the contemporary bedroom.

When planning the wiring of these lights, make sure you have switches by the door and the bed, so that you can illuminate the room as you enter, but also turn off all the lights in the room without having to get out of bed.

To make a bedroom a really relaxing place to be, you may also want to add a dimmer switch so that the main light can be reduced to just a subtle glow. This type of arrangement can also be beneficial in a baby's or small child's room, so that just enough light remains to provide comfort, and ease of access for an adult, without disturbing a child's sleep.

Task lighting

In sleeping areas, bedside lamps are a practical addition to a pendant or other ambient light. The bedside light can be in the form of a traditional ceramic or wood base and shade, a wall-mounted adjustable lamp, or a concealed light over the headboard. You can also have a light with a baffle that focuses the light on one side of the bed so that a partner sleeping on the other side will not be disturbed by the beam.

A dressing table needs its own light source positioned so that the light is not seen directly in the mirror because this will make it difficult for the viewer to see, but still targeted so that it illuminates the person who is using it.

Right: *Floor-level lighting can provide a stylish effect in a minimalist, contemporary bedroom.*

Below: *This light is attached to the wall next to the bed, therefore saving space on a bedside cabinet.*

Bedroom accessories

The bedroom is a place where many people indulge their decorating dreams, but it is also a personal space where you relax and unwind and should therefore be comfortable and well-organized. Apart from the larger items such as the bed and general storage, it is the small touches that will add to the intimacy and coziness. If there is space, a chaise longue or chair and footstool can be added so that you can sit or recline comfortably without having to get into bed. A wooden trunk or ottoman, with storage in the base, may also be placed at the foot of the bed and be used for laying down clothes or sitting on when putting on boots or shoes. Window dressings also play an important role—they should be dense enough to provide privacy and darkness to help you sleep, but decorative and attractive so that when they are pulled back during daylight they are a feature. Whether plain or ornate, the rod/valance area should be treated as part of the overall design and complement the fabric and style of the dressing beneath.

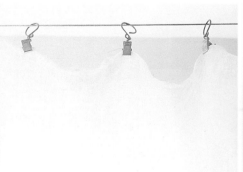

CLOCKWISE FROM TOP LEFT:

A motif has been picked out from the dominant fabric in the room and painted onto the corner of the valance to complement the drapes.

An Asian, embroidered door hanging has been used to soften and decorate the mantel above a fireplace in this bedroom.

A simple scheme with neutral colors and natural fabrics can be relaxing and calming.

This appliqué pillow brings together several shades of pink used in the room.

A bedside lamp is an ideal task light for reading in bed. Additional ambient lighting, such as this candle, can be used to create a relaxing atmosphere.

A simple opaque white canvas shade obscures the view in this minimalist bedroom.

Here, scented cedar blocks in a small fabric bag are hung around the neck of a coathanger. Their subtle scent will permeate the whole closet.

Cosmetic items such as this perfume bottle and matching glass pot can also double as bedroom ornaments.

Use scented paper to line any shelving that stores clothing. This will keep it fresh and will also add a pleasing but subtle aroma.

When in doubt, choose plain, simple, white bedlinen—you can never go wrong with it.

This metal wire provides an easy, no-sew method of hanging lightweight drapes.

Do not forget the smaller details. By choosing decorative knobs for your cupboards and drawers, you can lift and unify the whole scheme.

A paper bag filled with dried herbs, such as lavender, can scent your clothes. Alternately, you could fill it with mothballs.

Well-designed storage is absolutely vital in a bedroom. This partitioned cupboard provides neat, individual compartments for hanging items as well as folded clothes and accessories. This makes it easy for the owner to locate specific clothing.

Dining rooms

Planning your dining room

These days many homes do not have a separate dining room—a dining area tends to be part of another room, for example, the kitchen or living room. This duality of spaces means that the decoration of one will be influenced by the other, so schemes for these areas must be carefully planned.

Below: *Tall folding doors create an elegant divide between the modern kitchen and a classic dining room.*

Below right: *An arch, knocked through a rear wall, creates a passageway between the dining room and extended kitchen beyond.*

Opposite: *The colors of the spacious dining room and the adjacent kitchen complement each other so there is no visual barrier between them.*

Planning your space

The role of the dining room is continually being usurped by the kitchen, where a table caters for the needs of both scattered and regular family mealtimes.

The advantage of a detached dining room is that it can be laid in advance, and after the meal the door can be closed on the debris and forgotten until later. It is also removed from the clatter and preparation in the kitchen and provides a change of venue and ambience from the living room.

The separate dining room dates back to the 18th century when eating and drinking were taken seriously, so the dining room was considered of great importance and status. These days entertaining is still an enjoyable way of spending time with friends but there is little formality, and the explosion of interest in a more casual style of cooking and barbecues makes a separate or grand dining room a little out of place.

Delineating the dining area

The modern dining room is most likely to be part of a main living area or an adjunct of the kitchen. In both cases, the location and type of lighting will play an important part in altering the mood so that there is a change of ambience between a family breakfast, television watching, or

Protecting your dining table

You can buy lightly padded table protection by the foot in most good fabric stores and many furniture stores. This has an insulatory layer that prevents heat from damaging the varnish or finish, and prevents dents or marks from being made by heavy pots or knives. Over this you could put a plastic-coated cloth for day-to-day use.

Below: *This dining area is part of a family kitchen, yet the high-back, upholstered dining chairs and chandelier give it a distinct identity.*

Below right: *This open space is divided into separate rooms, but the wide open doorways give the impression of it being a single space.*

an evening meal with friends. In addition, the table setting style and the overall decor of the room will also be influential.

A change of flooring may also help to delineate the food preparation part of the room from the entertaining section. In the kitchen, the floor should be durable and practical, so stone, linoleum, or terra-cotta tiles are ideal, whereas in the dining area the floor could be warmer, welcoming, and stylish, so wood or a high-quality, polished limestone, perhaps with a rug or kelim, would be appropriate.

In many kitchens, a section of work area—an island or length of units and worktop—creates an actual, physical break between the two areas. This works well and creates the impression of having a distance between the dining and food preparation zones.

The dining table

The configuration and layout of the dining space should allow for a certain amount of flexibility, so that a family of four will be comfortable having lunch there, but a dinner party for eight will feel equally at home. An extending table will help to accommodate this, whether there are separate leaves to be inserted, or adjustable flaps that fold down.

There are some ingenious round table designs that enlarge by the addition of segments, like putting pieces into an orange. A simpler method is to have a larger disk, made in a cheap material such as particle board, that clips on top of the smaller table and can be disguised by a generous round tablecloth. The larger disk can be hinged in the center so that it may be folded in two and stored in a cupboard, under a bed, or in a garage until it is required.

Seating arrangements

Dining room seating is an important consideration. It is one thing perching on the edge of a wooden stool when you are gulping down breakfast, but quite another to be expected to sit through a lengthy dinner party on a hard stool with no back support.

Dining chairs should have a back to provide support for the diner, and if made of wood or metal, padding is important. You can also dress chairs up to give them a more formal appearance by adding a slip cover (see box, right, and pages 184–7).

Another option is to build a well-upholstered window seat or bench-style arrangement along a wall. This is ideal for children and will enable you to seat more people than you could in separate seats. The table can be placed in front of the window seat and extra chairs lined up around the edges.

Above: *A low wall separates the dining and kitchen area from the seating space beyond.*

Covering chairs

High-back padded dining chairs are comfortable but can be decoratively covered to make them a feature. The most simple dressing is a long panel of fabric, the width of the back and base of the chair. This drapes over the front and down the back of the chair and is held in place with simple ties at the top and base of the seat back. More tailored covers with skirts that cover the legs are also popular. These can be held in place by bright buttons or contrasting ties of cord or tape.

Above: The way you dress the dining table is as important as the decoration of the room as a whole. It should echo the style of the meal being served, whether it is formal or informal.

Below right: This dining area is at the front of this house, overlooking the street. However, clever use of half-shutters and crisp white linen drapes means that the view is obscured but natural light can still come into the room.

At-a-glance color guide

Red is a traditional color for dining room walls—it is a rich period color and looks opulent in candle or electric light. Chocolate brown, which has an element of red in its composition, is also a luxurious color against which crisp white linen and sparkling glassware look good. However, these rich, lavish colors lose something of their intensity in daylight so they are best used in evening-only rooms.

Color and style

When considering what colors or style options to use in a dining room, look at the other functions that take place in the space, and also how natural light and artificial lighting will affect the color and decor at different times of day.

Using color

If you have a separate dining room, you may like to look at richer, darker, more dramatic tones. Dining rooms are most often used at night so you can afford to indulge in all your favorite jewel shades.

Dark red, rich emerald green, and even chocolate brown can look wonderful under muted electric light and candles. Even minimalist and contemporary schemes can include a panel or single wall of these rich colors to spice up a simple setting.

For a living/dining area, choose a scheme that is suitable to both day- and nighttime living. Again, table dressings and lighting can help transform a dining area, but the wall color and floor covering should be compatible to both functions. If in doubt, opt for a neutral or plain scheme and then add details such as pictures, table lamps, and patterned pillows.

For a kitchen/dining arrangement, the emphasis should be on practicality—fabrics and dressings should be easy to remove and washable. In general, stick to light colors because they enhance a feeling of cleanliness and productivity. Choose a darker tone of the same color for the dining area because this will create a division but retain a link between both parts of the room. Or paint the kitchen in a single pale color and then incorporate this color into the dining area in conjunction with a darker tone of the same color or a paint effect combining the two shades.

There are certain colors that have an affinity with food and others that do not work as well. Deep purple is a color seldom found in kitchens or dining rooms; the sludgy shades of olive green, mouse brown, and mid-gray are also rarely seen. They may appear as part of a pattern or in a

worktop material such as slate or granite, but in quantity and on their own they can give an impression of grubbiness.

Even though you may vary the floor covering from one area to another and even dress up plain walls in the dining section, it is advisable to keep the ceiling in a uniform solid color, providing continuity and reflected light.

Style and furnishings

As well as linking shared spaces with color, it is advisable to keep to a similar style of furnishings. If the kitchen is futuristic in steel and glass, then the dining area should have complementary elements to reflect that look. If the sitting area of the room is in a neoclassical style, then the dining area should follow suit with columns, pilasters, and furniture in a similar vein. But if you have a separate dining area, in a room by itself, then you can opt for whatever style you like.

tiled tabletop with pickled driftwood edging

This tabletop can be teamed with the legs of your choice and used as a dining, coffee, or even outdoor table. Its tiled surface makes it practical to care for as well as heat-resistant. The ceramic tiles used here mimic more expensive sandstone or marble. Their irregular edges give them a handmade appearance and blend well with the driftwood finish of the wood edging. To give new planks a weathered finish, the grain of the wood was raised using a blowtorch, then the effect was toned down with white pickling wax. The wax protects the surface, too.

Materials

⅛-in. thick exterior-grade plywood for the base

Planks of wood slightly thicker than your tiles

Wood trim deep enough to cover the plank wood and edge

Pickling wax

PVA glue

Wood adhesive

Screws

Tile adhesive

Small "stone" ceramic tiles

Sandstone grout

Finish nails

Tools

Tape measure and pencil

Square

Handsaw

Miter saw

Blowtorch

Fine-grade steel wool

Soft cloth

C clamp

Electric drill

Notched trowel

Level

Flexible grout spreader

Calculating the framework

1 Sketch out the dimensions of your table, making sure that you will not need to cut any tiles. This will give you the measurements for the plywood base and the lengths of plank that will form the frame. Use a square or the edge of a handsaw to mark the 45° corner angles and use the miter saw to cut out your wood to form the four pieces for the frame.

Preparing the frame

2 Gradually singe the surface of the plank frame using a blowtorch on a low setting. The patterns in the grain will emerge gradually as the surface singes. Make sure that you do not forget to do the sides of the frame, too.

3 Apply pickling wax to the surface of the wood using fine-grade steel wool, working it well into the grain. Allow this to dry, then polish the surface with

Measure the size of the table, marking the 45° corner angles before cutting.

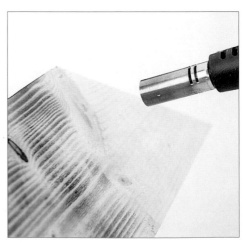

With a blowtorch, singe the surface of the plank frame until the patterns in the grain show.

Know your tools

• When using a blowtorch you should light it with care, following the manufacturer's instructions. Always wear heavy-duty gloves and a protective eye mask. To learn how to do the scorching method described in the project, practice on scraps of wood. This will allow you to see the length of time it takes to raise the grain without burning the wood.

• Always use a notched trowel when applying tile adhesive. This provides a grooved bed of adhesive that grips the tiles more effectively than a flat surface would.

• Flexible spreaders are used to apply tile grout once the tiles have stuck firmly to the adhesive. The flexible blade is used to force the grout into the spaces between the tiles. It can then also be used to remove any excess grout from the surface of the tiles.

a soft cloth to remove any excess pickling wax and to make sure you create a neat finish.

4 Seal the surface of the plywood with a coat of diluted PVA (1 part PVA to 2 parts water) and allow this to dry for approximately half an hour. Anchor the frame in place on the plywood base using wood adhesive. Clamp the frame with a C clamp until it sets, then drill a hole through the back of each corner and put a screw in place to make sure that you create a very firm fixing.

Preparing the surface

5 Apply a thick layer of tile adhesive to the plywood using a notched trowel. Cover the surface up to a height that will ensure that the tiles all sit level with the surface of the frame.

Laying the tiles

6 Bed the tiles firmly into the adhesive, checking regularly with a level to ensure that you achieve an even surface. Then make sure you allow the tiles to set overnight.

7 Use a flexible spreader to work the grout well into the tiled surface, making sure that

there are no gaps. Allow this to set, then polish off the excess with a soft cloth.

8 Singe and pickle the flat edge trim before mitering it to cover the edge of the table. Stick it in place using a thick layer of wood adhesive. Position small finish nails at regular intervals to make sure it is firmly secured.

Apply pickling wax to the surface of the wood using steel wool. Work it into the grain.

Glue the frame and plywood base together, clamp them, and insert screws in the corners.

Apply an even layer of tile adhesive to the surface of the plywood.

Alternative

If you would like to make a tiled table suitable for outdoor use, then buying a ready-made metal frame is the best option. Many small metalworking companies will be happy to make a table base to your dimensions. To apply an intricate design to it, you should use the indirect mosaic method.

Get your wood supplier to cut you a piece of exterior-grade plywood to fit snugly within the table frame. Seal both sides with PVA glue diluted 1 part glue to 2 parts water. Use colored pencils and a piece of squared paper to plan your design, calculating the exact number of mosaic tesserae needed. Cut a piece of heavy brown paper to the size of your tabletop, then scale up and transfer your design onto it. Stick individual tesserae, grooved side up, onto the paper using PVA glue. Spread tile adhesive onto the plywood surface. Carefully lift the paper and apply to the tabletop, paper side up. Allow to dry before wetting the paper in order to peel it away from the surface. Finally, grout around the tiles.

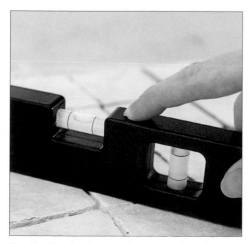

Lay the tiles in place and use a level to check you are achieving an even surface.

Grout over the surface of the tiles, making sure that you fill in all the gaps.

Glue the singed and pickled trim to the sides of the tabletop to finish it off.

suedette

dining chair cover with decorative trim

Any straight-backed dining chair can be instantly transformed with a simple slip-on cover. For a really luxurious look we have used a chocolate brown suedette, which is an imitation suede. Suedette is far more economical than the real thing, is easy to cut and sew, and will not fray. The trick to getting a really good fit is to make a muslin or paper pattern first. The leather thong lacing allows the material to be adjusted around the chair legs and also minimizes the amount of sewing involved. Decorative holes along the skirt and colorful feather trims provide a final flourish.

Materials

Muslin or paper make pattern

Dressmaker's pins

Suedette (around 5 ft.)

Cardboard

Eyelet kit (consists of eyelets, eyelet punch, and riveting tool)

13 ft. leather thong

Beads to trim

Tools

Scissors

Tape measure

Pinking shears

Sewing machine (or needle and thread for hand sewing)

Pencil

Hole-punching tool

Tailor's pencil

Making a template

1 Drape the muslin or paper over the chair and use scissors, a tape measure, and dressmaker's pins to cut and form the shape of the cover. For a snug, tailored fit, one long piece should be folded over to cover the front and back of the chair back.

The seat and skirt can then be formed by using additional pieces of muslin or paper.

2 Remove the muslin or paper from the chair and pin the pattern onto the suedette. Cut the pattern out of the material using pinking shears. Leave just

over 1 in. of fabric as an allowance all the way around in case there are any necessary final adjustments.

3 Turn the fabric inside out and pin it onto the chair, marking the position of the seams along the sides of the seat and back.

Lay the template over the suedette and cut out the material using pinking shears.

Once the fabric is pinned on the chair, mark the position of the seams using pins.

Sewing the cover

4 Sew the pieces together using a short straight stitch. Then press the fabric while it is still inside out using a cool iron. Turn the suedette the right side out and place it over the back of the chair to check the fit again. Make sure that the flaps meet neatly. Use scissors to trim any excess fabric as necessary.

Creating a pattern

5 Make a pattern of carefully measured holes with a pencil on a piece of thin cardboard and then use a hole-punching tool set on different settings to punch out the design. Use the cardboard as a template, placing it on the suedette. Mark the design on each flap using a tailor's pencil.

6 Turn the suedette over and use the hole punch on different-sized settings to punch out the design on the skirt.

Lacing the skirt

7 Using a tailor's pencil, mark six eyelet positions on each side of the skirt at 1 in. intervals. Punch these out with the hole punch. Thread lengths of leather thong through the holes to "lace" the skirt together.

8 Cut the ends of the thongs to length. Thread a silver bead onto each one, tying knots to secure the beads in place.

Sew the pieces of suedette together using a short straight stitch by hand or machine.

Once you have a template, mark your design onto the fabric with a tailor's pencil.

Punch out the design using the various sizes on your hole punch.

Alternative

If you prefer a more traditional look, why not adapt the pattern to add stylish covered buttons that fasten along the side of the chair? Covered buttons come in two parts—you simply cover the front piece in your choice of fabric before snapping the back in place.

Measure your chair and cut the fabric following the steps given in the main project, but add a slightly larger seam allowance. Then cut two additional pieces of fabric that will form side flaps to cover the back of the chair. Pin together inside out. Machine stitch the pieces together, hem the back piece neatly, and then turn the cover right side out. Position the cover in place over the chair and carefully calculate the positions of the buttons, making sure that they will provide a snug fit when fastened. Hand stitch them along the side of the cover. Stitch small loops of elastic in the corresponding positions along the length of the back flap. Slip the buttons through the loops to secure the cover in place.

Punch holes along the sides of the skirt and then lace them together with leather thongs.

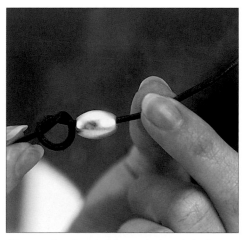

Place a silver bead at the end of each leather thong and secure it by tying a knot.

cotton drapes

with embroidered raffia motif

These simple drapes are the ideal way to dress a dining room window that overlooks a garden, linking inside and out. You can either make your own panels from scratch, following the steps below, or start with ready-made curtain panels and then just simply customize them. We used coarse string and raffia for the embroidered flowers, which have a naïve quality and add a pleasing textural dimension to the panels. Finishing them off with ribbon tabs is one of the simplest ways to suspend them from a rod.

Materials

Muslin or voile fabric
(you could use ready-made
muslin curtains)

Ribbon

Dressmaker's pins

Coarse green
hessian string

Raffia

Pearl buttons

Green ribbon

Tools

Tape measure

Scissors

Sewing machine
(or needle and thread
if hand sewing)

Tailor's pencil

Metal ruler

Darning needle

Creating the drapes

1 Measure the height from your curtain pole to the floor and add about 1 in. as a hem allowance. Cut the muslin or voile to form panels.

2 Cut lengths of ribbon to fit the top of the panels, then cut another eight 4-in. lengths of ribbon per panel. Pin these pieces at intervals under the long length of ribbon.

3 Sew the ribbons top and bottom in order to make sure that they are securely fixed in place. Next, create a hem along the bottom of each of the panels by using a straight stitch (this can be done by machine).

Positioning the flowers

4 Use a tailor's pencil and metal ruler to mark out the position of the flower stems on each fabric panel.

Hem the bottom of each panel using a straight stitch, either by machine or by hand.

Mark out the position of the stems on the cut panels using a tailor's pencil.

Know your materials

Cotton is a natural fabric that is available in a variety of different weights. There is a comprehensive range of plain and patterned finishes available and patchwork and most quilting suppliers will often offer a range of space-dyed cotton fabrics. Muslin is a fine soft cotton fabric with a fairly open weave that gives it a relatively gauzy appearance—this material is ideal if you want to make drapes that let plenty of light into the room. If you want to use an even sheerer fabric, choose from organza, voile, or chiffon.

Sewing the stems

5 Next, thread a darning needle with a length of coarse green string and sew along each of the stems using a large running stitch.

Making the flowers

6 Form the flowers using a length of raffia, which should be threaded onto a darning needle. Sew large loops of raffia to form the petals of the flowers. Finish each of them by knotting the raffia neatly on the reverse of the fabric. This will ensure that the flowers keep their shape.

7 Then sew a pearl button in the center of each flower head to complete the design. If you want to use this type of design in a children's room, there are many additions or alternatives to choose from. For example, you could customize it by using a colored ball fringe instead of buttons. Brightly colored raffia flowers and colored ribbon tab-tops would also work well.

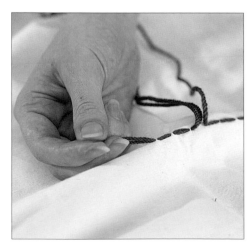

Sew along the stems with coarse green string using a large running stitch.

Make the petals by sewing large loops of raffia and securing them with a knot at the back.

Sew a pearl button in the center of each flower to finish it off.

Alternative

For a colorful alternative, you could always try dip-dying your piece of fabric. To do this, mix dye powder and the recommended fixative in a bucket, stirring well. Dip the ends of the fabric panels into the dye bucket and secure the top (on a washing line, for example). Leave in the dye for the manufacturer's recommended time. You will see that the dye begins to travel up the fibers of the fabric. Remove from the dye bucket and rinse under a running faucet until the water runs clear. Allow to dry completely.

Another method you could try is tie-dying. This is a technique that involves tying small bunches of fabric tightly with string. When dipped in the dye, the string acts as a barrier to the dye so that the areas covered by the string do not get colored. For a simple pattern of small circles, try tying small coins at regular intervals over the fabric. Dye, then hang on a washing line to dry before untying all the coins to reveal the pattern.

Whatever method you decide on, make sure that the fabric you are dying is compatible with your chosen dye. Also, try to choose a color that fits in with the overall decorative scheme of your room.

Occasional and small-space dining

Small and occasional dining areas are a feature of many homes. Although the lack of space can be restricting, careful planning and the use of furniture and fixtures designed to cope with such problems can make the best of what is available.

Design features

There are some design features that you can incorporate into your home that will enable you to make the most of the space that you have available or help you to create an occasional dining area, away from the main dining room.

Breakfast bar

This type of arrangement can be slotted in around other functions. For example, a peninsula worktop may also double up as a breakfast bar or occasional dining area. A worktop-only island unit can be covered with a cloth or mats to create a central dining point.

Beware when planning this type of arrangement that you leave enough overhang on the work surface so that the diner may pull their seat up under the worktop and sit with bent knees. It is also advisable to locate this type of eating area away from dishwashers and washing machines.

Breakfast bars or raised-shelf dining areas are best finished with rounded edges rather than angular ones. It is more comfortable for the diner to sit close to a round edge rather than jutting, angular corners, and if people bump into them, they will be less likely to hurt themselves.

Effective table designs

There are certain types of occasional dining furniture that are also very useful in small dining areas because they fold or stack away so that the maximum amount of floor space is available when the dining facility is not required. A clever system is a fake top drawer. This has a fake front panel that slips neatly into a standard unit of drawers, but when pulled out it opens up into a tabletop or dining surface (see box, left).

As well as the extending drawer table, there are standard foldaway tables, either semicircular or square, that are usually hinged

Right: Tall stools that can be pulled up beside an island unit to make a casual dining space work well in this colorful family kitchen.

to the wall and have an adjustable leg underneath that can be pulled out and fixed in place for stability. When you have finished, the leg is folded back and the table dropped flat against the wall. A similar type of arrangement can also be connected to the end of a section of worktop that has free space around it, possibly at the side of a passageway or entrance.

Tabletops can also be supported on hinges or a pulley so that they are raised and concealed in a cupboard, but then dropped and supported on a foldaway leg when needed. Another option is a wide, fixed shelf at the bottom of a row of shallower shelves. The narrower shelves above can be used to store books and china, but the wider shelf at the bottom is at a height to accommodate people eating. This works well along a flat wall but can also be used in a corner. Corners can be awkward spaces to use, but can be fitted with triangular shelves to provide storage.

Above: *The overhang of the surface of the unit in the foreground creates a breakfast bar, which is used in conjunction with stylish high stools.*

Left: *For more leisurely dining, chairs with supportive backs are preferable to stools.*

Chairs

Seating in small-space dining areas is often on high stools. These should have padded, sculpted, or at least pliable seats and backs, and most importantly, a foot rest. The main problem with sitting on a high stool is that you have nowhere to rest your feet, unless there is an integral foot bar or a bar is run along the lower section of the facing units.

The lower tables and surfaces will also require chairs. Again, the foldaway and stacking designs can be neatly stored but easily brought into use.

Making your dining space look bigger

In small dining areas you need to plan carefully in order to make the space feel larger and more roomy than it really is. There are several tricks of the trade that will enable you to do this.

Using mirrors

A mirror can be effective because it reflects light and offers a feeling of space beyond instead of a solid, definite wall. Mirrors can be set into panels in doors to give them a less dense and solid appearance.

However, a mirror must be treated with care, not only because it will shatter if a chair or the corner of a table is knocked against it, but also because too much mirror can make a small room become disorienting. Mirrors on opposite walls will create a continuous repetition of images that can have a dizzy and muddling effect, as well as giving a room something of a funfair or circus appearance.

Using glass

Another practical surface in a small dining area is glass because, like mirror, it does not appear solid or defining. Glass shelves, made from laminated and reinforced glass, can be used along a wall without making the space feel smaller, although what you stack or display on the shelves should be selected to emphasize this effect rather than conceal it. Glass, light-colored china and ceramics, and pale wood objects are best, rather than row upon row of books, which will be heavy in weight and give a dark and solid appearance.

Using color

Pale colors will also help to impart a feeling of space in a small dining area, so look for fresh, light colors such as yellow, cream, beige, blue, and almond green. Avoid dense and ornately printed fabrics, and for window dressings, a shade may save valuable inches compared with a heavily pleated pair of drapes.

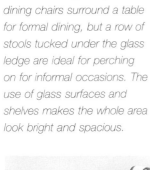

Below: The bright striped dining chairs surround a table for formal dining, but a row of stools tucked under the glass ledge are ideal for perching on for informal occasions. The use of glass surfaces and shelves makes the whole area look bright and spacious.

Floors and ceilings should be in pale colors, and you can rarely go wrong with a white ceiling and pale wood floors or pale stone tiles, both of which will help add to the feeling of spaciousness. If the floor and ceiling are dark, it can make a boxy and claustrophobic environment in a small space.

Clutter will also fill in the limited area you have, so pare down the amount of things you have on show. However, a balance must be found because a room devoid of objects or decoration will be boring and bland. A few carefully selected decorative objects will enhance but not overpower the room.

Playing with light

Lighting can also help make a small space seem larger. Small corner floor lamps can be placed in the corners of a room so that the beam shines directly up the wall from the floor, emphasizing the height of the space as well as illuminating the corners of the room and making them appear bright and defined.

A light placed over the middle of a centrally positioned table will also draw attention to the center of the room, and if the rest of the room is subdued, this will create a feeling of greater space as well as concentrate the focus on what is going on immediately in front of the diners rather than what lies behind them.

Building extensions

In some cases it may be possible to extend a small room to create a dining space. For example, if you have a side return from a garden, alley, or pathway, you could push the exterior wall out to incorporate this space. In situations such as this, it is often difficult to incorporate side windows into

the scheme because planning permission may be denied if it is felt that the side windows will overlook a neighboring property. Also, the view may not be worthy of the expense of installing a window. In these cases, a glass roof or panel can be the answer.

A sloping or arched glass roof, made up of reinforced panels, will allow light to flood into the dining area during the day and at night provide an interesting celestial "ceiling" to the room. Two factors that will have to be considered in this type of extension are ventilation and screening. The glass roof will not only allow natural light to penetrate the room

but also the sun. During the summer it may become incredibly hot, so louvers or a window section in the roof will allow air to circulate and help counteract the problem.

Also connected to the heat of the sun is its ability to fade and damage fabrics. A set of shades with canvas, wood, or special louvred slats will cut down glare, provide shade, and protect materials used in dressings in the dining area. Another option to maintain ventilation is a centrally positioned ceiling fan with variable speeds. This will give a vaguely tropical feel to a room but helps to stir the air and provide a cooling artificial breeze.

Above: *This sunroom extension has not only enlarged the kitchen area and made room for a separate dining space, it has also increased the amount of natural light in the main room.*

Display and storage

Display and storage in a dining area may, in some cases, be one and the same thing because useful items can also be beautiful. To keep the right emphasis, the pieces left on show should be selected for their decorative appearance rather than their utilitarian qualities.

Organizing your storage

The amount of storage that you need to allow for in your dining room depends on the layout of your house, whether you have a separate room for the purpose or whether it forms part of the kitchen or living area.

In the kitchen/dining area storage is paramount, not only to contain cooking ingredients and crockery but also to keep equipment and utensils under control. A cluttered kitchen will overwhelm a simple dining area, so it is best to keep kitchen surfaces as clear as possible—this will also provide more space on which to work.

If space is limited, you may need to store table linen and tableware in your living/dining room. It is particularly important to keep such items out of sight—otherwise, the living and relaxing area is in danger of becoming linked with the kitchen. While it is acceptable to have glass, bowls, pitchers, and decorative china on display in the kitchen/dining area, a living area is predominately for entertainment and relaxation.

Right: When planning your dining room storage, make sure that you have enough shelving space to keep all the accessories you may want near the dining table.

Storing dining equipment

Storage for dining-related items needs to be subdivided. Allocate a shelf for linens, tablecloths, and napkins, and another shelf for heat-resistant mats, napkin rings, and coasters. Cutlery is best kept in a subdivided drawer with separate divisions for knives, forks, and spoons. If the cutlery is of good quality, perhaps silver-plated or with a raised pattern on the handles, then the partitions should be lined with felt to stop them from being scratched.

A traditional canteen is another option. This is a box divided into specific areas to hold individual knives and forks. With knives, the blades slot into a niche at the top of the box and the handle rests in a slightly wider container at the bottom. There are also specific holders for forks and spoons.

Decorating storage units

Storage in a dining room does not have to be dull. You can decorate storage units to make them an integral part of your scheme.

Decorating cupboards

The front of a cupboard is like a blank canvas and can be decorated in subtle or ornate ways. Simple bead can be used to create a panel or the doors themselves could be painted in

Far left: *This cutlery pouch makes a decorative accessory to any table, but is also useful for a buffet party. If you present each guest with the cutlery they need for the meal in a single neat package, it makes it easier for them to hold and look after.*

Left: *A simple three-shelf hutch-top structure, placed above a boxed-in radiator, provides an attractive display unit for pieces of an antique dinner service.*

different colors. Alternately, you could transform the doors with a decoupage arrangement of black-and-white photocopies, postcards, insets made from panels of self-adhesive paper, or sheets of manuscript music, which will give the exterior of the plainest cupboard a lift.

Another option is a fabric panel. In traditional kitchens the material most often used was a simple checked cotton, but linen dish towels can be equally effective.

Dressing shelves

In a country-style dining room, simple wall-mounted shelves can become the decorative focal point of the room. A length of deep border lace can be pinned to the front edge of the shelf, or plain white paper cut in a simple zigzag pattern can also look charming. Even the more mundane materials such as newspaper and brown paper can be cut into an attractive fringe or edge, and have the advantage of being easy and cheap to replace.

In a contemporary setting, the nose of the shelf can be covered with a strip of copper or other fine metal. Thin copper sheet can be cut into narrow strips, beaten over the edge, and held in place with a few nails. The metal border can be left plain as a simple highlight strip, or punched to create a pattern or simple motif.

Display storage

Storage in a dining room can be made into a display feature. It is important to choose items that complement the design and decoration of your dining area.

Storing plates

In an informal or rustic-style dining area, plates can be displayed on a hutch or plate rack. In some homes a narrow shelf, with a groove or recess on the upper side, is sited around the top of the room. Plates can be arranged on this ledge and displayed at an angle, with the lower edge resting in the niche of the shelf and the back of the plate against the wall.

Some people hang decorative ceramic plates, serving dishes, or parts of old dinner services on the wall instead of conventional artworks. To create a more contemporary look, colored glass plates, chargers, or large decorative platters could be used.

Storing other utensils

Collections on hutches can be a mixture of various styles, colors, and shapes, or themed. Some people collect a certain type of china such as teapots or eggcups, and others gather a particular pattern or decoration of tableware, or even a particular designer's work.

The arrangement of china on hutches can also be informal, made up of a haphazard collection of sizes and styles. To get the full benefit of the pieces, taller objects should be kept at the back and smaller items in front.

Drinking glasses and glassware are most practically stored in cupboards. If you want them to be admired, have doors with glass insets, but without the protection of an enclosed space they will quickly lose their shine and become dull with dust and general atmospheric pollutants. Glass is at its best when brilliant and polished.

Making a plate rack

A plate rack consists of a rectangular, boxlike frame with corresponding pairs of dowel rods around ⅝ in. in diameter that are fitted opposite each other at the sides.

The distance between the rods (from front to back) should be sufficient to hold a plate or saucer approximately 1½ in. deep and the length between the two sides needs to be wide enough to accommodate a dinner plate about 1 ft. wide.

Below: *A wooden cube wine rack can be tailored to slot into most gaps between units.*

Right: *This cupboard has an automatic internal light so that when the door is open the interior is lit up, which makes it easier to locate the item you are looking for.*

Storing food

Fresh fruit and vegetables can be arranged to create an appropriate and attractive display. For example, in summer a glass bowl full of zesty lemons and limes will allude to freshness and piquancy; in the fall a glass or silver stand filled with dark red and green grapes gives a hint of opulence; and a cream bowl of globe artichokes can provide an interesting and alternative table center in the winter when flowers are less readily available.

Storing bottles and glassware

There are a number of types of wine racks available (see box, left). Only limited amounts of wine should be kept in the dining room, because the room is liable to be warm, which is not good for wine, and also because the bottles gather dust. A small display of a dozen or so bottles can look attractive and can be slotted in neatly below a console or side table, the bottom shelves of a bookcase, or in a disused chimney. Good wines should be kept in a temperature-controlled environment such as a cellar.

Other types of alcohol such as spirits and liqueurs may also be stored and displayed. Again, keep a few well-chosen bottles on show rather than a huge range.

Decorative or attractively shaped clear glass bottles with clear or color contents can be made into a feature if a subtle shaft of light is directed onto them. Glass decanters may also be arranged as ornaments.

Another place to display drinks and bottles is on a trolley so that they can be easily wheeled from one area to another. This is especially useful if you are serving drinks before dinner in the living room, but want to provide liqueurs or refresh glasses during dinner in the dining area. There are many types of trolleys available, from the classic beech laminate Alvar Aalto model to metal and wood designs. Choose one that is lightweight, easy to maneuver, and in keeping with the rest of your furniture and decorations.

Decorative display

Display in a dining room does not always have to be practical. In fact, you can create a decorative display feature that is the centerpiece of your scheme.

Minimal decorative displays

In a contemporary setting displays should be orderly, in keeping with the surroundings. There is an Asian custom whereby the prized artifacts and artistic possessions of the house are stored in a trunk. Each item is taken out in turn and displayed alone for a period of time so that its full beauty can be admired.

In a situation such as this, the few items that are put on show must be of high quality and of real interest because there is little else to draw the attention or eye away.

Left: *The narrow shelving unit creates a division between the kitchen/dining and sitting areas and is an ideal place to display decorative objects. The low dividing wall is a perfect resting place for dishes, plates, and cutlery rather than cluttering up the limited amount of work surfaces in the kitchen.*

Display backgrounds

The background against which a display is set is important. For example, in a rich- or deep-colored room, light colors, black-and-white prints or photographs, gilt frames, and mirrors will stand out very successfully. But if you put a pastel or subtly colored watercolor painting in a pale frame on a neutral or similarly colored wall, it will not be accented.

In the same way, a display of cream items against a cream wall will also be lost.

Against a plain or palely decorated background, displays and arrangements can be used to bring in highlights and stronger accents of color. For example, in a simple, off-white rustic dining room it can be a nice idea to create an arrangement of old handblown glassware and simple

terra-cotta bowls. The glassware will provide a green tint and the bowls a brownish hue.

These items can also inspire a table setting with a decorative linen cloth, white china, silver cutlery, and rich green napkins, while on another occasion the mood can be changed with a bunch of yellow flowers, a pale yellow cotton cloth, and green and white napkins.

Reducing shelf height

Big, deep shelves are fine for storing large items such as coffee pots and glass fruit bowls, but for smaller or flatter pieces such as saucers, plates, and cups, a deep shelf can make them more difficult to access and leave wasted space above and behind.

Reduce shelf height either by fitting another shelf in between or by hanging plastic-coated shelf dividers from the upper shelf. These clip over the nose of the upper shelf and hang beneath. Note, however, that these temporary shelves are not designed to support heavy weights.

exotic fabric

wall hanging with tassels

It is quick and easy to transform a neutral dining room using hanging fabric panels, which give parties an added sense of occasion. Semisheer sari fabric is used here because of its vibrant color. Contrasting pockets of sheer organza with iridescent bead trim can be used to hold menu cards, fragrant spices, or decorative skeleton leaves. You could vary the designs to suit different occasions—for example, use gingham and pockets filled with colorful sweets for children's parties, or velvet with fur trim and pockets full of mulling spices at Christmas.

Materials

Enough fabric to cover your walls

Gold thread

Bead trim

Dressmaker's pins

Contrasting organza for pockets

Gold-trimmed mirror decorations

Wood battens

Brass hanging rings (used for picture framing)

Brass picture nails or hooks

Paste gems or tassels

Tools

Scissors

Sewing machine

Paper

Iron

Hacksaw

Awl

Hammer

Preparing the material

1 Cut the material into panel lengths that will fit your room size (do not try to span one long wall with a single panel—it is easier to hang several side by side). Thread your sewing machine with gold metallic thread—you may need to adjust the gauge and remember to use the manufacturer's recommended needle size for metallic thread. Fold the border over on itself top and bottom, press, then sew along the length to form a channel. Pin the bead trim in place under the top channel, tucking the binding under the flap of fabric. Then sew a second line of stitches in order to secure it into position.

2 Use paper to make a square pattern, then cut three squares of organza per panel, allowing ½ in. hem allowance each side. Press with a cool iron.

Using gold thread, fold the border over on itself and sew along it to form a channel.

Using a paper template, cut out three squares of organza per panel, allowing for a hem.

Know your materials

Saris are excellent value for money when used to decorate a home because a single one provides around 33 ft. of good-quality fabric. They also come in stunning colors. They can be purchased from Indian and Asian fabric suppliers, but are increasingly available in large general fabric stores, too. Many saris have ornate woven metallic borders that add extra interest to the material and can be used as a feature in your design.

Saris make great lightweight curtain panels, simply draped or clipped onto a rod. For additional privacy, and to soften the light, you can also use them in conjunction with a shade. They can be used to dress a bed canopy or create a wall hanging in order to bring some instant color to a room.

Decorating the pockets

3 Cut lengths of bead trim to fit around the squares that will make up the pockets, and then pin the trim in place.

4 Sew the bead trim onto the pockets (you will need to position the machine foot on the left or right setting to avoid crushing the beads). Pin the pockets in place at equal intervals on the fabric panels, then sew them on to secure.

5 Sew mirror decorations onto the center of each pocket.

Attaching panels to the wall

6 Cut the flat wood battens to the correct length with a hacksaw and feed them into the channels at the top and the bottom of your fabric panels. Hand stitch the channels closed.

7 Use an awl to make small holes that drive through the fabric right into the battens. Then carefully screw brass rings so that they sit along the top of each of the panels.

8 Attach the panels to the wall using small brass picture nails or picture hooks, which you can either decorate with tassels (as shown here) or glue paste gems into the center of each one.

Pin the bead trim in place around the top of each of the organza squares.

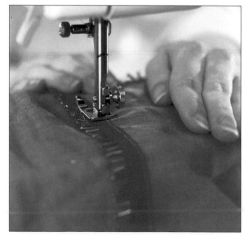

Sew the trim in place, taking care that you do not damage the beads.

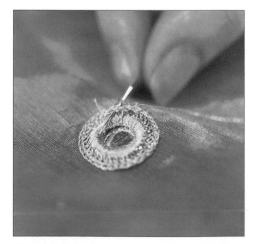

Now hand sew the mirror decorations onto the center of each square.

Alternative

If you prefer to create a more permanent fabric wall covering, there are various methods to choose from. It is possible to buy textile wallcoverings from specialty wallpaper suppliers. They are fairly expensive but durable—which means that they are often used in commercial interiors. Suitable fabrics include those with heavy weaves like hessians or slub linens with a high natural fiber content. They consist of a textured fabric surface with a paper backing and are hung in a similar way to standard wallpaper.

Another option, which provides a quick solution to a poor wall surface, is to fix slim battens along the top and bottom of the wall. The fabric should then be stretched tight and stapled or tacked top and bottom onto the battens. Each width of fabric should be overlapped slightly so that no gaps appear. Canvas or fabric with a high natural fiber content is an ideal choice for this. Once stretched, it can be sprayed lightly with water to cause it to shrink tight.

Feed your wood battens through the channels at the top and bottom of your panels.

Use an awl to make holes in the top of the fabric, then screw brass rings along the edge.

Use picture hooks to attach the panels to the wall. These can then be decorated.

lighting your dining room

Lighting a dining room requires several levels of illumination and ideally a dimmer switch so that the intensity of light can be fine-tuned to create the right ambience to suit different occasions. The focus should be on the table and the light must be distributed so diners can see each other and what they are eating.

Using candles

Great care should be taken when using candles, especially in glass containers because they may overheat and shatter, so only use containers that are specifically designed to hold candles and are wide enough not to be in direct contact with the flame. Never leave a naked flame unattended in a room. Scented candles are best avoided in a dining room or eating space because their perfume may interfere with the aroma of the food. The senses of taste and smell are closely linked and sweet perfume and savory aromas may conflict and be unappetizing.

Creating a mood

For general points about lighting design, see Effective lighting on page 134. In dining areas lighting plays an important role in creating the right mood. For breakfast time the light needs to be bright and invigorating to wake up sleepy people. In the summer natural light is best, so windows should have dressings that can be pulled well back to allow the light to pour through. In the winter artificial light takes the place of natural, so it is best to allow drapes and shades to block out the dark and cold.

Lighting for different occasions

A central light over the table can help to focus attention on eating and will illuminate the food and related items on the surface. Wall lights may also help to bring up the overall level of light in the room. Breakfast and lunchtime should not need much artificial light, apart from during a very dull day, when lights can be used to top up the amount of light present in the room.

A retractable center light over a table is a great way of changing the feel of a meal time. If the light is pulled up close to the ceiling, the spread of light is wide, covering most of the table with a

Right: *Light passing through this segmented lampshade creates a swirling pattern on the ceiling.*

Far right: *Nightlight candles in decorative glass containers and taper candles in classic sticks are an effective way to provide atmospheric lighting at the table.*

fan of illumination. On the other hand, if the light is pulled down closer to the table, the beam will be concentrated on a smaller area and make the atmosphere more intimate, ideal for a dinner party.

Dimmer switches are another useful way of changing the mood. For breakfast and family meal times, the light should be bright and clear so that the food and utensils are clearly visible. However, for smart lunch parties in the fall and early spring or an evening meal for adults, the lights can be dimmed to a low level and also be augmented by candlelight and low-level wall lights.

Reflected lights

In a dining situation, reflected light is subtle and attractive. This can be achieved in a number of ways, the most obvious being with a mirror. If you have one over a mantelshelf or on the wall behind a console or side table, you can arrange a group of candles so that the flames are reflected in it. This doubles the impact of the light from the flames and also creates an interesting feature.

Candles can be used in wall sconces, too. These are wall-mounted candleholders that have a back plate, which was originally used to prevent fat and wax from splashing on the walls as well as increasing the efficiency of the light. The back panel of a sconce is usually made from polished metal, copper, brass, or steel and it is sometimes made up of a shaped piece of glass or mirror.

Plain glass can also reflect a certain amount of light. If you place a small table lamp or candle in front of a window at night, the polished surface of the window will reflect light back into the room. The darkness outside will also make the light stand out as a feature in its own right.

Light shades

The shades you use on the lights will influence the level of light that comes through them. If you opt for a yellow-tinted glass shade, the light will assume a golden hue, while a white shade may mute the strength of light slightly but in general it will still be bright and clear. A dense shade will restrict the flow of light through the sides and concentrate the flow directly downward.

If the base of the shade is open, as in a standard curved pyramid-shaped shade, then the light will shine out of the base, and a small amount through the narrow top, in an increasingly wide triangular pool. A tubular shade will direct the beam in a downward direction, while a round or ball shade will not create a direct beam at all—the light will be emitted through the sides of the shade and will create a soft, overall glow, although there

will be an opening at the top of the shade to accommodate the light fitting and to allow heat to escape.

Light bulbs generate heat and therefore will increase the ambient room temperature during the course of an evening. Light bulbs should never be in direct contact with a shade or covering because, as they heat up during use, they may cause the material in contact with them to burn or melt.

Above: *These Chinese ceramic bowls, with patterns created by grains of rice, make an attractive table decoration when they are lit up with candles.*

Left: *In a large room a chandelier, such as this one with its ornate iron structure, can be a focal point and help to reduce the feeling of height and distance in the room.*

Dining area accessories

Accessories for the dining area really revolve around the tabletop and will reflect the type of dining, and perhaps even the food that is being served. For casual meals, the dressing can be less formal—for example, bowls for pasta or noodles, a knife and fork, a side dish for salad, and glasses for water and wine. Mats can be used instead of a cloth and colorful napkins are fun and functional. For more formal entertaining, however, the table is likely to be set with a cloth and a full complement of cutlery, crisp white napkins, and several glasses for water and various types of wine. The addition of candles, flowers, and other table decorations will depend on the amount of space you have on the tabletop and the time of day that you are entertaining. All these things will add to creating that special sense of occasion. Seating around a dining table should be chosen for its comfort as well as appearance. A rigid and upright chair with little or no back support will make diners restless during the meal, whereas a padded seat and flexible back will help them to relax and enjoy their time with you.

CLOCKWISE FROM TOP LEFT:

Decanting mineral water from commercial plastic containers into decorative colored glass bottles will add to the attractive appearance of your table.

Trays are old-fashioned but are still useful for carrying items to and from a table.

Various sizes and shapes of glasses are appropriate for different wines and drinks.

Table surfaces such as glass and wood may need to be protected from sharp blades and hot dishes, otherwise they could get marked and damaged.

Do not make a table center decoration so big that people sitting opposite have to strain to see each other or find it difficult to hold a conversation.

The other furniture in a dining room is as important as the table—think about coordinating the materials they are made from as well as using the same handles on all storage items.

This voile envelope contains the cutlery for a single place setting. It can be a useful way of allocating

cutlery for a buffet party, so that each guest has their own special container to pick up.

In a more informal dining area, perhaps one that is attached to a kitchen, stools and a breakfast bar work well for everyday eating.

Do not forget to think carefully about every aspect of your dining area—even light switches can be chosen as decorative embellishments.

A small plant such as this cactus can be made more dramatic and have larger impact if set in an oversized dish or bowl.

Think about the type of seating that will suit your dining space—stools are an effective way of making the most of limited space.

This table has modern elements with leather mats and napkin rings, yet still retains a classical feel.

A decorative gilded Moroccan tea glass makes a perfect holder for a nightlight candle.

Candelabra can add a touch of romance and glamour for evening dining.

Kitchens

Planning your kitchen

The kitchen is the heart of the home—it is where people tend to congregate, drink coffee, and chat, but it is also where food is prepared, stored, and cooked. Standards of hygiene in a kitchen should be rigorous, and safety is a factor that must be taken into consideration both in planning and decoration.

Kitchen layouts

Galley kitchens are long, usually narrow, passageway-like spaces where work surfaces and cupboards are lined up along opposite walls, as in the galley of a ship.

Island kitchens are generally found in large rooms where a central block of cupboards and worktop has been installed to make it easier to create the work triangle. The block of cupboards is referred to as the island, because it sits alone on the floor area and is not attached to any other section.

Planning your space

The role of the kitchen has changed in the last 30 years. It used to be a room with just one function but it now often has to be multifunctional.

Whether you are designing a kitchen from scratch or altering or adapting an existing one, it is best to be aware of the basic rules. The most important of these is that you should always take professional advice and help with plumbing and electrical wiring.

The work triangle

It takes time and effort to create a well-designed layout for a kitchen. Each one is unique in shape and size and will also have its own variety of problems that have to be solved. The standard rule to use as a starting point is to make sure that you create the work triangle. This maps out the three main working areas in a kitchen—the sink, the oven/burner and refrigerator. These areas should be sited at the points of an imaginary triangle so that you work efficiently between each point during the preparation of a meal. Beside each point on the triangle it is advisable to have some sort of worktop.

This work triangle should not be interrupted by a main traffic pathway, so do not position it between two doorways. The space between each point should be easily accessible and they should not be too far apart. If the distances between the refrigerator

Right: *There is easy access between the different working areas of the kitchen and the island unit provides plenty of work surface.*

Opposite: *The design of this small kitchen makes the most of all available space. The sliding panel at the back of the room folds back and connects to the living room.*

When choosing appliances, you should be guided by the amount of space you have and the way that you eat and entertain. If you are mainly a takeout eater, then you probably will not make much use of a semiprofessional oven. If you live alone and have a dishwasher, then a double sink with integral waste-disposal outlet and double drainer may be beyond your needs.

Right: *Here, the upper cupboards are long and narrow, which makes the room seem taller. The glass fronts stop them from appearing too heavy.*

Below: *Where wall space is at premium, this type of open shelving, with a row of hooks for cups underneath, is effective.*

and cooking and washing surfaces is substantial, and you cater for a large family or regularly entertain lots of people, you may find a trolley useful to bridge the gap. A butcher's block or island is another option.

It is also wise to keep the refrigerator/freezer and oven apart, because although both are already insulated, the heat emitted by a high-temperature oven may affect the freeze and chill mechanisms and efficiency of the cooler machines.

Storage considerations

When planning your storage, be sure to take into consideration the doors on the cupboards and appliances. Allow plenty of space for each one to open and to make sure you have easy access to the inner depths.

Make sure that you allocate suitable storage beside each element of the kitchen. By the refrigerator/freezer you could, for example, have storage for fresh fruit and vegetables in wicker drawers or racks. By the dishwasher you may find cupboards to stack china and drawers for cutlery and glass useful (see Display and storage, pages 218–19).

Fitted or unfitted?

There are two basic types of kitchen cupboards: fitted or unfitted. You can choose whichever you prefer, or opt for a combination of both. The fitted kitchen generally gives a more tailored appearance to the room, whereas the unfitted allows more versatility and variety.

In small kitchens, fitted cupboards can be structured to make the most of all the limited space available. Freestanding cabinets usually look best in a large kitchen. Here, a hutch can be placed along one wall and a collection of cabinets and tables used to create a variety of working areas. Freestanding furniture can be a good option if you live in rented accommodation, because you can then take the them with you when you eventually move.

Unfitted schemes allow you more time to accumulate the various pieces you want. With this type of kitchen, you can freely add to it as and when your budget permits and when you come across an attractive piece. A fitted kitchen, on the other hand, is usually bought and installed in one go, so you need to be sure that you have the money to pay for it all at once or commit to a monthly payment scheme.

You may decide that you want a combination of fitted and unfitted furniture. It is usually best

to make sure the areas where the machines or major plumbing is involved are fitted. For example, items such as a wall-mounted oven and the sink need to be in a stable structure to support the plumbing and waste points. However, general storage and a table area can easily be unfitted.

Installing your kitchen

Unless you are competent to do this kind of work, leave the installation of a kitchen to the professionals. The process is often filled with problems and requires technical knowledge.

Consult the electrician, plumber, and cupboard installer before they start and make sure that each knows what the other is doing. If they work individually rather than being employed by the same company, try to get them to agree

a timetable so that they do not get in each other's way and so that they work in a logical order.

When installing a kitchen, you should do all the groundwork first and then add decoration. This is because the wiring and ducting for pipes and vents are best done before any flooring or tiles are put in place. Get the oven, extractor fan and hood, burner, sink, and radiators plumbed and wired in before you paint and tile. The refrigerator/freezer can be put in later because it only requires an electrical outlet and, sometimes, access to a water inlet.

Most fitted cupboards have a base plinth that can be put in place after the flooring has been laid. The plinth fits between the base of the cupboard and covers the adjustable legs that support most base cupboards.

Filling the gaps

Very few kitchens are perfectly symmetrical and able to accommodate a precise number of regular-sized cupboards. The basic cupboards are base- and wall-mounted and come in standard sizes, but most manufacturers produce others, such as spice cupboards and wine racks, that can be used to complete a scheme.

Most of the standard, factory-made units have a chipboard, plywood, or particle-board carcass with a melamine or similar facing on the side. Drawers and door fronts can be made of a wide variety of finishes—they are simply attached to the standard carcasses. Inside the carcasses, you can have a fixed shelf or variable shelves that can be moved up and down to meet your storage needs. Corner cupboards may have swing shelves that pivot around a central pole—these enable the full depth of the corner to be used. Some cupboards come with a single drawer, while others have a complete set that run from top to bottom.

Left: *One of the advantages of a fitted kitchen is that you can have cupboards specially made to fit the space available, such as the narrow corner ones in this kitchen.*

Below: *These stylish fitted kitchen cupboards are tailored to follow the line of the opening that leads from the kitchen to the dining room.*

Below right: *This kitchen is typical of the semiprofessional style—its focal point is the large steel-clad burner and industrial-style vent. By raising the solid cupboards on tall legs, it appears less dominant because there is space and light beneath.*

Styles of decoration

Once the practicalities have been sorted out, you can turn your mind to color and decoration. There are various styles of kitchen to choose from, so you need to think carefully about the look you want to create and how this fits with the various roles your kitchen needs to be able to fulfill.

Semiprofessional kitchens

The semiprofessional style of kitchen is modeled on the steel-clad industrial kitchens of professional chefs. In its ultimate form the scheme is white, steel, and clinical, but it is easily adapted to a home setting by using color, wood, and softer elements.

The primary pieces of equipment are the industrially inspired stove, large refrigerator/freezer, and clean, long expanses of work surface. This is a kitchen for keen cooks. The professional stove usually has double the capacity of the standard appliance and you can add a plate-warming feature and eye-level grill.

Keeping your kitchen safe

Make sure that you always have a fire blanket and a small handheld extinguisher near the burner and oven. Also install a smoke detector or alarm in an area away from the main cooking facilities.

If children have access to the kitchen, install door-fastening devices to cupboards. Attach guard rails around burners and ovens, and if possible, a safety gate across the door.

Do not keep sharp knives in a cutlery drawer. Wall-mounted magnetic bars are a good idea. Another option is a knife block, which keeps knives in order with the blades covered but the handles free.

Left: *This metal-clad kitchen has a sleek, modern style.*

Below: *One way of softening the industrial look is to introduce wood, such as this work surface.*

Bottom: *This single-sheet, steel backsplash is easy to wipe and polish because it has a continuous, smooth surface.*

To go with these large and serious pieces of equipment, you need an equally large refrigerator, again steel-clad.

To link these steel-clad machines, the work surface and backsplash of the kitchen is often made of steel as well. This type of worktop usually has to be specially made, ideally from a single sheet of steel, so that there are no unsightly lumps or joints in the middle of a run of work surface.

This style of kitchen is very hardwearing and long-lasting due to its industrial background. The household versions of the appliances are not made to such high mass-catering, specifications, but they are still sturdy and will therefore also have a long and productive life in the average home's kitchen.

Using such a large amount of steel in a room can make it feel cold and hollow, so it is important to balance this by introducing natural elements. An occasional warm, wood cupboard front, wood flooring, or a panel of color will help. The colors you choose should work with the coolness of the steel, so blues, soft shades of lavender, and even orange can look good. The flooring can be wood, but if you want to keep strictly to the industrial feel, look at polished cement, gray slate, stone, or a textured, industrial rubber sheeting.

If this style of kitchen is part of a kitchen/dining room, try to avoid too many soft and fluffy elements in the dining area. Echo the clean, uncluttered lines of the kitchen and use similar colors. Simple geometric patterns will complement the modern, no-nonsense look.

Above: *Bright colors in a kitchen work well to soften the sometimes clinical look of modern design.*

Right: *The sink and traditional-style lever faucet in this kitchen are typical elements of country-style decoration.*

Simple modern kitchens

A less severe version of the semiprofessional kitchen is the simple modern style. This creates a light, airy surrounding with color and space. It is still streamlined but has a certain softness to it. Here, the layout is practical and functional but elements of color are encouraged. The doors of the cupboards are generally plain or have a minor panel detail, but they are dressed up with interesting and functional knobs or handles and a colorful laminate or finish. The flooring may also be colorful but washable—for example, linoleum in a complementary shade to the cupboard doors that incorporates a patterned layout of checkerboard tiles or a laser-cut overall pattern may be used.

This style can be based on a palette of two or three colors, or two colors and a lighter or darker tone of one of them.

If you are in any doubt when you are first devising a scheme, you should start by keeping it very simple. You can always add more decorative elements later, but if you put too much in to begin with, then it will be much more difficult to subtract any later. Simple is usually best.

Country style

Another look that is popular is the country style. Even in urban homes there are kitchens that look as if their doors open onto green pastures instead of a busy highway. The rural idyll provides inspiration for a number of interpretations. For example, folk style incorporates tongue-and-groove paneling, brick or flagstone floors, a dominant enameled range such as the classic Aga, with a shelf or fire surround with plenty of utensils, crockery, and other items on show.

Country style can be pared down to a neater, more spartan Shaker or Scandinavian interpretation, or taken to Mediterranean climates where the walls are roughly plastered and painted. White teamed with cobalt blue accessories follows a Greek influence, while terra-cotta and brightly handpainted plates evoke Italian or Spanish settings.

Two areas that are usually constant in the country genre are the oven and sink. The oven is often an enamel-fronted range or Aga, and dominates a wall of the room. The sink should be an old-fashioned deep, rectangular, white ceramic style. With this type of sink, you may also opt for the old-fashioned faucets.

The color schemes you choose for the kitchen should complement the genre of country style that you have chosen. Cooler shades such as gray, muted green, and pale gray-blue indicate a Scandinavian-style approach. Stronger tones such as deep greeny blue or ox-blood red mixed with warm cherry wood and a leaning toward the neat and tidy indicate a Shaker-style kitchen. A more cluttered and colorful range of inspirational pictures with a cottage garden feel and a diverse range of colors is of the English rural vein. Terra-cotta mixed with either green, red, yellow, and strong blue will hint at more distant shores and the warmth of the Mediterranean lands.

For a contemporary take on this old-fashioned style, and to avoid creating a pastiche, extract the elements that you like best and work around them. For example, warm colors and textures, especially those like the adobe walls of traditional South American homes, will suggest heat. Instead of putting your bottles of olive oil in the cupboard, leave them on a shelf. Pots of fresh basil and oregano on the windowsill will provide a subtle hint, and some nice, clear glass Kilner jars containing various dried pastas will also allude to their country of origin.

Traditional kitchens

The last style is the traditional kitchen. In its purest form, this is a working kitchen like the semiprofessional kitchen, but instead of taking stainless steel as its main feature, wood is dominant. The wood can be natural, painted, or even stained, and is mixed with other established materials and finishes such as ceramic tiles. Slate, stone, and glass are also present.

In some cases wood and even old wood is simulated with modern materials and finishes to create a viable traditional appearance. Particle-board cupboards can be routed to create imitation tongue-and-groove and paintwork may be rubbed down around the corners and in areas where signs of wear would naturally appear.

The basic traditional kitchen is once again a simply decorated room, but it is up to you to accessorize and embellish. However, although this type of kitchen is meant to feel "lived in," you should never let the amount of accessories you have get to a level where they begin to interfere with the function of the room.

At-a-glance color guide

Kitchens are best decorated in light, fresh colors on the walls— secondary color can be introduced in cupboards and soft furnishings.

The semiprofessional kitchen (see pages 214–15) is usually white with plenty of stainless steel, but to soften this look for the home add elements of wood and splashes of color such as orange or blue.

The simple modern kitchen (see opposite) can incorporate a scheme of two colors and tonal variations of the main colors.

The country-style kitchen (see opposite) generally mixes white or cream with pea-green, sky blue, cherry-red, or sunflower yellow, unless you opt for a Mediterranean scheme where terra-cotta takes the place of the white and lavender blue and olive green become the complementary colors.

Traditional style (see left) often mixes wood with slate, stone, glass, and ceramics, and revolves around a natural color palette rather than fashionable colors.

Left: A Scandinavian country setting where the dominant material is wood.

217

Display and storage

In a kitchen storage should be allocated so that the items are close to the place where they will end up being used most often. For example, keep spices near the burner where they will be shaken into saucepans, and spatulas and wooden spoons near the work surface where you stir ingredients.

Storing pots and pans

Care should be taking when storing pots and pans. If you stack fry pans or shallow pans on top of one another, place a double thickness of paper towel between the two to prevent the top pan from damaging the enamel or nonstick surface of the lower pan. Before storing woks and cast-iron pots, dry them thoroughly and brush over the surface lightly with cooking oil.

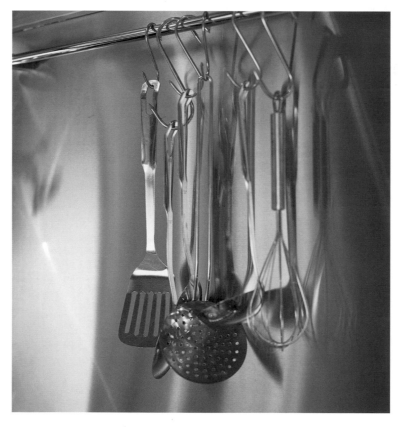

Above right: Butcher's hooks are used to hang steel utensils close to the burner where they will be most frequently used.

Storing and displaying kitchen equipment

Kitchen cupboards are important areas for storing equipment, pots, pans, and canned food, but there are also many display opportunities around the room.

Storing utensils

In most kitchens a number of frequently used utensils are kept out so that they are always at hand, so this inadvertently leads them to being on display. The way in which these things are contained or shown will depend on the style and decoration of kitchen that you have chosen, but here are a few suggestions.

Spatulas, wooden spoons, and light wooden utensils can easily be kept upright in a glass, ceramic, or metal container that is positioned on a worktop.

Rails or rods and butcher's hooks are popular hanging options. You can use a wooden rod in a country- or traditionally decorated kitchen, or steel in a more contemporary one. Butcher's hooks are S-shaped, made of steel, and come in two sizes—the large is big enough to support pots and pans, whereas the smaller size is ideal for suspending spoons, spatulas, and whisks.

When hanging heavier items, you should make sure that the rod is strong enough to support the weight. If you use a long rod that is holding heavy weights, then you may need to put a couple of extra support brackets, fixed to the wall or ceiling, along its length.

If you want an alternative to a rod, then you can use a chain. This chain should be made of a strong metal with good-size links. The chain can be hung horizontally between two points or cut in varying lengths that are individually hung and allowed to fall vertically.

Storage containers and units

Storage jars need not always be shut away in a cupboard. Think about displaying them on a shelf to add a decorative feature and also to allow easy access to the items stored within them, such as coffee, tea, and sugar. Give such jars a sense of unity by choosing a matching set such as steel and glass or white ceramic containers.

Glass containers are extremely good for display as they show the contents from top to bottom.

Traditional wicker and reed baskets are fine for general storage but they do hide most of their contents behind dense sides, so you should only use them in cases where you do not mind concealing what is contained within them.

Plate racks can be fitted inside a cupboard or on the wall over the work surface. These enable you to slot washed, flat tableware between the sections in order to leave them there to dry (see Storing plates, page 193).

Displaying equipment

Although the clean worktop approach is advocated in modern kitchens, a few useful pieces of equipment can be left on show to soften the edges and provide the feeling of a lived-in space.

Salt and pepper grinders are often placed on an open shelf so that they are easily accessible because they are in constant use. They come in a variety of shapes and sizes but a matching pair of chrome, glass, or wood pieces will look very appealing in any kitchen. Choose a pair that will go with your overall color scheme.

Classic pieces of equipment such as the Philippe Starck Alessi juice squeezer, a cafetière, or French coffee percolator are common show pieces. A neat espresso coffee maker and a kettle are also fashionable kitchen equipment.

The rule with this sort of accessory is that it should be both useful and beautiful. If you are leaving it on display, then make sure that you choose the nicest shape, the best finish, and also the one that has the most interesting lines, because it will become part of the look of the kitchen.

Storing and displaying food

Fresh fruit and vegetables can bring a pleasant splash of color to a kitchen and will also be a constantly changing embellishment as you replace what you have eaten from the display. To display fruit and vegetables well, look at openweave metal baskets that allow the fruit to show through and also breathe, and glass bowl containers. The disadvantage with glass

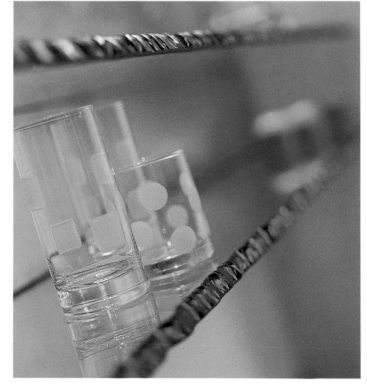

bowls is that they restrict the airflow to the lower fruits, which means that they will ripen and rot much more quickly. Make sure that you use fruit and vegetables within a few days, before they start to wrinkle or go moldy.

wall writing

paint effect

Painted lettering is a cheap and effective way of adding wit and humor to a wall. Writing in a foreign language always looks far more stylish than your mother tongue, which will also add a touch of glamour and mystery to something as mundane as a recipe. The writing is achieved by using cotton swabs and water-based glaze. If you are confident of your own handwriting style, you can work freehand, but for a neater, more controlled look use an overhead projector, which will allow you to project a guide onto the wall. Projectors can be rented from good tool rental companies.

Materials

Pale blue latex paint for your basecoat

Acetate projector paper

Water-based glaze in slate blue

Cotton swabs

Water-based satin varnish

Tools

Paintbrush or roller

Computer and printer, or permanent marker pen

Soft-bristled brush

Overhead projector

Varnish brush

Preparing the surface

1 Apply the pale blue basecoat to the wall and allow to dry.

Creating the recipe acetate

2 Type out your chosen recipe on a computer using a suitable font and print it out on acetate paper. Alternately, you can handwrite onto the acetate using permanent marker pen (as in this example).

Transferring the recipe

3 Use a broad, soft brush to apply the glaze to the wall using random strokes.

4 Place the acetate sheet on the projector and adjust it so that the recipe fills the wall space. Work quickly, "writing" in the wet glaze with a cotton swab. Use a new swab as soon as the one you are using becomes clogged.

5 Once dry, protect the recipe wall by applying a coat of water-based satin varnish using a varnish brush.

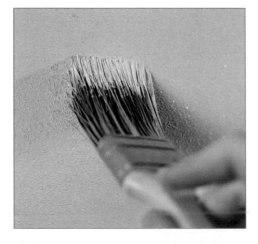

Apply the basecoat over the whole wall using a brush or roller, whichever you prefer.

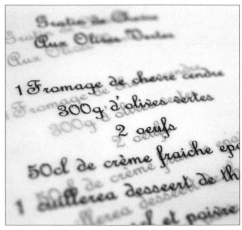

Type your recipe and print it out onto acetate paper, or write directly onto the acetate.

With a broad, soft-bristled brush, apply the glaze to the wall in random strokes.

With the writing on the acetate projecting onto the wall, "write" in the glaze with a cotton swab.

Once the writing is dry, protect the wall with a coat of water-based satin varnish.

revamped

kitchen cabinets with wood veneer

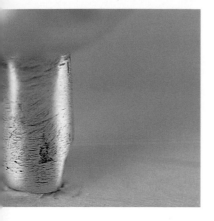

If you are tired of your existing kitchen cupboards, you can revamp them in a number of ways. A simple way of giving plain flat doors a quick facelift is to stick thin wood veneer over the melamine surface. The beauty of this treatment is that the doors look as if they are solid wood. There is also a huge variety of different veneers available so you can choose the color and grain that most appeals to you. A couple of coats of marine varnish gives the veneer a tough surface. Simple chrome, pebble-shaped handles provide a contemporary touch.

Materials

Wood veneer

Contact adhesive

Mineral spirits

Marine varnish

Knobs or handles of your choice

Screws

Tools

Flexible sanding block

Pencil

Metal ruler

Sharp craft knife

Adhesive spreader

Pile of books or something similar

Cloth

Fine-grit waterproof sandpaper

Varnish brush

Drill and wood bit

Screwdriver

Preparing the doors

1 Clean each melamine door well to remove any grease and grime. Use a flexible sanding block to "key" the surface.

Cutting the veneer

2 Place each door face down on the sheet of veneer, and using a pencil, draw around the doors to mark their outlines on it.

3 Carefully cut out the veneer using a metal ruler and a sharp craft knife (see picture bottom left, page 224). Handle the veneer with care as you do this—it is brittle and marks easily.

Attaching the veneer

4 Spread a thin, even layer of contact adhesive over the front of one door and the back of its corresponding veneer and allow to dry until just tacky. Carefully lower the veneer into place over the door. Accuracy is very important at this point as the

Once you have cleaned the surface of the doors, use a sanding block to create a "key."

Place each door in turn on top of the veneer and draw around it with a pencil.

Know your materials

The best way of fixing veneer panels in place is to use contact adhesive. This is a very pungent glue that should be used in a well-ventilated space. (Always wear a face mask for extra protection against fumes.) It is important to spread a thin layer evenly on each surface to be stuck, as the bond is instantly formed between the two layers. This does mean that repositioning is impossible, so take great care when placing the veneer on the door. Once stuck, even pressure should be applied over the whole surface to stop areas rising or bubbling—use a layer of heavy books or magazines and allow to dry for the manufacturer's recommended drying time.

glue forms an instant bond, making it difficult to reposition the veneer. When in place, cover with a cloth to avoid marking the surface and weigh the veneer down evenly with piles of books.

Finishing touches

5 When the front of the door is dry, cut thin lengths of veneer

that are slightly wider than the sides of the doors. Spread both the door side and thin strip with glue and stick the first one in place. Use a sharp craft knife to trim away the excess for a perfect fit (it is a good idea to use a new blade for each cut). Wipe away any residue of glue with a cloth dipped in a little mineral spirits

because this will mark the finish if left. Continue this process until you have covered all of the doors.

6 Sand the veneer using fine-grit waterproof sandpaper for a super-smooth finish and wipe it down with a little mineral spirits (do not use water or this will cause the veneer to swell). Use a clean varnish brush to apply a thin layer of marine varnish over the surface and sides of each door. Allow to dry, then sand lightly with waterproof sandpaper before adding another two coats of varnish for an extra-hard finish.

7 Mark the position of your knobs or handles, then drill using a wood bit.

8 Screw the knobs in place. Hang the doors back up and tighten the hinges.

Use a metal ruler and sharp craft knife to cut out the various pieces of veneer.

Cover the veneer surfaces with contact adhesive using an adhesive spreader.

Create thin strips of veneer to cover the door sides. Glue, stick in place, and trim to size.

Alternative

For a more industrial look, you can use a similar technique to cover existing cabinets in sheet metal. This is not a cheap option and should only be considered if your cabinets are of high quality and are still in good condition. For a really professional finish, it is best to take your cabinet doors to a metal supplier who will be able to "wrap" the cabinet doors in thin metal sheet to give a perfectly smooth finish. If you want to try doing it yourself, get your choice of sheet metal cut to fit the front of the cabinet doors. A solid metal sheet can be stuck in place using contact adhesive applied to both surfaces. It should then be weighted until dry. If you have chosen a pierced design, this method will not work so you should use small tacks or screws to secure the metal sheets along the edges of the cabinet doors instead. Make sure that the metal you have chosen is rust-resistant—if in doubt, seal with a coat of clear lacquer varnish. Finish off with contemporary knobs or handles.

Once you have created a smooth finish, apply a thin layer of marine varnish to the veneer.

Drill the holes for your knobs or handles using a wood drill bit.

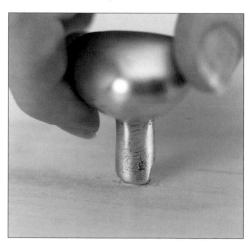

Screw all of your chosen knobs into position on the doors before rehanging them.

225

toughened

glass backsplash with tile design

Toughened glass provides a good alternative to tiles acting as a backsplash in a kitchen or bathroom. Glass suppliers can cut glass to your measurements and bevel or polish the edges to make it safe to handle. Ask for the glass to be drilled so that you can secure it in place. You can back the glass with the design of your choice. Here, a checkered aluminum-leaf design was used, which gives a modern tiled appearance that echoes chrome utensils. Rubbing the leaf with fine-grade steel wool gives the leaf a distressed look, allowing the backing to show through.

Materials

Length of predrilled toughened glass

Lining paper

Water-based gold size

Sheets of aluminum transfer leaf

Fine-grade steel wool

Clear wax polish

Blue latex paint

Plastic screw anchors

Mirror screws

Tools

Soft cloth

Scissors

Square

Pencil

Small paintbrush

Drill

Masonry bit

Screwdriver

Preparing the glass

1 Clean the piece of glass thoroughly to ensure that there are no greasy marks on it, then polish with a soft cloth.

Designing the backing

2 Using a pair of scissors, cut a length of lining paper the same size as the backsplash. Mark out a grid of squares about the size of kitchen tiles with a square and pencil. Make sure that there are no cuts in the design.

3 Place the glass backsplash carefully over the grid, making sure that all the edges line up exactly. Use the grid as a guide, and with a fairly small paintbrush, apply a thin layer of water-based size over each alternating square.

4 Allow the size to dry for the recommended time until it becomes clear. If necessary, cut

Clean the glass to remove all greasy marks and fingerprints, then gently polish with a soft cloth.

Using a paintbrush, apply a thin layer of water-based size over alternate squares on the glass.

Know your materials

Glass provides a hygienic, easy-to-clean alternative to tiles in both kitchens and bathrooms. Although it needs to be handled with care, glass is also extremely resilient when used correctly. A good glass supplier should be able to recommend the correct thickness for your project and cut and drill it to the size that you require.

All interior glass must carry an official safety mark to prove that it is toughened for use in the home. It is important to ask for glass that has a polished or beveled edge because this removes any sharp edges. You could try using glass with an etched pattern or Georgian wired glass, which would make attractive alternatives.

the aluminum transfer leaf to the required size with a pair of sharp scissors. Apply the sheet of aluminum transfer leaf carefully, making sure that it lines up exactly with the square that you have already marked on the lining paper.

Applying the transfer leaf

5 Rub the back of the sheet of aluminum transfer leaf carefully. You must make sure that it adheres firmly to the water-based size. Then gently peel off the backing paper, making sure that you leave the aluminum transfer leaf in place.

6 Dip a small piece of fine-grade steel wool in a little clear wax polish and use it to rub the back of the aluminum transfer leaf gently. This action will lift away small areas of the

transfer leaf and will allow some of the backing to show through.

7 Using a small paintbrush, apply the blue latex paint over the back of each square of the aluminum leaf and then allow the leaf to dry.

Fixing the backsplash

8 Position the glass against the wall and use a pencil to mark the drilling point. Use a masonry bit to drill a hole and insert a plastic screw anchor. Screw the backsplash in place using a mirror screw with a chrome cap.

Apply a sheet of aluminum transfer leaf to the lining paper, making sure it adheres to the size.

Peel back the lining paper carefully, making sure the transfer leaf remains in position.

With a piece of fine-grade steel wool dipped in clear wax, rub the back of the transfer leaf.

Alternative

To create a traditional tiled backsplash, you could use irregular broken tiles or small mosaic tesserae cut with tile nippers to form organic patterns. You will need to start with a completely smooth, clean wall. Plan your design first by producing a sketch with colored pencils on squared paper. Use the direct mosaic method, which involves transferring your design directly onto the wall in pencil. Apply waterproof tile adhesive onto the back of each tesserae or tile fragment to build up the design one piece at a time. You will find it easiest to start by sticking down the pieces that form the outlines of the shapes within the design, then fill in large blocks of color around them. Place whole tesserae first, then use tile nippers to cut smaller shapes to fit the design.

Using broken tiles or pieces of china is a good way to achieve a design inexpensively. Break them up by placing them in a strong plastic bag or wrap them in a dish towel. Use a hammer to break the items into small, irregular pieces.

Paint the back of the transfer leaf with some blue latex and allow to dry.

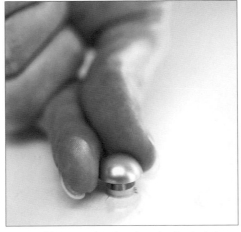

Finish off by screwing the glass backsplash to the wall using mirror screws with chrome caps.

lighting your
kitchen

Task lighting that illuminates the work surfaces of a kitchen is a top priority—after all, this is the place where you will pour hot liquids and use sharp knives. But the kitchen may also be used as a dining area or place to have coffee with friends, so a softer, more ambient level of lighting will also be required.

Natural and artificial light

It is extremely important to provide effective lighting in every part of the kitchen. For general points about lighting design, see Effective lighting, page 134.

Using natural lighting

It used to be a rule that kitchen designers invariably put the sink in front of a window so that the person washing up had something to look out on, but with the advent of the dishwasher this is no longer a priority. Daylight is still a prized commodity because its access and flow is usually restricted by wall-mounted cupboards and machines. To get around this, an increasing number of people are putting transparent roof panels and windows in the kitchen ceiling. This is a perfect solution in an extension or single-story dwelling.

In an apartment block or house with upper levels over the kitchen, it is often not possible to carry out this sort of improvement so other options have to be explored. Shiny surfaces are good at reflecting light but they can be hard to keep in good condition. Pale and white-based colors will help, as will tidy worktops. By keeping clutter to a minimum you will make your room appear to be lighter.

Right: A large window can be an asset in a kitchen because it allows plenty of natural light to enter. An adjustable shade will help soften the light if it is too bright.

Below: This lighting feature at the base of an island unit faces toward the dining area and creates an unusual display in the evening.

Window treatments can also contribute. Opt for shades or sheer drapes that can be pulled back rather than heavy window dressings, which restrict light and may also be a haven for dirt.

Artificial lighting

An overall ambient light is useful—when first entering the kitchen this will give you a general view and be adequate for a simple or direct assignment. To work within the kitchen, you will need task lights that focus a steady and even beam of light on the work surface.

Task lighting is usually positioned under the lower edge of wall-mounted cupboards and should run the length of the cupboard in order to allow the light to be distributed across the whole of the lower surface.

Spotlights or recessed ceiling lights provide a good level of light over large areas. This type of light needs to be carefully positioned and angled to avoid the beam casting a shadow of the person over the work area. Pendant lighting is also a useful addition if placed over an eating area.

Light fixtures and accessories

Under-cupboard lights are often small strip lights. Fluorescent tubes were once the main source of light here but now main-supply halogen tubes are more popular.

For pendant and wall lights, it is best to avoid shades that are delicate and fragile because they are difficult to clean, whereas metal, enamel, glass, and ceramic can be easily washed down.

If the kitchen is a large room or a kitchen/dining space, it may be worth having two or three different circuits of lights connected to individual switches. Then you can switch off the main kitchen lights but leave an ambient lighting level in the dining area. It is also a good idea to have a switch that turns off all the lights by the main door.

Above: *Fiberoptic lighting set into the glass work surface and lower edge of the cabinets gives a constant level of light over the whole area.*

Left: *The linear lighting along the side walls illuminates the worktop from both sides instead of from directly overhead. This type of lighting will mean that you can avoid casting shadows over food while you work.*

recycled

slate and zinc bulletin board

This stylish and useful bulletin board exploits the beautiful weathered finish of old roof slates, which make an ideal chalk-board frame. Within the frame there is a zinc panel onto which postcards, recipes, invitations, and other pieces of paper can easily be attached with magnets, making it ideal for use in the kitchen or the office. Let the roof slates dictate the size of your bulletin board so that you will not have to cut them down to size. The predrilled holes can then be used to anchor the slates in place on the backing with a few galvanized nails used for roofs.

Materials

Slate roof tiles

Plywood

Sandpaper

Slate gray paint

Sheet of galvanized metal

Contact adhesive

Screws

Galvanized roof nails

Chalk

String

Magnets

Tools

Pencil

Metal ruler

Jigsaw

Medium-sized paintbrush

Electric drill

Screwdriver

Adhesive spreader

Pair of gloves

Piece of wood

Small hammer

Measuring the frame

1 Calculate the dimensions of the frame by laying out the slate roof tiles on the piece of plywood. With a pencil, draw around the slate tiles as a guide, then using a long metal ruler, measure ½ in. in from the edge and mark out the frame.

2 Cut out the frame carefully with a jigsaw. Then use a piece of sandpaper to remove any rough edges.

Painting the frame

3 Using a medium-sized paintbrush, paint the whole frame with a couple of coats of

slate gray paint and then allow to dry for a couple of hours.

4 Once the paint is dry, turn the frame over and place the sheet of galvanized metal over the hole (it should be large enough to overlap the edges of the hole by a about 1 in.). With an electric drill,

To measure the size of the frame, place the tiles on the plywood and then draw around them.

Using a jigsaw, carefully cut out the frame and then gently sand to get rid of any rough edges.

Know your tools

Power tools make most home-improvement projects quicker and easier. If you do not own any, it is a good idea to borrow them from a friend or rent them from a tool rental store. This will help you to get used to using them before you invest in tools of your own. The most useful power tools are the jigsaw and electric screwdriver/drill.

Jigsaws have detachable blades that can cut various materials with accuracy. (When cutting most materials, it is advisable to wear eye protection and a dust mask.)

A combination electric screwdriver and drill is a dual-purpose tool. Detachable drill bits are available for making holes of various sizes in different materials and a range of screwdriver bits can also be attached for speedy screwing. Choose a model that has a reverse action so that you can unscrew with ease, too.

drill, then countersink a hole in each corner and screw in place.

5 Spread some contact adhesive onto the front of the frame and also onto the back of the slate tiles. When using contact adhesive, make sure you use gloves to protect your hands. Allow the adhesive to dry a little (do not allow it to dry completely because it needs to be tacky in order to carry out the next step).

Assembling the frame

6 When the adhesive is still tacky, position the slate tiles onto the frame and press firmly in place with a piece of wood. Make sure that you wear gloves to do this. Allow the adhesive to dry, then with a small hammer, tap a galvanized roof nail through the holes in each slate tile.

7 Attach a large piece of white or colored chalk to a medium piece of string. Tie the string around one of the galvanized nails to secure it in place.

8 The frame is now ready to be used. Using magnets of your choice, position postcards, recipes, pictures, and any other pieces of paper that you want to keep onto the frame.

Paint the plywood frame in a couple coats of slate gray paint and allow to dry thoroughly.

Using a screwdriver, screw the sheet of galvanized metal firmly in place.

Apply some contact adhesive to the back of the frame and the slate tiles.

Alternative

As an alternative, you could create a stencil design on your kitchen bulletin board. In this dramatic piece, the elements of air, earth, and water are represented by doves, grapes, and fish. To make this, choose an appropriate size of $\frac{1}{2}$-in. thick particle board. Use a mini-roller and tray to apply two coats of blackboard paint or black matte latex. Allow to dry. Stencil a flock of doves at the top of the board. Place a grape leaf stencil in the top lefthand corner. Stencil a bunch of grapes underneath and repeat two-thirds of the way down the board, then create the shoal of fish. To protect the pattern, gently brush on a coat of matte water-based varnish using a synthetic paintbrush. If you want to use different colors, experiment with variations in pearlized colors, such as jades, pinks, and silvers.

As soon as the adhesive is tacky, position the slate tiles onto the frame and press in place.

Once the tiles are in place, tap a nail through the tile holes to attach them to the frame.

Kitchen accessories

These are mainly practical pieces of equipment that are constantly on display in a kitchen. This could be because they are frequently used and need to be easily accessed or because they are bulky, heavy, and difficult to store and retrieve. Where possible, keep kitchen accessories off the worktops because they will restrict the amount of surface you have to work on and may also become spattered with ingredients when you are preparing food. Store your utensils and equipment in good working order so that they are always ready for use. If items are always left out, cover them with a cotton cloth or washable cover to protect the working parts from general kitchen grease and condensation. Small items such as knives should be kept in a knife block or on a wall-mounted magnetic strip—leaving sharp knives in drawers can be dangerous. Wooden spoons and spatulas can be kept in a ceramic or metal holder with the handles downward and the ladle or paddle section upward so that it is easy to identify each one.

CLOCKWISE FROM TOP LEFT:

Retro-style products, such as these chrome pieces, look as though they are vintage but are in fact manufactured to the highest modern standards.

Traditional wooden chopping boards are still very popular. You should have separate ones for cutting different types of food, such as raw red meats, chicken, onions, garlic, and fruit, so that tastes, aromas, and enzymes do not get transferred.

Clean, sparkling glassware is attractive and may be left on display, but be aware that it could become smudged and marked if left too close to an oven.

Items that are in daily use, such as a toaster, may be left on the work surface for easy access.

Lever faucets are very easy to turn on when you have sticky or flour-covered hands.

It is best to keep all your knives in a wooden knife block, out of harm's way.

Stainless-steel utensils can be hung from a simple rack near to where they will be used.

This old butcher's block has seen many years of use but is still a welcome addition and feature in most styles of kitchen.

Copper pans are treasured by professional chefs because the metal conducts heat quickly, but they must be kept well-polished if they are to be left on show.

A draining rack or surface is extremely useful positioned next to a sink.

Store like things with like so that you automatically know where they are. For example, place teapots beside the cups and saucers because you will need them all at the same time.

Colored glassware adds an unexpected decorative element in a practical environment.

Simple handles are best in a kitchen because they are easy to hold and pull when your hands are wet or greasy. They are also easy to wipe clean.

Pepper and salt grinders do not need to look mundane. There are many to choose from, so find one that echoes the style of your kitchen.

Bathrooms

Planning your bathroom

The bathroom is more than just a place to carry out your daily washing and cleaning ablutions—it doubles as a sanctuary of rest and relaxation into which you can withdraw after a busy day, a place in which you can unwind and pamper yourself.

Planning your space

The bathroom needs to be an adaptable space, with chameleon qualities. A well-designed bathroom should be a bright, invigorating, and a high-speed cleansing space in the morning, but also a calming, tranquil oasis

Below: Bathrooms planned on a linear scheme, so that all the main appliances run along one wall, make the best use of long, narrow spaces.

for a soak in the bathtub later in the day. So planning the design, layout, and decoration of a bathroom is important.

First, identify your needs. If you prefer a shower, fit a separate shower stall into the bathroom or another space and leave the bath-only bathroom as a backup or visitors' facility. Or if you have a limited amount of space in the bathroom, install the shower over the bath to provide a two-in-one resource.

Where possible, try to alleviate the pressure on a single bathroom with the sole toilet by installing another toilet and a small handbasin elsewhere. Handbasins can be installed in bedrooms and even self-contained shower stalls may be plumbed into an alcove or a built-in closet space in the bedroom to take more pressure off the main bathroom.

When planning the layout and design of your bathroom, first find out and locate the following utilities because the plumber is bound to ask. Where is the access to main water and drains? What is your tank capacity and where is it situated?

Family bathrooms or main bathrooms need to be practical and easy to maintain. It is a busy room where steam and damp are present on a daily basis so good ventilation is important. Ventilation

can be provided by gadgets such as a panel fan, which is inserted in a window or ducts recessed into a false ceiling—this will disperse the dampness as well as prevent mold from growing on grout or the shower curtains.

An effective bathroom layout

The main bathroom should be planned so that there is space to move without bumping into things. The layout of traditional bathrooms is usually planned around the largest piece of built-in furniture, the bathtub.

The bathtub is often plumbed in at the far end of the room with its longest side running parallel to the longest wall. At the foot of the bath is the toilet and beside that the handbasin. The basin and toilet are usually located nearest the door as they are used most often. This linear layout provides a corridor of space in front of each item, making them accessible.

In a square room the bathtub could be along one wall with the toilet and basin opposite, leaving the third wall free for the door and the fourth for storage or a shower.

Space-saving ideas

There are two types of bathroom suite—freestanding and wall-hung. With freestanding items, the basin, toilet, and bidet are mounted on coordinating

pedestal bases, while with wall-hung items the fixtures are attached directly to the wall, which leaves the floor space much more clear.

Wall-hung items can make a small room feel more spacious because of the empty floor area—also you can allow for some overlap, which may just help you squeeze in an extra item. For example, a handbasin can overlap with the edge of the cistern of the toilet, or can extend out over the end of the bathtub.

The small, modern cisterns now made for toilets mean that you can hide the unprepossessing water container behind a wall panel or a tongue-and-groove section so that it is not on view. With a panel, marble slab, or any such covering it will, however, be necessary to make a section removable to gain access to the cistern.

Another option is to mount the basin on or in a cupboard, which provides extra storage space, too. The basin can rest on top

of the surround or surface, or even be countersunk so it lies beneath.

En-suite bathrooms

The en-suite bathroom has also risen in popularity. This linked facility provides a direct connection to the bedroom. In some older homes, people sacrifice a second bedroom or study to have the luxury of this extra bathroom, and in modern apartments, they are often standard in the main bedroom.

Safety features

Light switches need to be carefully positioned to comply with building safety standards. Standard plate switches should be installed on the outer wall, not in the bathroom. If the switch is in the bathroom, it should be activated by a string pull set into the ceiling. The lights themselves should be contained in sealed units.

Only use electrical appliances that are specifically designed for use in a bathroom, such as designated shaver outlets.

Nonslip mats and textured strips that adhere to the base of the bathtub are ideal for homes with young children or older people. If children have access to the bathroom, make sure that medicines and cleaning products are placed in a wall-mounted cupboard that has a childproof lock on the door.

Aroma and texture

The bathroom is a place where aroma and texture play an important role. Scented candles and bath oils can add to the pleasure and therapeutic effect of a bath, so choose scents associated with relaxation such as lavender, camomile, mandarin, and orange. In the mornings, shower gels with citron, bergamot, lime, rosemary, mint, or pine essence will help invigorate you.

Texture in the form of towels is also important next to naked skin—for a gentle, calming rub down, use deep-pile towels, but for a stimulating and speedy dry, waffle cotton or linen towels are a good options.

Below: *Double basins can streamline preparation time for a busy working couple.*

En-suite bathrooms are often linked to, or part of, a dressing room or closet area, and in these cases the decorative theme can take a lead from the bedroom and continue into the bathroom, so keeping a common or complementary color and pattern theme.

If space is at a premium, consider sliding doors instead of conventional opening doors between the bedroom and this space. Sliding doors or panels take up less space and can be made with an opaque section at the top so that natural light from the bedroom can filter through to the bathroom, making it feel more light and spacious.

Wet rooms

Another recent trend is for wet rooms. These are small or modest-sized rooms that are completely tanked and tiled. A waterproof liner must be laid before tiling and a gentle slope built into the floor so that the water will drain away easily through a single outlet. Wet rooms are large showers without the restrictions of doors, curtains, or panels. They can also be fitted with steam attachments so that they can double up as a steam room. In this type of setting, it is common to find a small wooden stool or built-in, tiled bench area so that the bather can relax in the warm, moist environment.

Decoration and style

A bathroom is a private space where you can indulge your fantasies and decorate in a style that gives you pleasure.

Practical decorating

Whatever style of decoration you opt for, make sure that you bear in mind the practicalities of cleaning and the main purpose of the space. A quantity of fancy or ornate decorative objects will be time-consuming to clean, and thick-pile carpet will be difficult to vacuum thoroughly. There are specially designed acrylic carpets, but it is a floor covering that is best avoided for the bathroom.

Good ventilation is paramount because the fabrics stored and displayed, such as drapes, upholstered furniture, and clothes, can be ruined by steam and damp. This also applies to linen closets or storage where towels and bedding are kept because warmth and damp can give rise to mildew.

Waterproof and water-resistant materials play a major role in bathroom decor. These used to focus on the standard ceramic tiles and mirror, satin-finish paints and vinyl wallpapers, as well as reinforced glass, but some industrial materials have also made their way into this setting.

Stainless steel is now used to form bathtubs and basins as well as panels and shower trays. Polyurethane sheeting, even corrugated as in the roof building material, can make an unusual panel for the side of a bathtub or even a sturdy door to a shower stall.

Acrylic, fiberglass, and resin materials are used in the construction of preformed fixtures such as the all-in-one basin and surround or bathtub with integral shelf or wide lip around the perimeter. Materials once regarded as cold and uncomfortable in the bathroom have also had a reprieve—underfloor heating makes stone and even marble a viable floor covering in this space.

Tiles have also developed from the plain-colored square or those with a transfer motif. Nowadays there is a wide interest in mosaic, whether laid randomly in a mixture of several shades of one color, or pictorially. There are metallic and iridescent finishes, tiles with insets of metal and relief patterns, and encaustic tiles with flat matte finishes, all available in a wide variety of shapes and sizes.

Large sheets of reinforced glass are now very popular as backsplashes around basins and bathtubs. Curved opaque glass panels are used to create shower stalls and basins. Wood that is specifically dried and finished for bathroom use is also gaining recognition—it has long been used in saunas and spas because it adds a warm and earthy element to what could be a cool and clinical room.

Using color

The color scheme that you use in your bathroom is a personal choice, but blues and greens are

and Victorian interiors—dark wood and rich colors were in vogue then. Art Deco style with its angular shapes and black, white, and chrome schemes can also be attractive and opulent, or you could go back to the founding fathers of the bathing culture and study Roman references, with details such as mosaics and sunken bathtubs. Your bathroom could also be inspired by the style of other countries and cultures. For example, Turkish and Moorish civilizations made great use of colorful and decorative ceramic tiles. Turkish steam baths are found around the country and many are decorated with blue, white, green, and brown tiles in delightful geometric designs. Moorish tilework can be seen in homes in southern Spain and north Africa, and again pattern and color are dominant.

Modern indulgent schemes tend to be more streamlined than traditional styles—lighting plays

Left: The minty green color used here adds a fresh touch to this contemporary white and stainless steel bathroom.

Above: In a wet room you can install a bench along one wall, and then cover it with tiles.

Below: A timeless, classic roll-top bath, with central faucet and overflow fitting, rests on a rich blue ceramic tiled floor.

generally regarded as appropriate watery colors, reminiscent of sea, sky, lagoons, and other aqueous features. Yellows and oranges are bright and warm, while deep colors can be dramatic and indulgent in a bathroom setting. Although colored bathroom suites were all the rage during the 1960s and 1970s, there has been a return to white ceramic, which is fresh, clean, and adaptable. White bathroomware is also safe—it will work with every color and is compatible with every style or decorative theme.

secondhand, through antiques stores and specialty suppliers.

To create an indulgent traditional style, look at Edwardian

Indulgent-style bathrooms

Traditional indulgent bathrooms can follow a period style, with features such as a roll-top bathtub, a Victorian basin on a pedestal with an integral decorative backsplash and shell-like soap recesses, and a toilet with high wall-mounted tank. These items are all available, either as reproductions or

Above: This classic faucet and shower stall would complement a traditional-style bathroom suite.

Below right: The towel rail around the side panel of this bath is adapted from a shower curtain rod.

Opposite: The water tank for this toilet is concealed behind a slate-clad box. Slate is also used to line the shower area.

an important part in creating the indulgent mood, as do the accessories. The finish and accessories should be luxurious because the setting will be plain.

Streamlined bathrooms

In a traditional streamlined bathroom, the basic furniture designs may still allude to an historical period. But in this case, the room will be decorated with lighter, brighter colors and adequate storage will ensure that surfaces are left clean, uncluttered, and easy to wipe down. Additional furniture will be kept to a minimum and the layout designed specifically to assist quick and efficient use. However, in the evening, lights can be dimmed, candles lit, and the atmosphere changed to one f indulgence and relaxation.

The modern streamlined bathroom is almost clinical in its efficiency and minimalist lines. The materials used are businesslike and utilitarian and there are absolutely no fancy frills or floral prints. This is a place where morning ablutions are carried out at top speed and there may be a floor area where an exercise mat or equipment is used. In the evening, this space can be made

softer by dimming lights and putting aromatherapy oils in the bath water or steam shower but it will retain its minimalist, uncluttered appearance, creating a restful and undemanding environment in which to unwind.

Bathroom fixtures

The first elements of your bathroom that you need to plan are the fixtures. Be aware of plumbing and space limitations when you make these plans.

Bathtubs

There is a wide variety of different styles to choose from. Bathtubs are usually plumbed along one wall. If, however, your room is spacious, you may choose to have a freestanding bathtub in the center of the room. A freestanding tub is luxurious in its use of space, giving a feeling of opulence simply by taking up so much room. However, with a freestanding bathtub the plumbing

and waste pipes must be laid under the floor because they cannot be run along a wall.

Sunken bathtubs are an alternative option. You will need to consult a professional if you plan to install this type of feature. Jacuzzi, whirlpool, and spa baths are luxurious choices for those who like to spend many hours in a bath. Again, these systems need to be installed by a professional.

There are also smaller-than-standard baths: these half- or stiz baths are popular in Europe. The sitz bath is designed so that it is short but deep, with a step or seat cast into the center. The half-bath is a compromise, but with a shower overhead it can be used as a deep shower tray or an occasional bathing place.

Handbasins

The handbasin that you choose should complement the style of bathtub that you select. Basins come in a wide range of different

and a glass door, then there are a number of screen options available.

For a shower over a bathtub you could opt for a fixed screen, standard or bifold doors, or a series of sliding panels. These will be made from textured plastic or reinforced glass. To make these screens watertight, there needs to be a flexible rubber seal along the bottom edge of the section that meets with the bathtub.

For a freestanding bathtub in the center of a room or a corner bathtub, a separate screen or screens makes a sensible option. The showers for these tubs can either be ceiling-mounted or on a stand or rod that comes up from the center of the faucet.

Another option is a ring, like a mosquito net arrangement, suspended from the ceiling. From the ring the curtain or curtains are suspended and the bottom edge of the plastic liner is tucked neatly inside the edge of the bathtub so that the water is contained.

There are a number of standard fittings that can be installed between two opposite walls, or a straight wall and an adjacent one. The basic shower rod is either straight (to be attached to facing walls) or L-shaped (so that it can be attached around a bathtub with access to adjacent walls).

The simplest of these is a telescopic, extendible tube with suckers at each end. You simply extend the rod until it is the right length for the gap, lock in place, and then slide it into position on the wall—no nails or screws are required. The other option is the fixed rod, which will need to be secured with screws.

Toilets and bidets

An unlikely area for decoration but one that should not be ignored is the toilet seat. The standard seat is a dull, plain plastic rim protector and lid, and the classic version is of polished wood, which provides a warmer and more comfortable surface to sit on.

Above: *Bathroom design is now focusing more on style and aesthetic appeal than just utilitarianism. This fine wood basin and elegant chrome stand are an interesting sculptural feature for a bathroom as well as being somewhere to wash.*

Right: *Ladder-style, wall-hung radiators not only heat the bathroom but also double as a towel rail.*

styles, either floor- or wall-mounted. A popular shape for the contemporary bathroom is like a large bowl that sits on a support. Basins are also available in different materials such as wood, which has to be treated so that it does not warp or bow when it comes into contact with water.

In small or second bathrooms you can use "rinse" basins—these are just large enough to be used for handwashing or teeth rinsing, but not hairwashing. There are certain styles that have an integral return or backsplash so tiling is unnecessary.

Showers and screens

If you do not have a preformed shower stall or a shower built into a corner with two tiled walls, a fixed glass panel,

In the traditional-style bathroom there are a number of options for the arrangement of faucets and related accessories, but the accepted layout in this setting consists of separate hot and cold faucets and a plug on a chain. The classic faucet design is the cross bar, often with ceramic hot and cold disks.

The modern bathroom pares down this equipment and can be as minimalist as a lever with an integral spout with the waste lever included in the back of the spout arch.

In contemporary bathrooms, these accessories are most often in chrome, but in the traditional bathroom brass is an option. These days many reproduction brass faucets come with a lacquered finish, which means that the shine stays bright and does not need to be polished.

Towel rails

Another element of the bathroom is the towel rail, which now falls into the useful and beautiful category. Towel rails have gone from being a necessity to a star feature in the bathroom, with a wide selection of attractive designs to choose from.

There is also an amazing variety of heated towel rails available. The most popular and straightforward style is the wall-mounted ladder, which supplies heat and provides a place on which to hang and dry towels. These come in a variety of colors and finishes and have horizontal bars that are grouped in sections of varying widths.

Another design is the S or snake. This can be either attached to the wall so that it is fixed in position or on brackets so that it can be swung out at a right-angle to the wall. Make sure that the towel rail is not positioned where you may brush up against it while drying and burn yourself.

Left: *This polished slate panel acts as a backsplash as well as a surround for the wall-mounted faucets and spout.*

Above: *The sandstone walls used here mellow the overall sleek look created by the stainless steel accessories.*

Below: *Many contemporary bathrooms feature basins that are styled like bowls sitting on a tabletop or surround.*

The current vogue is for more decorative finishes on toilet seats and these range from gimmicky, with beer or wine labels suspended in clear, solid plastic, to photographic images such as tropical leaves or blooming flowers. There are also photographic techniques that reproduce images of materials such as marble or granite onto a plastic or resin surround.

Another item of bathroom furniture that is popular throughout Europe is the bidet. This is an underrated piece of equipment that can be useful in homes where there are young children or elderly people who find a bathtub or shower too difficult. It can also provide an effective footbath for refreshing your feet at the end of a long day.

Faucets and other accessories

In the modern bathroom the faucets and other accessories are an important part of the overall design. They make a statement because the rest of the fixtures and the general decoration are usually very simple and plain.

Among contemporary designs there are many faucets that have utilitarian roots—for example, the lever. This simple metal paddle, which is connected to the spout or water faucet, has been refined from the originals found in industrial washrooms and at hospital sinks.

Faucets have also migrated away from the basin surround and are now likely to be wall-mounted directly above the basin and accompanied by the spout, which arches gracefully at the end.

framed mosaic
backsplash panel

This mosaic panel is an attractive alternative to tiled walls, and can be positioned behind a bath or basin or simply hung on the wall like a picture. Any type of mosaic tile can be used—an unusual iridescent glass mosaic that catches the light beautifully is used here. Although the materials of the panel are relatively expensive, one of its main advantages is the fact that it is portable. You can choose a trim to complement your design—a simple wooden frame stained with a dark walnut varnish that offsets the pale colors of the tiles works well in this example.

Materials

Waterproof plywood

Sandpaper

PVA glue

Sheets of mosaic tiles

Grout

L-shaped trim

Panel adhesive

Walnut satin varnish

Tools

Metal ruler

Pencil

Jigsaw

Tile adhesive

Paintbrush

Notched trowel

Sponge

Flexible grout spreader

Soft cloth

Small paintbrush

Miter cutter

C clamp

Preparing the panel

1 First, plan the size of the mosaic panel carefully so that you can avoid cutting any mosaic tiles. With a long metal ruler and a pencil, mark out the dimensions of the panel onto a sheet of plywood, making sure you allow for a border trim all the way around the panel.

2 Cut out the panel carefully using a jigsaw. Then, using a piece of sandpaper, remove any rough edges from it.

3 Seal the plywood with a solution made from 2 parts PVA to 1 part water and allow to dry thoroughly.

4 Using a notched trowel, apply a layer of tile adhesive to the sealed sheet of plywood. (Make sure that you wear gloves when you do this.)

Fixing the mosaic tiles

5 Place the sheets of mosaic tiles face down into the adhesive, pressing them down

Using the mosaic tiles as a guide, mark out the dimensions of the panel onto the plywood.

Using a notched trowel, spread tile adhesive evenly over the sealed sheet of plywood.

Know your tools

• Having a set of good-quality clamps is essential for many woodworking projects because they hold glued joints together, exerting pressure until the glue has dried enough to form a strong bond. (They may be called C, G, or D clamps.)

• The miter cutter used in this particular project is the type often used by picture framers. It allows for fine adjustments of the blade, thereby ensuring a perfect angled cut. Miter cutters can be bought from all home-improvement stores.

firmly to make sure they adhere to the panel. Allow the mosaics tiles to dry overnight.

6 Use a wet sponge to soak the paper backing of the mosaics. Allow the water to sink in for a few minutes before peeling away the backing.

7 With a flexible grout spreader, force the grout well into the gaps between the tiles. Wipe away any excess grout, then allow it to dry completely.

8 Polish the mosaic tiles with a soft cloth until they shine.

9 Using a miter cutter, cut an L-shaped trim to form the frame, stick in position with some panel adhesive, and clamp in place until dry. Color with a varnish of your choice.

Place the mosaic tiles carefully onto the tile adhesive and press them firmly into place.

Soak the paper backing of the tiles, then let the mosaics sink in before peeling off the backing.

Using a flexible spreader, force the grout well into the gaps between the mosaic tiles.

Alternative

You may prefer to tile directly onto your bathroom wall. To do this, you must first make sure that your wall is perfectly smooth and that the surface has been properly sealed.

Mosaic tiles are usually supplied with paper or mesh backing, which enables you to work with squares of about 1 ft. at a time. If you are tiling behind an existing basin, it is advisable to start in the bottom righthand corner and work your way along and then up. If you are tiling a whole wall, then use a level batten nailed to the wall as a guide. Always order 10 percent more tiles than you think you need, to allow for mistakes or breakages. If you are using blends of more than one color, it is wise to mix the sheets up well to ensure a good color mix.

When your tiles are hung and grouted, you should seal the gap between any bathroom furniture and tiles with silicone sealant. This forms a flexible watertight seal between the fixtures and the tiled surface.

Wipe away any grout, allow to dry, and then polish the tiles with a soft cloth until they shine.

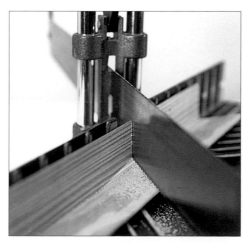

Using a miter cutter, carefully cut an L-shaped trim to fit around the border of the panel.

exotic fabric
shower curtain

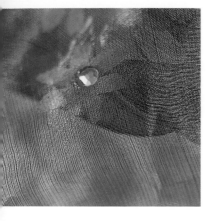

Shower curtain designs only seem to cater for lovers of shiny plastic with amusing or nautical themes—there are few that add instant glamour to your bathroom. This decorated organza shower curtain is both pretty and practical as it is backed with clear plastic. The two materials are joined at the top, allowing you to separate them so you can shower with the plastic layer inside the bathtub or shower stall, while the delicate fabric remains dry on the outside. Small glass and diamanté beads attached all over the surface of the fabric with iridescent fabric glue provide embellishment.

Materials

Organza fabric

Clear plastic

Ribbon

Curtain weight

Iridescent fabric glue

Small glass beads

Small diamanté "gems"

Curtain rings

Tools

Dressmaker's pins

Tailor's chalk

Metal ruler

Scissors

Sewing machine (or needle and thread for hand sewing)

Eyelet kit (consists of eyelets, eyelet punch, and riveting tool)

Measuring the shower curtain

1 Measure the distance from your shower curtain rod down to the floor and then add about 1 in. to allow for the hem. Join both materials together using dressmaker's pins, making sure that the clear plastic is on top. Next, use tailor's chalk and a long metal ruler to mark a straight line, and then cut the material to the required length using a pair of sharp scissors.

Sewing the shower curtain

2 Turn over the bottom edge of the material and press down on it to flatten it. Next, use a sewing machine set on a medium-sized straight stitch or a needle and thread to sew a length of ribbon along it. This will then form a channel along the bottom of the material.

3 Cut a length of curtain weight and feed this through the channel. Secure the curtain weight with a couple of small stitches by hand at each end. Carefully trim the sides of the shower curtain.

Using a pair of sharp scissors, cut the material carefully along the marked straight line.

Pin the length of ribbon along the bottom of the material and sew in place to form a channel.

Know your tools

• Clear plastic suitable for shower curtains is sold in fabric stores and is often used as a table covering.

• Organza is a lightweight material woven from metallic threads, giving it a shimmering quality. It is fairly slippery, making it awkward to sew. Set the gauge on your machine to a setting suitable for lightweight fabrics and use a needle designed for metallic thread. When sewing the layers of plastic and organza, it is best to practice on some scrap pieces first until you find the ideal gauge settings.

Decorating the shower curtain

5 Using an iridescent fabric glue, attach some small glass beads and diamanté "gems" to the organza. Because it will come in contact with a lot of water, make sure that the fabric glue is waterproof.

Fixing the shower curtain

6 Use the eyelet punch to make holes at even intervals along the top of the curtain.

7 Using the riveting tool, fit small eyelets into each of these holes.

8 Thread the curtain rings through the eyelets and hang the shower curtain from the shower rod. Rings with decorative glass droplets are used here to provide an extra-glamorous finishing touch.

4 Turn over the top edge of the shower curtain material and once again press down on it. Then cut another length of ribbon to fit over it. Make a sandwich of the ribbon, the organza, and plastic material and pin them all carefully in place. Stitch along the top and bottom of them with the sewing machine set on a medium-sized straight stitch or use a needle and thread.

Cut a suitable length of lightweight curtain weight and thread through the ribbon channel.

Turn over the top edge of the curtain and stitch the ribbon, organza, and plastic together.

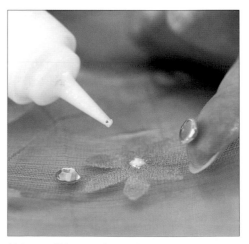

Using an iridescent fabric glue, attach some diamanté "gems" and glass beads.

Alternative

Simple recessed shower stalls with sleek glass doors look particularly effective in contemporary surroundings where a fussy shower curtain would look out of place. Many homes have a cupboard or alcove that could be transformed into a shower area. Take advice from a reliable plumber who will guide you through the process. Ventilation and ease of running pipes to the site are the most important things to take into consideration. It may also be worth installing a pump to increase the water pressure.

To make the area watertight, you will need to install a shower tray or tile the floor area and add drainage. For the walls use conventional ceramic, mosaic, or stone tiles (you could consider waterproof lining panels in a number of different materials, including hardwood or glass).

If you cannot find an appropriate ready-made glass door to fit your alcove, many bathroom manufacturers will be able to custom-make a frame and door to fit.

Make holes at even intervals along the top of the shower curtain with the eyelet punch.

Use the riveting tool to fit the small eyelets along the top of the shower curtain.

Thread the curtain rings through the eyelets and then hang the shower curtain from the rod.

recycled glass bead curtain

Bead curtains make a delicate alternative to lace or voile and catch the light beautifully. Their moisture-resistance makes them an ideal choice in the bathroom. Beautiful recycled beads in watery shades of blue and green were used here. It is important to make sure your wire or string is sturdy enough to support the weight of the beads. A fine-gauge, heavy-duty wire with small "crimping" beads to hold the glass beads in place were sufficient in this example. Use a strong piece of dowel or metal rod to hold the individual strands and hang from curtain rod brackets.

Materials

Glass beads

Strong bead wire

Crimping beads

Dowel

Silver spray paint

Wood drill bit

2 long nails

Metal washer

Tools

Pliers or scissors

Handsaw

Pencil

Drill

Vise

Hammer

Measuring the curtain

1 Measure your window or doorway in order to calculate the exact number of bead strands that you will need for the curtain. Next, figure out the necessary length that each strand should be and then cut the appropriate number of lengths of wire by using your pliers or a pair of scissors.

Threading the beads

2 Use a glass bead to anchor the bottom of each length of wire, threading it through a loop and then using pliers to secure a crimping bead around the wire to hold the glass bead in place.

3 Thread the remaining beads in place. While doing this, you can either build up a pattern or use them completely randomly if you prefer. When you reach the end of the bead string, use a crimping bead to secure the last glass bead in place (see picture bottom left, page 258).

Preparing the dowel

4 Use a handsaw to cut the dowel to the length that you require.

Cut out the number of lengths of wire that you need with scissors or pliers.

Anchor the bottom of each length of wire with a glass bead. Secure it with a crimping bead.

Know your materials

Spray paint is available in a wide range of different colors and finishes. It is ideal for providing even paint coverage and is often used for stenciling. Hold the can at a sufficient distance from the surface you are painting and do not attempt to put too much paint on at any one time or you will end up with runs and drips. Make sure the area around the item is well-masked because spray paint can travel into the smallest of areas. Use only in well-ventilated conditions and always wear a safely mask.

5 Use spray paint to apply a coat of silver paint to the dowel and allow it to dry.

Attaching the bead strings

6 Mark the position of the bead strings at intervals along the length of dowel. Grip the dowel in a vise and drill the required holes using a wood bit.

7 Thread different-shaped beads onto a slim nail and then hammer the nail into the end of the dowel to form a finial. Do the same the other end.

8 Anchor the strings of beads by feeding them through the hole in the dowel. Add a metal washer and then loop the wire around a small glass bead and hold in place with a crimping bead.

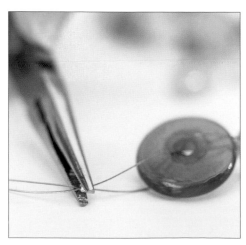

Thread all your beads on a piece of wire, and use a crimping bead to secure the last one.

Once you have cut the piece of dowel to length, spray it with silver spray paint.

Measure and drill holes in the dowel for the lengths of bead to be suspended from.

Alternative

When it comes to screening windows and doors, anything goes. You could combine traditional wooden slatted blinds with an elaborately decorated sheer drape to create a multilayered effect. Dress the curtain by stitching decorative beads or mirror pieces at random intervals or attach tassled hems along its lengths. The light will be reflected off these decorative features back into the room.

Use your imagination to come up with your own ideas when dressing windows. You could use any material that can be attached to a length of string or wire. For a hi-tech solution, try shiny compact disks threaded onto strong nylon thread—their shiny surface reflects colored prisms onto the walls of the room. For a whimsical, nautical look, try decorating with shells, sand, and small pebbles gathered from the beach. Use a small drill bit on a low speed to drill holes in shells carefully. Use rustic garden string to complete the look.

Thread beads on a thin nail and then hammer it into the end of the dowel as a finial.

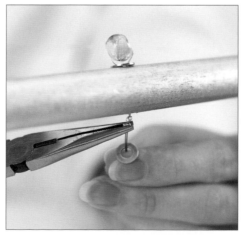

Once the bead strings are in place, attach a metal washer and crimping bead to secure.

lighting your bathroom

Bathroom lighting needs to be focused on individual areas—for example, the mirror over the handbasin where shaving or makeup applications takes place. There should also be lighting focused on a shower stall or bathtub so that you can see gels, soaps, and shampoos.

Right: As well as a good-sized normal mirror, it is also useful to have a magnifying mirror in the bathroom.

Below: Lights can be placed directly over a bathtub and shower—such fixtures will need to be installed by a professional electrician.

Planning your lighting

For general points about lighting design, see Effective lighting, page 134. Lighting in a bathroom needs to be located so that it focuses on the needs and moods of the person using the space. In the morning and evening, good lighting above or around the mirror is a priority for shaving, applying makeup, and cleaning.

Practical lighting

Even if there is a good-sized window in the room, you will probably need additional electric lighting. This can be provided by targeted spot or task lights on the ceiling that are directed onto the mirror in front of the basin. Make sure these lights are directed to shine into the

mirror so that it is reflected back onto your face. If the light shines down too steeply, it will light your back.

A strip or row of bulbs may also run along the top and sides of the mirror so that the light is evenly distributed and regular. Wall-mounted side lights with adjustable arms or heads can also be effective.

With the halo or surround of light on the edge or front of the mirror, it can be more effective to have low-voltage lights rather than high-voltage ones because the latter will create an intense unflattering light that will make you look pallid. The right level of good-quality light will give an accurate color rendition and color temperature, which are important, especially if you are using the lit area to apply your makeup.

For close inspection, there are magnifying mirrors that have integral surrounding lights so that the illumination is directly positioned to shine onto the face or section of the face that is being examined. These enlarging mirrors are wall-mounted and the electric cables are enclosed in the casing of the arm or support.

Decorative lighting

Floor lights are becoming increasingly popular in contemporary bathrooms. These lights are contained in sealed casings and are used to uplight a shower stall from the outside, or in the side panels of the bathtub. They can also be used in the corners of the room to emphasize height and space.

Shelf lighting is sometimes used in the bathroom. A single, long glass shelf can be used to support decorative objects, and by positioning a small light below or on either side of the shelf, you can create an effect

where the shelf appears to glow. This can be eyecatching when the rest of the room is in a subdued light.

Lighting in a shower stall is best done with ceiling-mounted spotlights or enclosed lights such as a nautical bulkhead light. Spots or directional lights can be positioned directly above an enclosed stall, or angled to shine through the glass or side panel of a shower a shower over a bathtub.

Above: *In this small bathroom, in a converted attic space, dormer windows have been set into the roof to provide good natural light.*

Left: *Here, the lighting not only makes it easier to see but also highlights and makes a special feature of the glass basin.*

Bathroom storage

A variety of items and products need to be stored in a bathroom—towels should be kept aired and dry, whereas bottles of shampoo and bath products are often slippery, soapy, and damp and therefore need to be kept separate and contained so that any drips or leaks are not allowed to travel.

Storage units

Storage can be provided either built-in or freestanding. Built-in cabinets can provide storage in places such as under the basin, in linen closets, and even under window seats. They are particularly helpful in small bathrooms where furniture can be custom-made.

Large items of storage can be subdivided into narrow shelves for smaller objects and wider ones for bulkier things. Even within deep shelves, you can section the space with baskets or boxes to keep smaller objects in order.

In some bathrooms there will be a boiler or water heater, which is a bulky, rather unattractive thing.

Above right: Traditional racks that hold soap and sponges are still widely used.

Right: In a shower, the shelves should also be constructed so that water will drain off them rather than sit in stagnant puddles.

Depending on the type of boiler, it may be possible to disguise it with a built-in cupboard but check with a professional before doing so because some require ventilation.

If you do not have a boiler and would prefer freestanding options, there are many available. These vary from modern designs with light wood or steel frames and glass panels to the more traditional armoire with short legs.

Baskets are useful but natural rattan or woven coconut fiber types should be used for dry things, rather than wet. Baskets can be used to hold waste as well as dirty linen.

Left: *The glass shelves in this room are backed by the glass wall of the shower stall and are used to display a collection of old perfume bottles. The shelves are a decorative rather than practical feature, but help to create a barrier between the bathing and showering elements without cutting down on the flow of light from the window beyond.*

Above: *Baskets are useful for containing laundry and towels because they allow air to circulate around the fabrics inside, allowing any moisture to evaporate.*

Small storage solutions

Different types of small storage solutions are needed in a bathroom to cope with the variety of items that are kept there. For example, children's bathtime toys will be wet after playtime but can be stored in a nylon net bag or similar soft, mesh container and left to drip-dry over the bathtub or basin. They are then easily retrieved for the next set of water activities.

Other items that are in frequent use, such as soap and sponges, are often damp and should be kept on or in a holder that has a grill structure or a punched base so that the excess moisture flows away or evaporates.

A basket or tray will make a neat container for items that need to be taken out from a cupboard regularly.

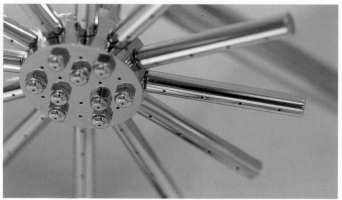

Bathroom accessories

Bathroom accessories should be functional as well as attractive. First, you will need to choose the main items, such as faucets and towel rails, that are part of the general furniture of the room but may also be made into a feature. For instance, the style of the handles on the basin and bathtub faucets or the structure and finish of a towel rails will have visual impact on your whole decorative scheme. Then there are the secondary accessories, such as soap dispensers or dishes, holders for tissues, cotton balls, and toothbrushes, as well as mirrors for closeup use. As a rule, try to choose small accessories that have a similar or matching finish to the rest of your scheme. Keep decorative items in the bathroom to a minimum because they will gather dust. Try to avoid glass and fine ceramic or china containers, unless they are high up on a shelf. Plastic and metal are good robust materials for bathrooms, but check that there is a sealant or varnish on the metal so that it does not tarnish or rust.

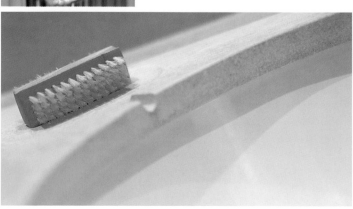

CLOCKWISE FROM TOP LEFT:

This is an old-fashioned style of shower lever with a white ceramic handle and would fit into a bathroom decorated in a traditional period style.

A star-shaped showerhead will give a wider area of spray than most other types.

This contemporary bowl-style basin is made of colored glass to complement the rest of the decorative scheme of the bathroom.

Stacks of neatly folded towels can be a useful as well as attractive addition to a bathroom shelf.

Smooth, curved handles on drawers and shower stalls are easier to grasp when your hands are wet or slippery with body lotion or bath oil.

A modern take on the traditional bath rack with an integral magnifying mirror.

Ceramic and glass containers are attractive but should be carefully positioned so that they will not be knocked over and broken by the edge of a towel or a passing hand.

Ladder-style, wall-hung radiators can be plumbed in level with the wall so that they take up a minimal amount of room.

These wall-mounted, decorative, X-shaped faucets and spout are plumbed in above a sink—their crisp, clean lines complement the stark but functional slate back panel.

This neat metal grid is the outlet for water in the base of a shower stall—the gullies in the tiles and a slight incline direct the water to this point.

In contemporary bathrooms materials such as glass, cement, steel, and wood are often used—here, a specially treated wooden sink is un unusual and eye-catching feature.

Many modern materials can be molded and cast into shapes. This runaway for excess water has been designed as an integral part of the basin surround.

Clip-on towel racks can be bought to fit onto most styles of wall-mounted radiators.

A corkscrew radiator is a fun-looking, useful addition to a bathroom.

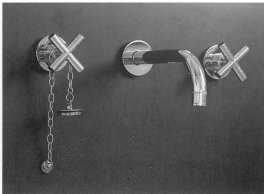

Work and play areas

Planning work and play areas

If you have space to spare in the house, think how to put it to best use. If you work from home, you will require a dedicated work space or you may want to set an area aside to pursue a hobby. Older children may need a quiet place to study, while younger children will always want somewhere to play.

Working and playing in the home

The number of computers used in the home is fast catching up with televisions. More home-working is being done on computers by people who are self-employed or job share. Household accounts and mailing lists are also stored on computers, which can be a helpful way to avoid clutter and run a home efficiently. Many schoolchildren also use them on a regular basis to help them with their homework, to play games, and to email friends.

Home-working is becoming an increasingly popular alternative to regular office life for both domestic and financial reasons. Financially, it costs a company far less to employ someone who works from their own home, and this option is made possible because of the quick and easy interaction offered between home/office and clients by video phones, email, and computer technology.

And just as it is important to have a dedicated work space, so an area dedicated for play can be a great bonus in a family that has children. A playroom or den will be a specific place where toys and games can be kept, which then leaves the main living area predominantly for adult relaxation.

damp, provide adequate ventilation, and if you want to plumb in an additional toilet and handbasin, get access to the waste and water pipes. In an attic conversion, you have to watch out for similar things—ventilation is important because rooftop rooms can become very hot and stuffy during the summer, and again, if you want to plumb in restroom facilities, you need to find out the proximity of the main pipes and drains.

An attic conversion with roof windows can make a useful extra space, whether it is transformed into a work area or used for a play or hobby room where painting, sewing, or photography can be enjoyed. The sloping edges of the roof, which are too low to stand up in, can be utilized for storage, with low cupboards or sliding shelving systems on castors. The shelving system can be constructed so that it is of a triangular shape with decreasing shelf sizes so that it slides in under the slope of the ceiling

Opposite: A colorful scheme can be invigorating in a work space, but avoid fussy wallpapers with distracting patterns.

Left: An attic conversion with glass insets in the roof has provided a light-filled and spacious artist's studio.

Below: This curving desk gives a student ample work space in her bedroom.

Planning your space

Because of the increase in home-working, more people are seeking out a space from which to conduct their business. Some opt for a converted garage, a basement development, attic extension, or separate outbuilding, while others take over a spare bedroom or divide off part of a large room. Alternately, such areas can be made into a playroom.

If you use a basement or attic, you will need to consider three important aspects: access, structure, and headroom.

Access is usually via a staircase, for which a rectangular space of 10 x 3 ft. will be necessary for standard vertical stairs, whereas a spiral can squeeze into 5 sq. ft. But a spiral staircase, with its triangular-shaped steps, can be less easy for very young children and elderly adults to manage.

For a basement development, the floor joists of the room above may need to be strengthened, and in a small cellar part of the floor may have to be excavated to provide sufficient head height and to lay down a waterproof membrane. You will require planning permission, as well as structural and architectural advice, for such large-scale alterations.

In a basement or cellar, you also have to be able to gain access to natural light, overcome

269

Above: *Wire and cable management is a necessity in modern home offices. Here, a specific hole has been provided in the desktop so that cables can be fed out and down to the electrical outlet rather than squashed between the back of the desk and the wall.*

Right: *This neat study area has been created in the space at the bottom of a basement staircase. Good electrical lighting is important here because there is no natural light available.*

rather than along it. With the limited head height in these areas, recessed spotlights in the ceiling can save valuable inches. In a single, long open space, folding doors or partitions can be used to subdivide the room, but you should also try to keep available the option of opening it up again.

Small rooms should be kept light and airy and decorated simply to make the most of the limited amount of space, and in basement conversions, to make the most of the light available. Do not be tempted to use this additional space as a junk room to store bits of furniture that you do not want elsewhere in the house. Instead, be specific and invest time and money in selecting light-framed, lightweight pieces. You may also find that you need to be careful when buying larger pieces of furniture—you must certainly check that you will be able to get them up or down the staircase into your room.

It is possible that you will have to buy a desk that comes in sections to be assembled once it is inside the room. In small rooms, you can save valuable space by having furniture specially designed and built-in, although this will probably cost you more.

Where a standard table may have an overlap or lip that leaves a gap between the wall and the base, you can have a specifically designed table made to butt directly up to the wall. Foldaway furniture can also be useful in rooms where space is limited as it can then be folded flat when it is not in use but is also very easily opened out when it is needed.

Creating space within a room

Working from home requires discipline, and where possible, it is best to allocate a separate room to this activity. If you cannot afford to dedicate a whole room, then create space within an area of a room that can be used without disturbing others. It is also important to be able to separate work and home life so that you can concentrate on each part as and when you are involved with it.

If children are using the computer to do homework, they should be free from outside distractions, so the space should be out of the main thoroughfare of the home or the bustle of the kitchen. This will enable them to concentrate on their task and give it their full attention. If the computer is used for games, then others will also appreciate the fact that the "beep beeps" and general games activity are isolated from the area where they may be trying to relax or listen to music.

If your work area is part of a larger room, you can create a way of containing it—this can be done with screens, panels, lightweight movable bookcases, or even a series of Venetian blinds or pull-down shades. These room dividers do not have to be permanent, but can be flexible so that they provide privacy and seclusion only when it is needed.

Left: *Adjustable seats allow you to tailor a sitting position to suit your stature—this gives better ergonomic support and helps to relieve physical tension. A seat with wheels can also be useful if you need to turn or move around to collect papers or files.*

Practical considerations for a work space

There are practical and health implications that should be taken into consideration when planning your work space.

When computers and VDUs (visual display units) are used in a regular office environment, it is the employer's duty to make sure that health and safety regulations are followed, but at home it is up to you. The location of the computer screen should, where possible, be sited near a window and natural light, but the screen must be angled in order to avoid glare that is hard on the eyes and may obliterate parts of the screen.

Do not have the ambient light level in the room too low. The levels of light in the room and the screen should be comparable.

Your desk should be adjacent to shelves or storage where frequently used files or reference materials are stored so that they are easily accessible. If your work involves a lot of paperwork, then

Making decorative screens

Screening off an area or corner of a room can be done in a number of ways.

There is the standard panel screen made from a wood frame with a wood, fabric, or other type of panel. There are also curving screens made from small strips of wood that articulate and undulate like an old-fashioned roll-top desk. These are more flexible than the frame screen and can be used in difficult areas and around odd shapes. Alternately, you could use a bookcase or a row of tall, bushy plants to make a screen.

you may find it useful to have a desk that has an extra long return, such as an L shape, that provides you with an adjacent surface on which to collate or arrange the documents you are dealing with.

Try to keep the desk free of small items that get lodged under books and papers. (See Storage and display, page 278.)

Good ventilation is also essential in a working space to avoid stress and fatigue. If the room becomes too warm and soporific, you will be in danger of falling asleep. Heat will build up from the VDU and electric lighting so keep the door open and leave a window slightly open.

Machines such as computers, faxes, printers, copiers, and phones always involve a spaghetti of wires and cables. Arrange these wires in order and keep them neatly coiled or wrapped around a cable manager; this will protect the wiring from damage and prevent people from tripping over them. It will also make it easier to identify a single line should you want to remove it.

Seating is important. At home one chair tends to be used for all situations, but the home office chair should be adjustable so that the height and position can be tailored to suit each individual in the household that will be using it—from child to adult.

To get the correct position, sit on the seat and adjust it until, while still seated, your horizontally outstretched arms are roughly at the same level as the bottom of the VDU casing, your eyes are at the same level as the top of the VDU, and your feet are flat on the floor. If you work in a seated position for long periods, you may find that a foot rest is comfortable.

When using a keyboard, your hands should not be too bent at the wrist and the keys should be easy to tap softly. To avoid eye strain and headaches, make sure that the screen is at a comfortable distance from your eyes. This is around 2 ft., but less is acceptable if using a laptop.

Practical considerations for a playroom

A dedicated playroom can be brightly painted, imaginatively decorated, and completely child-friendly, rather than having to be compromised because it is in a space shared with adults. You should definitely avoid having prominent sharp corners on furniture. Where possible, sand or rub the points down until they are more rounded and soft, or stick on plastic corner caps to prevent small children from banging their heads or limbs against them and being bruised. The same applies to work areas because adults may bang their legs or hips against a table edge or cupboard corner as they rush about.

Below: A study area does not have to look like an office—it can fit with the style of the rest of the room. Here, a Scandinavian period-style room works easily around this elegant desk.

Left: A work area should be bright and airy. Make the most of all available light by positioning your desk near a window. Make sure, however, that there is no reflected glare on your computer screen.

Color, light, and atmosphere

Both work and play areas benefit from being light and airy—they are places where the mind and body need to be alert and active and the decor and surroundings should help to promote this outlook. The space should be conducive to concentration, but not be dull or boring. If you have converted a cellar or attic space, you will need to make the most of any available light and use every trick in the decorator's book to make the space seem spacious.

First, keep the ceiling plain or simply patterned and decorate the walls and ceiling in a light color. Smooth wall surfaces will also reflect light more efficiently than rough or textured ones. If you do want to introduce a strong or dark color, use it on one wall only, as a special feature panel, and preferably on the wall that has a window set into it so that the light from the window will counteract any darkness. Dark colors can be oppressive and depressing, and vibrant reds, pinks, and oranges

too hot and lively. This could make you feel agitated, distracting you from your work.

Solid colors or light, geometric patterns are best for a work space. If you make it too floral or bedroom-like, it will detract from your sense of purpose. For business visitors, fussy floral papers may give the impression that you are less than serious, or not focused on your work. Light, fresh colors such as lemon, green, and blue, or neutrals such as beige or oatmeal, are clean and appropriate.

At-a-glance color guide

Walls in a study should be plain rather than fussy. Restful colors are good for keeping you calm, but should not be so subtle and restful that they make you sleepy. One option is to mix bright and pale colors. Paint one wall a vivid and exciting color such as blue or green, and then paint the other in a much paler tone of the same color. In a dark room, a light or white ceiling will help reflect the available natural light, as will gloss-painted white window frames and surrounds.

273

striped room-
dividing shades

Most of us need an area in which to complete paperwork. If your work area is in the corner of a room used for another purpose, these shades are ideal for screening off a messy desk or hobby area. Making your own shades allows you to tailor them to fit your space. Most medium-weight fabrics can be made into shades by using a fabric-stiffening solution. Choose a fabric of a sufficient width to avoid joints that would prevent the shade from rolling up neatly. If the area that you wish to cover is wider than your fabric, make several shades that will give access to different areas.

Materials

Roller kits for making the required number of shades

Cotton fabric

Fabric-stiffening spray (with flame retardant)

Masking tape

Latex paints

Fabric-painting medium

Thread

Tools

Tape measure

Square

Scissors

Pencil

Junior hacksaw

Tailor's pencil

Small paintbrushes

Iron

Staple gun

Needle

Preparing the materials

1 Make a drawing of the area to be covered with accurate width and height measurements. Decide where you will fix the shades and calculate how many roller kits you will need. Use a tape measure, square, and scissors to cut the fabric. Mark the lengths of dowel using the width of the fabric as a guide.

Cutting down to size

2 If necessary, trim the lengths of dowel that are supplied in the roller kit using a junior hacksaw.

3 Spray the material with a suitable fabric-stiffening spray. This will also prevent any cut edges from fraying, and make the fabric flame-retardant.

Drawing the stripes

4 Using a pencil, mark out stripes of different widths and apply strips of masking tape to the edges.

Adding the colors

5 Use around six colors of latex paint mixed with a fabric-painting medium and paint the stripes. Allow the stripes

Measure the dowel using the width of the fabric as a guide to fit the size you require.

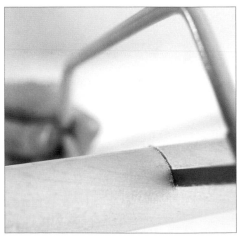

If the lengths of dowel are too long, use a junior hacksaw to trim them down.

Know your materials

Roller kits can be purchased from most large furnishing stores. They are a good-value option if you have large windows, and they also allow you to use your own choice of fabric. The kits supply the winding mechanism, a wood or metal roller, the brackets to attach the shade to the window, and a string pull. Some kits also include the stiffening spray needed to make your chosen fabric more rigid. If possible, try and get one that also gives the fabric a degree of fire retardency.

to dry in between colors for the recommended time before reapplying strips of masking tape.

6 When all the stripes have been painted, iron on the reverse side, making sure that the instructions on the fabric-painting medium are followed. This is to ensure that the paint is colorfast.

Assembling the shade

7 Attach the fabric to the roller mechanism using the adhesive strip provided. Reinforce this with a staple gun if your shade is long and heavy.

8 Using a needle and a piece of coordinating thread, sew a channel for the rod at the bottom. Feed the rod through the channel and then slot it in place. Finally, attach the pull cord supplied with the roller kit.

Spray the material with fabric-stiffening spray suitable for shades to make them fire-retardant.

Use a pencil and a ruler to draw stripes of different widths onto the fabric.

Paint the stripes and use masking tape to achieve clean lines.

Alternative

If you want a more permanent, formal way of dividing your room, consider fitting a series of doors that can be folded back to create one large room when required. These doors can run on small wheels that slot into tracks on the floor and ceiling. Alternately, they can be hung on sets of door hinges and anchored in place with simple bolts that slot into plates on the floor. Ready-made bifolding doors and tracks can be bought from home-improvement stores, or you could search for reclaimed doors. Paneled doors can be customized by removing the top panels and replacing them with fretwork or glass. This allows plenty of light to filter through while still giving each side of the room a degree of privacy. Fretwork screen panels can be bought in a variety of designs and materials, including particle board, hardboard, and pressed metals. Glass panels can be bought from a glass supplier who will cut them to fit. You can choose from plain, frosted, or colored or stained glass panels.

When the stripes are dry, iron on the reverse side to make sure the paint is colorfast.

Attach the fabric to the roller mechanism using the adhesive strip provided in the kit.

Sew a channel at the bottom of the shade, then feed the rod through and slot in place.

Storage and display

In work and play areas storage is important. In a work space you will need to have reference books and files at hand, and in a play area different types of toys and games should all be kept in their own containers or drawers so that they do not get lost or form an untidy jumble.

Work space storage

In a work space the most important thing is to avoid too much clutter. Keep things that you need at hand and store items that are seldom used on upper shelves or more distant cupboards and file cabinets. Avoid a buildup of files, boxes, and paperwork around you because it can make you feel trapped and overpowered by your surroundings. The best way to keep paper under control is to edit it regularly—never let an "In" tray build up to the stage where it overflows into a second basket.

If your desktop is organized, it also makes it easier to cope with things that pass over it. A good basic stationery kit such as paper clips, eraser, stapler, and sticky tape should be kept in a divided or sectioned drawer because this will enable you to know exactly where each thing is and it will be easy to lay your hands on them when you need them.

Small items such as paper clips and bulletin board pins can be effectively stored in clear glass jars with screw-on lids. The lids keep the contents firmly inside but the glass sides make it simple to identify the contents. Clear plastic containers can be useful but the lids tend not to stay as firmly in place as the old-fashioned screw type, and in time thin, shiny plastic may become brittle and crack.

But a working space does not need to be dull and regimented. In fact, stationery and office accessories is an area where color, pattern, and design have recently made a huge impact.

Right: A file cabinet can be positioned underneath your desk, which will make it easy to reach paperwork and also makes good use of space.

Below: Box files are extremely useful and can be labeled so that you can locate items very quickly.

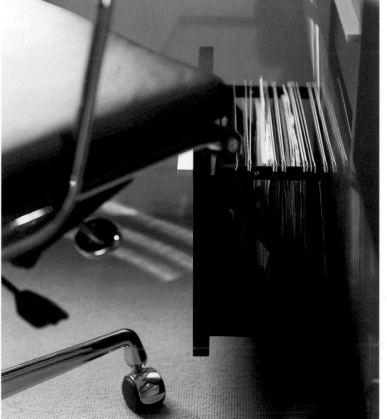

Files that were once covered in a standard gray or dull casing are now widely available in brightly colored covers, which can make it easier to identify an individual file at a distance. Instead of buying a dozen files in the same uniform finish, have different-colored ones so that you will be able to memorize what color relates to a particular topic. This will also give your work space a more lively appearance. Or you can create your own (see box, page 280).

Another useful piece of apparatus can be a wall grid. This may be made of wood or metal and is a panel of bars onto which items can be hung. Wall grids are generally more robust than bulletin boards, and with small butcher's hooks can be a good place for hanging tools such as scissors, hammers, and spanners.

Larger sections of wall grid can support small shelves and may be used in the area of wall in front of a work station. The various hooks and attachments can then be used to display stationary elements such as sticky tape, labels, a clock, craft knife, rulers, and so on, putting everything on display and immediately at hand. This type of arrangement is better for a wall by a desk or secondary work station rather than the primary one, because the equipment hanging in front of a person trying to work may become distracting and make the space feel reduced and cluttered.

If a lot of storage and shelving is necessary in your work space,

you can make it seem less dominant by painting it the same color as the wall. This will make the shelves appear to be an integral part of the wall rather than a feature that is set against it.

Useful work space furniture

If your work requires you to gather information, swatches, or reference material from elsewhere and bring it back to your desk, a trolley may be a useful addition to your furniture. The trolley can be used to transport material from one area to another in one move rather than your having to go backward and forward several

Above left: *Storage specifically designed to hold certain items, such as tapes and CDs, not only contains them but also makes them easier to view and select.*

Above: *This is another example of a specially designed cabinet. It neatly contains a CD player, CDs, and videos.*

Left: *In a small study reinforced glass or plexiglass shelves are useful because they provide ample storage but do not appear too heavy or block out light.*

Decorative labels for storage boxes

Labeling and identifying the contents of boxes and files is important so that they can be easily seen. For business files, use clear white labels with bold black printed letters. If files or boxes are used in a damp or moist environment, or will be lifted with wet hands, then cover the labels with a strip of clear adhesive plastic. For young children of pre-reading age, color coding can be helpful— dolls' clothes in a pink box, toy soldiers in a red one, and books in green, for example—or you can cut out appropriate pictures to make it easy for them to see what belongs where.

Right: *This storage system has a variety of sizes of shelves and forms an efficient office space along just one wall.*

Below: *Magazine holders come in a variety of materials, colors, and finishes so they can coordinate with your decorative scheme.*

times with armfuls of files. The trolley can also be pulled right up to your desk where you can easily access the documents, thereby using the top of the trolley as an extension to the desk.

As well as modern office equipment, old or antique pieces can be useful as well as interesting and attractive. Old wooden store-display systems with glass-fronted drawers can make a pleasant change in a home office and will blend in more easily with traditional furnishings and fabrics. Map chests, with their rows of large, flat drawers, not only provide ample storage

but are usually of such a size and construction that the top can be used as an additional work surface, a partial room divider, or even a place to put a kettle or coffee machine.

Just as the map chest can be used to create a low or partial divider, a small bookcase can be used in the same way. These low barriers help to divide work from home space but do not cut off the flow of light or line of vision. A three-shelf bookcase, up to 3 ft. high, can be secured to the floor and an adjacent wall to make sure that it is stable. The side facing the work space will display the

shelves and provide storage, whereas the back will face into the other half of the room and may be concealed by the back of a sofa or painted to match the wall in that area. (See page 270 for more ideas on how to create a separate space for your work area.)

Display in work spaces

Although the primary function of your work space should be practical, there is no reason why you should not create a display of a few ornaments to create a comfortable, welcoming environment. If you have a bulletin board beside your desk, you will also be able to place things such as a calendar, family photographs, and useful phone numbers on it. This can be livened up with posters, too. Be careful not to let your work space become too cluttered though.

Storage in play areas

If a child's bedroom doubles as a play area, by putting toys away in boxes out of sight at the end of the day you are removing the temptation for a small person to get out of bed once the door is closed at night and continue playing. Good toy storage can help young children because they learn about discipline and tidiness, too. It also helps to keep the floor area clear when games time is over, so that if there is a change from day- to night-time activity the space will quickly and easily adapt. Adults also need to be able to check on sleeping children without falling over rollerblades, toy trains, or treading on a favorite doll or toy.

Plastic crates with lids that stack neatly one on top of another work well in a child's room. These can be arranged along a wall and labeled so that the contents are easily identified without having to open each box. Drawers on wheels or castors can be slotted under a bed, and narrow shelves are ideal for books and small toys, such as soldiers, small cars, or dolls.

If a small child learns that his or her toys are always returned to the same box or bag, they will quickly learn the routine. This will also save the parent or helper the thankless task of searching endlessly for a specific item.

Having easily accessible storage should stop smaller items or play things getting separated or lost. For a slightly older child's

bedroom, you could store smaller items, such as paintbrushes and crayons or favorite soft toys, in a wall or door hanging with pockets. This is simply made from a strong cotton fabric such as canvas, or even a more interesting material such as denim (see box, right). The panel can be fixed to the wall or the back of the door by hooks and eyelets or with a strong piece of cord attached to each end of the top piece of dowel and looped over a couple of strong hooks. The pockets can be made in contrasting colors to that used for the back panel or decorated with felt letters, cutout pictures of the things that are stored in the pockets, or decorated with buttons to add interest.

Display in play areas

In a child's room storage can also double as a display area. For example, a troop of cowboys can look fun if they are displayed on a shelf in a room where the theme revolves around the Wild West. If Barbie is the dream doll of the moment and the bedroom is painted pink in her honor, then the doll herself should be on show to be a part of the overall scheme.

Display areas can also be informative. A bulletin board for school certificates or good reports, as well as homework and activity timetables, will be useful. Pictures may also need to be pinned up—by using a cork bulletin board you can protect the wall surface from holes.

Making your own hanging storage

First you need to cut a long rectangle of your chosen material. If you are thinking about hanging it behind a door, then take the dimensions of the door and reduce it so that the back sheet is about 2 ft. shorter than the door measurement from top to bottom and about 9 in. narrower at each side. Hem the back panel and make a channel top and bottom to hold a length of dowel the same width as the material. Slide the dowel into the channel and sew over the ends of the fabric to keep it in place.

Measure the items you plan to put in the pockets and cut the material to the same size with an additional generous hem allowance. Hem the top edge, then turn in the sides and bottom of the pocket and sew onto the back panel.

Left: *This tall system of shelves in a child's bedroom not only stores toys and books efficiently but also displays them attractively.*

281

tongue-and-groove display panel

Lightweight slatted panels are ideal in a home office or a study with changing storage needs. These panels were made using tongue-and-groove floorboards, with the tongues removed. The ingenious part is that the grooves provide an anchor for shelves and pictures, which can be hung at varying heights. Simply unhook and rearrange to change the layout if required. The panels can be attached directly to the wall, or for a less permanent version, onto vertical battens attached to the wall. Use picture hooks made to fit over a picture rail to suspend pictures.

Materials

Wood battens

Softwood tongue-and-groove floorboards

Wood screws

Shellac

Water-based primer

White water-based satinwood paint

Wood glue

Tools

Handsaw

Workbench

Tape measure

Sharp plane or jigsaw

Sandpaper

Electric drill

Countersink bit

Paintbrush

Hacksaw

Screwdriver

Measuring the area

1 Decide on the height and width of the screen. Using a handsaw, cut the wood battens and floorboards to the required dimensions.

2 Secure each floorboard in turn on a workbench, and with a sharp plane or a jigsaw, remove the tongue.

Securing the floorboards

3 Lay out the cut floorboard lengths, allowing a ½ in. of space between each one. Place the vertical battens in position at each end. If you are making a wall more than 13 ft. wide, you should add another central batten for extra stability.

4 Drill and screw through the back of the batten into each floorboard using a countersink bit, making sure the screw head sits beneath the surface of the wood.

Using a handsaw, cut the battens and tongue-and-groove floorboards to the required size.

Secure each floorboard to the workbench and remove the tongue with a jigsaw.

Know your materials

Tongue-and-groove floorboards were used here because they are stronger than tongue-and-groove wall paneling and the deeper groove along their length was perfect for hanging picture hooks and shelves from. It is important to treat the knots (the rounded marks where branches were) with shellac. This seals the knots and prevents resinous sap from bleeding through the paint and spoiling the finished look.

5 When all the floorboards are secured to the battens, turn the panel the right way up and sand thoroughly. Using an old paintbrush, apply shellac to any knots in the boards (this will prevent resin from bleeding through the paintwork and spoiling the finish).

Painting the floorboards

6 Apply a coat of water-based primer followed by two coats of white water-based satinwood paint and allow to dry.

Making the shelf

7 Use another floorboard (with the tongue removed) to make the shelf. Cut two pieces of the same length and butt together to form the back and base. Cut two identical squares with the corners cut off to form the sides. Glue and screw together. Treat with shellac, then prime and paint white.

8 Use a hacksaw to cut a length of L-shaped metal trim to fit the top of the shelf.

9 Drill, countersink, then screw the longest edge of the metal trim in position on top of the shelf. This will slot neatly over the floorboard lengths and anchor itself in the groove.

Use a countersink bit to screw through the back of the batten into each floorboard.

With a paintbrush, apply shellac to any resinous knots to prevent resin from bleeding through.

Apply a coat of primer and then two coats of paint to the boards.

Alternative

One of the most attractive methods of storing CDs is to slip them horizontally into a grooved panel of wood. Hardwoods with an attractive grain look best, but if you want to make one you will need a router with a groove-cutting bit. You can adapt this idea, making a simpler version by adding pieces of dowel to the front of a flat panel.

Sketch out the rough dimensions to plan the quantity of materials you will need. Get a panel of wood or particle board cut to fit your space, and sufficient square-section dowels cut to the same width. Make sure that the dowels are deep enough to hold the CDs firmly in place. Use a soft pencil and square to mark the position of the dowels on the back and front of the panel, making sure that each is a CD width apart. Spread a thin layer of wood glue over one side of each dowel and position them all. Tap a row of thin finish nails through from the back of the panel to hold the dowels in place. Finally, attach the panel to the wall with screws or mirror plates at each side.

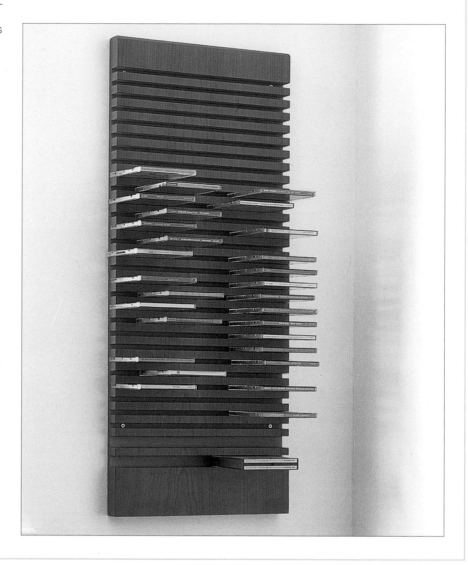

Use another floorboard to make the shelf, then treat with shellac, prime, and paint.

Use a hacksaw to make an L-shaped metal trim to fit the top of the shelf.

Drill, countersink, and screw the longest edge of the metal trim in place on top of the shelf.

lighting for work and play

The type and arrangement of lighting that you choose for both work and play areas are important. Work areas should be bright and airy, conducive to concentrating on the task at hand, while in children's rooms safety is a priority.

Below right: A movable task light that will focus light directly on paperwork or a screen is a basic necessity in a working or study environment.

Work space lighting

The computer screen should, where possible, be sited near a window and natural light, but the screen must be angled to avoid glare that is hard on the eyes and may obliterate parts of the screen. Do not have the ambient light level in the room too low. The levels of light in the room and the screen should be comparable.

A specific adjustable work light is essential to supplement fading daylight. A standard table lamp with a shade or a central room light is not good enough because it may cast shadows on the screen, making it difficult to see. Desktop or task lights, such as recessed and directional spotlights, will also be needed in order to light up the rest of the desk surface.

Playroom lighting

It is best to provide high-level ambient light for a play area so that the lower levels of the room are as cable-free as possible. Use childproof safety covers on the electrical outlets to deter small fingers from investigating the holes, and equip light fittings with safety plugs that have partly sheathed pins.

It is best to avoid small china-base table lamps or anything that is easily broken—instead opt for robust light fittings. There are

many specially designed for children's rooms, available from many different stores.

Lights not only provide illumination but can also be a fun and interesting part of the scheme, particularly in a play area. For example, crescent moon and colorful umbrella-style paper shades are available.

If the children using the play room spend most of their time at floor level, then you will need to have a good, broad-beam overhead light such as recessed spots in conjunction with wall

lights. The wall lights can be contained in enclosed shades, so that there is no direct access to the bulb and so that the bulb is contained should it blow.

If the play area doubles up as a work room for an older child or adult, adjustable task lights could be attached to the wall so that they can be positioned over a desk or work area without being in the way of the play area. This type of work light should be angled so that the beam shines diagonally across the papers on the table, to focus on the work.

Customizing files

In your home office you can customize your files with decorative paper, such as silver, glossy pastel shades, or colored self-adhesive plastic and choose colors that represent the topic contained within the file. For example, you could use blue for water-related subjects and green for landscape gardeners or grass-seed suppliers.

Left: *A desk is best positioned near a source of natural light. Here, mirrors are used to reflect and make the most of the light.*

Below left: *Task lights should provide a good, even level of light but should not be too strong or create glare, which can be hard on the eyes.*

Using natural light

It is best to keep window dressings simple to make the most of natural light. In a work area an adjustable shade or Venetian blind is ideal because it can be used to shield bright, direct sunlight, yet can be rolled or pulled up out of the way on darker days.

In a play room, opt for simple drapes, shades, or something like a folded Roman blind that can be effective and attractive. The latter should be placed at a level out of the way of sticky fingers. If the play area is really more of an adult recreation room, you may need to tailor the window treatments to suit the hobby. For example, if photography or making family videos is an abiding hobby, then blackout shades may be needed.

Creating your own decorative shade

Customize a lampshade for a child's playroom by painting the outer surface or sticking on cutout shapes. You could try cutting out motifs from extra drape or bedding material and applying these to the shade. If you are using a floral motif, leave a little of the edge of the petal hanging over the lower edge of the shade for a decorative finish. Always buy a shade that has been safety tested and only decorate the outside of it.

Workplace accessories

Work areas within the home should be softer and more comfortable than a commercial or business space, yet they do need to function efficiently. Storage and good planning are the keys to success, and a built-in desk can convert a wasted space under a staircase or at the end of a corridor into a useful additional room. Because these are domestic environments, you can have fun with accessories such as files and pencil holders and can indulge in bright colors and fun schemes. However, they should not be too extravagant or they might distract you. Once the desk and storage space have been allocated, the next most important items are ventilation, lighting, and seating. Ventilation is important if you are using electrical machines because they generate heat and may make a room stuffy and dry. Target lighting, provided by an adjustable spot or desk lamp, will be vital for good viewing and also for the care of your eyesight. Finally, an ergonomically designed, adjustable chair is vital for good posture and support.

CLOCKWISE FROM TOP LEFT:

An old pewter tankard doubles as a pencil holder—this is a practical yet quirky storage solution.

Smooth edges, such as those on the arm of this chair and the desk edge, make a more pleasant and safer working environment.

Good storage is essential to keep things in order and easily accessible, especially in small spaces.

The shelves of bookcases can be arranged so that they accommodate specific sizes and types of books.

Transparent shelves do not appear as heavy or dense as solid wood or particle board, and in a small room can make it appear more spacious. However, you should only use reinforced laminate glass or plexiglass for this type of construction.

Small file cabinets can be used as a desk base. This also means that frequently used files and papers can be kept close at hand.

Clear labeling will make it much more easy to identify the contents of your files and drawers.

Glare on a computer screen can make it difficult to focus on, so have an adjustable side light and shades at the window to allow you to achieve the right level and direction of light for your working environment.

Bright, light colors can be very invigorating when used in a study or workroom.

If you do a lot of paperwork, make sure that you have plenty of tabletop or desk surface in order to lay out the material.

Coordinating stationery can make a desk area visually pleasing and inviting.

This neat study area has been built in at the end of a corridor, but still provides adequate and dedicated working space.

Work lights need not be dull—this modern design has an adjustable head that slides up and down the main steel support.

Old cabinets can be used as storage for paperwork or toys. The solid front panels can be removed from the doors and replaced with fine wire mesh or even pleated fabric to give a more homely feel.

Connecting areas

Planning connecting areas

Passage and hallways are an often overlooked part of the home, yet they are very important, not only because they link one room to another but also because, if they are decorated in an attractive, clutter-free way, they can make the experience of passing through them more enjoyable.

Hallways, landings, staircases, and passageways link rooms and various levels in a home, but are often narrow, dark, and difficult to make the most of. If you have a long corridor, try to subdivide it into three parts, such as the entrance hall, the inner passageway or corridor, and the end, so that in each section there is a focus.

Hallways

The area immediately inside the front door is a busy place where people arrive and depart, where mail is received, and coats, boots, hats, and gloves are often kept. It is also an area that forms a barrier between the outside world, a place of transition between the reality of working life and the cozy, domestic interior.

To accommodate the transition and these functions, you should create a space that is tranquil and organized. To cope with the comings and goings in this area, there should be a variety of storage and a place to sit while putting on and taking off shoes. It should also be decorated so that it appears bright and inviting.

Accessories

The first accessory in this entrance area is usually a roughly textured mat on the floor immediately inside or just outside

Right: Glass panels above the two main doors off this passageway allow natural light from the rooms on the other side to penetrate this windowless, internal area.

Below: Lighting is extremely important within a hallway. Here, low lighting that is situated just above the baseboards illuminates the passageway.

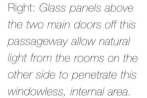

the door. The inner floor in this area should be covered with a practical finish—something that can be easily cleaned. Stone, wood, flagstones, or tiles are good but can be softened or brightened with a runner, which must be made safe to use with a good, nonslip backing.

The floor covering should be strong and resilient because there will be a lot of wear and tear. As nice as a pure wool carpet would be, it may mark quickly. You can opt for a wall-to-wall carpet but put a rug or mat over the area immediately inside the door, or a runner that covers

the central track from the doorway, thereby protecting the carpet that is underneath.

Passageways

Corridors and passageways. are in the "center" of the home and will invariably have doorways that open into and out of this space, but it is less frenetic and busy than the front door area.

The corridor or passageway is not often filled with people— if it is busy, people are usually just passing through, so it can be an area where some privacy can be had while making a telephone call. To accommodate this, another

table and chair would be useful. The table may be needed for telephone directories, a phone book, a message pad, and a pen. A table lamp may also be helpful. If you do not have enough room for a table, then a couple of shelves could be fixed to the wall instead.

Depending on the size of your passageways and corridors, you may find it useful to have pieces of furniture arranged as drop-off or staging points. For example, if you have a kitchen on one side of a passageway and a living/dining room on the other side, a low table or a small chest by the living/dining room door could be very useful for resting a tray of plates or a hot dish while you open the door.

In a long passageway, a resting point outside a bedroom door may also be handy for putting things on while distributing clean linen, light bulbs, books, or other items along the way.

Left: *Hallways need to be practical, so a piece of storage that can hold coats, shoes, and other items is a great addition.*

Above: *Folding doors that concertina back on themselves are useful to divide areas where space is limited.*

A chest of drawers can also be a worthwhile addition in a corridor or passageway linking bedrooms. The linen for the various rooms can be stored here. After laundering, all the sheets can be returned to the same central container. As a general rule, all the furniture in passageways should be light, narrow, and well-spaced so that the corridor is not an obstacle course.

The end point

The third zone is the end of the corridor or passageway—this should be made a focal point rather than dismissed as a dark or dreary place. If you come in through the main door and look down the corridor, the eye should be greeted by an appealing sight.

This area should be well-lit so it is easy to see, and the length of distance can be assessed. Knowing where the corridor or passageway ends gives a psychologically comforting idea of where you are and what lies between you and the end wall.

Landings

If the hallway or passageway passes through a landing area, around a corner, or past a bay window, there may be additional space or width at this point. In this case, the area may be used to create a cameo setting. This can be a simple chair and occasional table with books and magazines, or a large piece of sculpture. If the area is big enough to accommodate a good-sized table, wall-mounted bookcases, and a chair, it could also be used as a study or casual working space.

Staircases

Staircases often lead to and from hallways and connect one level to another. Stairs need to be well-lit and should have a handrail or

Top: *A curving wall is an interesting architectural feature in this area.*

Above: *A wall-mounted table forms a decorative feature in this landing.*

Right: *Shield-like lights and stenciled gilded wallpaper add interest to a long hallway.*

Opposite: *Staircases can be sculptural features, as in this dramatic example.*

structure that encloses the steps, providing a safe support should anyone accidentally trip or slip. In some homes a skylight or a few windows on an upper level may provide natural light for the stairs.

By setting light wells and dormer windows into the roof, you can provide an invaluable source of daylight. The window need not open but can be a fixed panel, and if it is not overlooked, does not need to be screened. In a period home these roof lights were known as lanterns and were often interesting shapes such as

ovals divided into triangular segments, like an orange. This type of skylight created a feature in an otherwise bland area.

The sides of the staircase can be filled in with reinforced glass panels, with fine spindles of metal or wood or traditional turned rails, to let more light circulate.

Carpets, runners, and floor coverings used on stairs must be firmly held in place. With runners, stair rods can be used to keep them secure.

A bookcase could also be custom-made to fit under a

staircase. This is another awkward space that needs to be used carefully. Another option, depending on the size, is to box in this space to provide a separate toilet or a general store for vacuum cleaners and cleaning products. Otherwise it can be left open and shelved, dressed with a table and chair, or filled with a good-sized wine rack.

Decoration and style

As corridors tend to be in the inner part of a home, they are often windowless and dark, so you will have to rely on decorating tricks and techniques to make the place seem light and airy.

A traditional but practical form of decoration in hallways and stairwells is the use of the chair rail. This is a narrow, raised wood batten or molding, often with a rounded or decorative finish. Below the chair rail the wall can be papered with a thick protective finish and painted in a dark, even gloss paint that will withstand inadvertent kicks and scuffs. The upper level can be painted in a light, bright color, thereby giving the upper part of the hallway a feeling of spaciousness.

This type of scheme can be given an unusual Asian twist by painting the lower level of the wall in black and the upper levels and baseboard in red. This chinoiserie style reflects the lacquerware favored in China and can be lit with ceiling-recessed downlighters for a dramatic effect. Also any gilt- or silver-framed pictures or mirrors put on the walls will stand out and sparkle against the background.

The "print room"—another technique that can be used to decorate the hallway—is a useful 18th-century device that can be given a modern twist. To create a traditional print room, the walls of a small room or vestibule were

painted in a mid-tone to strong color, and over the dry paint black-and-white prints of scenic views, portraits, or landmarks were pasted. The prints were then framed with borders to look as though they were actual paintings. This technique can easily be adapted and photocopies or black-and-white photographs could be used in a similar way.

A mirror is also an attractive feature at the end of a passageway, but avoid a single full-length mirror because it can be unnerving to watch yourself advancing. An oval mirror or a collection of different shapes and sizes of mirror can be arranged in an unusual and interesting way.

Linking spaces

As a corridor is a link between rooms, it is advisable to keep its decoration simple. An ornate or floral wallpaper may make the space seem smaller and may also be overpowering. However, plain walls need not be dull—they can be easily decorated with pictures and mirrors or real or imitation wood paneling.

Long passageways or connecting areas are a great place to hang a coordinating series of pictures, prints, or paintings. A set of black-and-white photographs, a series of prints or characters, or even a collection of plates or framed scarves can create interest as well as form a link from one end of the space to the other. Even if the pictures are not from the same series they can be linked by subject matter—for example, flowers and butterflies.

Another way of linking a space is by using a frieze or by painting the baseboard in a bright or dominant color so that your eye follows it around a corner or up to another level. A carpet, runner, or floor covering of the same color and pattern will also help to give an area unity, but in long passageways this can exaggerate the length and make it feel longer. In cases like this, it is best to have a series of mats or rugs that create pools of interest in sections or areas along the hallway.

Opposite top: A rectangular window has been set into the top of a long wall that covers two levels of stairs. The window is a feature on the otherwise blank wall and it gives a vista out onto the upper level.

Opposite bottom: Safety is an important factor on stairways. Here, fine, high-tension steel cables take the place of traditional rows of banisters and spindles, providing a secure barrier at the side of the stairs.

Left: Open-tread stairs allow light to pass from one floor to another and also appear less solid and bulky than enclosed treads.

Below: The internal wall that once formed a corridor between the kitchen and the adjacent room has been knocked down to hip height, creating an open passageway.

Connecting area storage

Connecting areas, such as hallways and passageways, are usually busy places where much of the day-to-day activity of a household will take place. As such, storage here must be space-efficient and flexible to the needs and requirements of all the family.

Right: For hall storage a narrow enclosure with a decorated opaque glass panel conceals coats and hats perfectly.

children's clothes can be kept at a height they can reach, while the adult clothes are at an upper level. This configuration also gives you double the hanging capacity in the same amount of space. The most effective arrangement is to stagger the hooks by placing the lower hooks halfway between the upper hooks. This also stops the garments from hanging directly over one another.

Smaller items such as gloves, hats, and scarves are better kept in a drawer or on a shelf so that they do not become entangled in the larger pieces of clothing. For hats and bicycle or motorbike helmets, a shelf above the coat hooks is a practical solution. Umbrellas are best in a stand. An old chimney pot or a tall cylindrical container is ideal.

Shoes and boots are more difficult to accommodate. They should be stacked in pairs and contained in a low box-style construction, subdivided into compartments. Each pair of shoes can fit into its own niche but boots may have to be rolled or folded. If the box is on the floor, firmly fixed to the wall, the top may be softened with long padded cushions and used as a seat.

If the shoe-box seat is not an option, then a straight-backed chair or stool is an ideal alternative. Any seat in this

Storing books

Hallways and landings are ideal places for storing books because they require only a narrow shelf, which can be tailored to fit into confined or difficult spaces. Even larger books can be accommodated—if they are too tall for the shelf, they can be laid down on their side or stacked horizontally.

Storing coats and shoes

You will need a variety of different storage options in your connecting areas. A coat rack is a common feature here. The traditional way to cope with this is to put a strong wood batten on the wall and attach a row of hooks to it. This serves the purpose but is not very inspiring or attractive. To liven it up, the

batten could be painted and the hooks made of brass. For a more modern design, the batten could be in steel or plastic and the hooks an unusual contemporary material, such as wood or chrome. The levels of hanging could also be varied so that short items can be hung halfway down the wall and longer ones above.

Such hanging arrangements are good for families, so that the

Left: *Mirrored insets in these cupboard doors reflect the* light, *making the room appear more spacious.*

area should be functional: it only needs to be comfortable enough as a temporary rest. If you have a porch or bay window, you may also consider building in a window seat that is hinged so that the base could be used as a storage place for shoes.

An alternative is a low, two-shelf system along which shoes can be arranged in lines. This can be made with planks of wood or rods. The rods at the back can be slightly raised so that the heels of the shoes rest over them.

Shelving

A table or shelf will also be practical and provide a place to put mail. The table should be of a narrow console style that lies flat against the wall. Hall tables often become a focus for clutter, junk mail, and debris, so you need to be disciplined about keeping it tidy if you choose this option.

A shelf can be small, neat, and attached directly to the wall above a radiator in a hallway. Radiators are often positioned by the door so that on arrival the reception area is heated and comforting.

The shelf may also help to guard people from direct contact with the heat of the radiator and it will also stop small objects from falling down behind it (see box, right).

Keys are another item you will need in this area. It is where you keep the car keys as well as those for the house and office. A small wall-mounted key rack can keep everything in place and at hand.

A key rack can be simple, such as a cork panel with rows of small hooks, or more elaborate, such as a little cupboard with a door that closes to hide the keys.

Installing a radiator screen

The easiest way to make a screen is to use a box made of particle board, chipboard, or wood to fit around your radiator and attach to the wall—you could employ a carpenter to make this for you. Once the frame is in place, you can fill the front panel to hide the main expanse of the radiator with a number of different materials. Expandable, wood garden trellis is a cheap and easy option—this can be painted or stained any color and then inserted into the surround. Metal grate, especially with a brass finish, often has attractive motifs. Fabric is another option: this can be used as a straight, tightly stretched panel, or pleated so it has a drape-like appearance. Avoid a solid front because this will restrict the flow of warm air and reduce the efficiency of the radiator.

leaf and

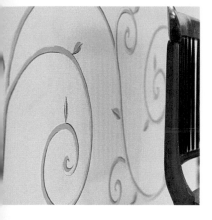

vine design

Inspired by the flowing shapes of wrought-iron and plasterwork used throughout history, this design is perfect for adding interest to a dull hallway. Traditional stenciling techniques are used to repeat the motif, but both the size of the pattern and the muted color scheme give a contemporary feel. Using subtle shading and highlighting techniques to mimic the way that light falls gives a three-dimensional illusion. The pattern is cut out of two large sheets of stencil card and designed so that it repeats itself when the card is repositioned.

Materials

Masking tape

Two large sheets of stencil card (24 x 34 in. sheets were used here)

Green latex paint for basecoat

Darker green latex paint for the vine

Gray/green latex paint for shadows

Off-white latex paint for highlights

Matte water-based varnish

Tools

Roller and tray

Thumbtack

String

Pencil

Craft knife

Stencil brushes

Artist's brushes

Preparing the surface

1 Mask off the area above the effect, then apply the basecoat and allow this to dry. Lay two sheets of stencil card on a flat surface, and with a thumbtack and string, make a compass positioned between the two sheets of card.

2 Draw the first circle with a diameter half the width of the card. Reposition the thumbtack and draw two more circles either side of the first, just touching it.

Making your design

3 Use a pencil to draw a line that joins up the circles to form an undulating pattern that will form the stem of the vine. Use French curves to follow the pattern, giving the vine its width.

4 Use templates to form the curling ends of the vine and to add random leaf shapes.

5 Use a craft knife to cut out the design, making sure you leave "bridges" where necessary to keep the stencil intact.

Applying color

6 With masking tape, position the stencil on the wall and apply the vine color with a dry stencil brush using a stippling action. Position the second sheet of stencil card so that it joins up with the first pattern and stencil. Repeat this process until the whole wall is stenciled.

7 In order to paint the shadow, decide which direction the light is coming from and use a

small artist's brush to apply a thin dark gray/green line along the areas of the vine that would naturally be in shadow.

8 To add the highlights, use a small artist's brush to apply an off-white shade along the areas of the vine where the light would fall. If you have a natural light source in your hallway or room, such as a window, work with it rather than against it. This will mean that the painted highlights and shadows on the stenciled vine will fall in the same way as they would naturally when the light falls on real three-dimensional objects.

9 When the surface is dry, varnish it with several coats of matte water-based varnish.

Using a thumbtack and a piece of string, draw the circles of the design on the stencil card.

Use a sharp knife to cut out the design, making sure there are "bridges" where necessary.

Apply the vine color carefully with a small, dry stencil brush and using a stippling action.

wall montage
of black-and-white photographs

Rather than leave treasured photographs languishing in a drawer or photo album, why not use them to transform a wall? The black-and-white images featured here were enlarged and tinted using a computer, scanner, and printer. Alternately, get this done at a photographic store, or you could enlarge images and alter their tonal values on a photocopier. The paper images can be applied directly to a wall using wallpaper adhesive, or you can stick them to a piece of primed hardboard that can be screwed onto the wall.

Materials

Sufficient paper images to cover your chosen area

PVA glue or artist's spray adhesive

Wallpaper paste

Matte or satin water-based varnish or artist's spray adhesive

Tools

Guillotine or craft knife

Metal ruler

Paintbrush

Square

Pencil

Adhesive brush

Bucket for mixing

Soft cloth

Cutting the images

1 Use a guillotine or craft knife and metal ruler to cut out the images. Make sure that all the squares are an identical size.

Fixing the ink

2 To make sure that the ink on the images will not run, fix it by brushing on a solution of 1 part PVA glue to 2 parts water. Test a small area first, and if the ink starts to run while brushing on the PVA solution, use artist's spray adhesive instead.

3 Using a square and pencil, divide the wall into square sections of around 10 sq. ft.—this will vary according to the size of your images. This will allow you to work on one section at a time.

Pasting the images to the wall

4 Take the required number of images to fill one square on your wall, making sure that the

Use a guillotine or craft knife to cut the images so that they are all square and the same size.

Brush the images with a little PVA solution or use artist's spray adhesive.

Know your materials

Artist's spray adhesive is used to fix artist's chalk and charcoal drawings. It also works well on computer printouts and photocopies where the ink could run if stuck with paste. The spray is available from art and craft stores and should be applied evenly in a well-ventilated room. To avoid breathing in fumes, wear a mask. If you prefer, you could use a solution of 1 part PVA glue and 2 parts water.

images are varied in terms of color, subject, and tone. Paste the back of the images using standard wallpaper paste and a soft brush. Allow to soak for at least five minutes (this allows the paste to be absorbed into the fibers of the paper, which will then swell) before applying to the wall using the pencil lines as a guide.

5 Smooth any wrinkles or bubbles of paste by gently rubbing the image with a soft cloth, making sure that you work from the center of the image outward. Allow the montage to dry thoroughly overnight. If any of the edges have lifted during this time, you can simply apply some extra paste with a small brush and

then smooth over the surface once again using a seam roller or cloth.

6 Protect the images by varnishing with a matte or satin water-based spray adhesive (to avoid brushmarks). Alternately, apply a conventional varnish with a clean, good-quality paintbrush.

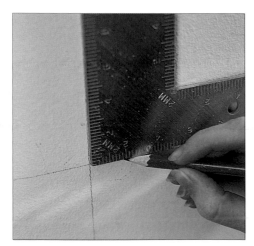

With a square and pencil, mark out the area on the wall where the images will be stuck.

Using an adhesive brush, paste the back of the images with standard wallpaper paste.

To remove any wrinkles or air bubbles, rub the images gently with a soft cloth.

Alternative

If you do not want to stick images directly onto your wall, it is still possible to create a striking graphic display by mounting and framing your photographs. This works most successfully if all the images are black-and-white and of a similar size. Simple black lacquer frames make a strong statement without detracting from the images themselves. Special nonreflective plexiglass can be used in rooms with strong natural light because this stops glare on the images. Plexiglass is a safer option than glass, especially in the bathroom, although it is more prone to scratching.

Arrange the images on the floor to decide on their positioning. To align the frames perfectly, use a tape measure and level and lightly mark the position of the nails in pencil on the wall. Make sure you use the correct picture nails and hooks for the type of wall you are hanging on (different varieties are available for solid and partition walls). For accurate results, check that the hanging wire is positioned at the same point on each frame.

Once finished, use water-based spray adhesive or varnish to protect the images.

floor storage

system with numbered sections

This floor storage system is ideal for keeping a busy household in order. Give each member of the family a number, or exchange the numbers for initials. It is ideal in the hallway, providing ample storage for shoes and bags. The construction is fairly simple but requires accurate cutting with a jigsaw. Sheets of particle board are sold in large sheets that are heavy and awkward to handle, so make sure you have help to lift them. A method called reverse stenciling is used to apply the numbers, then the whole object is varnished to withstand wear and tear.

Materials

3 lengths of 1 ft. 4 in. long, ¾ in. thick particle board

Screws

Wood putty

Fast-drying primer

Latex paint in coffee and cream colors

Spray adhesive

Satin water-based varnish

Tools

Pencil

Jigsaw

Sandpaper and sanding block

Flexible sanding block

Electric drill

Countersink bit

Scissors

Stencil brush

Paintbrush

Making a template

1 Make a paper template of the curved uprights. The height and the depth should be about 1 x 1 ft. Use the template as a guide to draw around. You should be able to fit five uprights along one length of particle board.

2 Cut the design out carefully with a jigsaw, then remove all the rough edges with sandpaper on a sanding block.

3 Using a pencil, mark the position of a slot running from the back to the middle of the three uprights, 1 in. up from the

bottom. Use the particle-board base as a width guide for the slot. Mark a corresponding slot on the particle-board base, running from the front to the middle.

4 Cut out all the slots and then sand all the rough edges with a sanding block.

Make a template of the curved uprights and use it as guide to draw around.

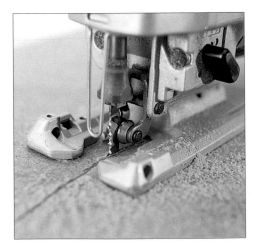

Cut the shapes out carefully with a jigsaw. Remember to wear a mask when doing this.

Know your tools

For this project we used a flexible sanding block. Because of its spongy texture it can be pushed into awkward corners and crevices. If you have a large area to sand you could use an electric sander, which does the job quickly and efficiently. For a really professional finish you should always complete the sanding by hand, with a fine-grade abrasive paper. For a super smooth paint finish, sand lightly in between coats with wet and dry paper. This will leave your paintwork completely free from brush or roller marks and will also get rid of any accidental runs or drips.

Assembling the pieces

5 Slot the uprights and the base together. They should fit snugly without moving.

6 Hold the back piece in place and mark the position of the uprights with a pencil line. Drill, countersink, and then screw each upright firmly in place. Attach the side uprights in place in the same way. Fill all the screw holes with some wood putty, then sand the whole thing using a flexible sanding block.

Applying primer

7 Prime the whole thing with a fast-drying primer, then sand lightly with a piece of coarse-grit sandpaper.

Adding the numbering

8 Paint the back of each section with some cream latex paint and then make sure you allow this to dry for the recommended time.

9 Use a computer and printer or a photocopier to enlarge the numbers 1 to 4. Use scissors to cut them out to form a mask, then use a little spray adhesive to attach the numbers to the back of each of the sections.

10 Use coffee-colored latex paint to cover the edge of each number with a stencil brush before finishing the painting with a larger brush.

11 Before the paint has dried, peel off the numbers to expose the base color. Varnish the numbers with two coats of water-based varnish.

Using a pencil, mark out carefully the position of the slots to be cut out with a jigsaw.

Slot the upright parts into the base and make sure that they fit snugly.

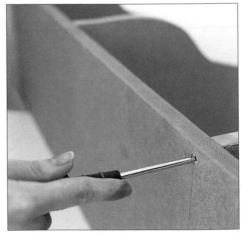

Screw each upright firmly in position and then fill all the screw holes with some wood putty.

Alternative

If you prefer minimal, uncluttered storage, consider transforming an alcove into a built-in cupboard. This streamlined example incorporates shallow shelves for storing shoes. Below this is a shelf doubling as a place to sit, beneath which is a cupboard for larger items like bags and suitcases.

The simplest way of creating this type of storage is to customize kitchen or other built-in cupboards. If you prefer to start from scratch, plan your design on paper, measuring the height and depth of the items you wish to store. Attach brackets or battens on the wall to hold the shelves, adding a larger shelf to form the seat. Screw vertical battens along each side wall in front of the shelves to attach the doors. Use kitchen cabinet-style concealed hinges to fit the doors level with the wall. Mark the positions of the hinges and use a special cutting attachment on an electric drill to cut holes for them. Make the doors from sheets of particle board and finish with your chosen color and handles.

Using a large paintbrush, prime the whole thing with fast-drying primer.

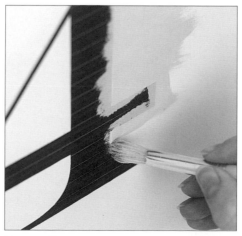

Use a coffee-colored latex paint to cover the edge of each number.

Before the paint has dried, peel off the numbers to expose the base color underneath.

lighting
connecting areas

Connecting areas and hallways are best lit by wall or ceiling lights because this will reduce the number of restrictions at floor level. Uplighters reflecting off a white ceiling will double the impact of the light source. Decorative shades can also be used to bring interest and decoration to a long passageway.

Using wall lights as a decorative feature

Wall lights can be used decoratively by creating a frame to surround the light so that it looks like a picture. Taking the light fitting as the center point, create a frame around it using bead or flat-backed beveled wood, and paint the frame in a stronger shade of the wall color, a contrasting tone, or a metallic finish such as bronze. Inside the frame put a mount board or a panel of another color, or if the rest of the wall is plain, a piece of decorative wallpaper. This will build up an eyecatching surround to the light and make it more than just a source light.

Right: *A band of decorative mirrors, close to the top of the walls, reflects the illumination given out by the ceiling light and amplifies it several times.*

Far right: *Wall lights are practical in a hallway as they can be fixed above head height, and if the beam is focused on the ceiling, they will supply a soft, indirect light.*

When entertaining or holding a party, the vestibule or initial section of the hallway is the first part of your home that guests and visitors see and experience so it should have a warm and welcoming appearance. To achieve this, the lighting should be adequate but not overbright.

Ambient lighting

In the evenings, guests arriving for a dinner party could be greeted by a low ambient light augmented by a large candle or an arrangement of candles. The smaller tealight candles can be set in glass votive holders, which will add extra interest. However,

candles should always be placed in safe, sturdy containers. At night you can place candles in front of mirrors in connecting areas so that the flames are reflected and create twice the impact.

Faux skylights

Lighting is important in a corridor because there is seldom much, if any, daylight. In a modern home you can use large panel lights on the ceiling that look like skylights.

When the light or lights are switched on they will provide a bright but diffuse light, which will illuminate an ample area beneath and create the impression of there being a window above. The light could be put on a dimmer so that during daylight hours the strength of light could be equivalent to natural light outside, but in the evening dimmed to a subtle glow.

Wall lights

Wall lights are another possibility for lighting linking areas. In a long corridor you will need a combination of wall lights to create an ambient atmosphere, and ceiling lights or lamps to make sure that the floor and lower levels of the passageway are lit.

There are also torchlike wall lights that resemble a handheld flare and simple semicircular plaster bowls that can be painted to blend in with the main wall color in the hallway.

In a rustic setting curved terra-cotta roof tiles, like those seen on Italian villas, can be hung on the wall with the underside facing forward. In this curved area a small dish or candleholder can be attached and a taper, tealight, or pillar candle lit. Alternately, the tiles could be drilled and wired to take a small electric bulb. There are electric candle-style bulbs that have a built-in flicker and are hard to distinguish from the real thing.

Recessed lighting

Another possibility for decorative lighting, which can be used in an older home, is to put a long but narrow tubular bulb behind the cornice or in a picture rail recess to direct light upward and cast shadows of the decorative edge of the plasterwork.

Spotlights

A line of recessed spotlights is an effective way of lighting a corridor. They can also be set on dimmer switches so that the level of light can be varied.

You may like to put them on separate circuits so that a pool of light can be directed onto an object or arrangement at the end of the hall, while the front and middle parts are in darkness or more subdued illumination. However, make sure the beam of a spotlight is not shining directly into the face of a visitor.

Picture lights

Picture lights add to the overall level of ambient light in a corridor as well as highlighting the pictures hung on the wall. Picture lights can be fine, linear, modern designs, no bigger than a fountain pen, or traditional, larger brass versions. Both versions need to be wired from the baseboard up to behind the pictures. This will require channels to be cut into the plaster of the wall that, after the wires have been placed, will then be replastered and smoothed. The overall effect can be used to create a miniature gallery.

Below left: Spotlights recessed along the edge of the floor by the baseboard are a way of introducing artificial light to a passageway.

Below: Recessed ceiling lights supplement the natural light source from the windows in the dining area.

ndex

Acknowledgments

To AWJ—absolutely essential

Many, many thanks to the owners and designers of the properties featured in this book, and to the following who helped with our additional styling and location hunting: Jane Taylor and Corrine Day at Heals; Jo Leyland at Purves and Purves; Di and Eva at Sheila Fitzjones; Sam and Kate at Parker Hobart; Melissa at Halpern; LK Bennett, Kings Road, London SW3; Karen and Jennifer at Damask; and Liberty Parker at Habitat. And extra special thanks for Jean Johnston's invaluable help in crosschecking pictures, for Ray's polishing abilities in the kitchen, and for Charlie's cheerfulness and clothes folding—what a team!

LOCATION CREDITS

The author, photographer, and publisher would like to thank the following companies and individuals for allowing photography of their homes and business premises.

Key

R = Right   L = Left   B = Below
T = Top   D = Detail   M = Middle

Tara Bernerd

(interior design/development)
2 Bentick Street, London W1U 2JX,
020 7009 0101

and John Hitchcox

(architectural design/development)
Yoo The Banking Hall, 20–28 Maida
Vale, London W9, 020 7266 2244
pp7, 106 (B), 107, 125, 296 (B)

Bulthaup Kitchens

1 North Terrace, Alexander Square,
London SW3B, 020 7317 6000
and 37 Wigmore Street, London W1,
020 7495 3663
(architectural design by John Pawson)
pp2–3, 208–9, 214, 219 (T), 231 (B)

Chesneys

194–101 Battersea Park Road,
London SW11 4ND, 020 7627 1410,
www.antiquefireplace.co.uk
pp86 (L), 87 (BR), 90–1, 93

Damask

Broxholme House, New Kings Road,
London SW6 4AA, 020 7731 3553,
www.damask.co.uk
*pp140 (L), 142 (TL), 150 (T),
167 (TR), 263 (R)*

Diligence

Providence House, High Street,
Stockbridge, Hampshire SO20 6HP,
01264 811 660
fireplaces on pp86 (T) and 110

Lisa Dodds (artist's own home)
*pp15, 110, 130, 131, 135 (T), 244 (B),
269 (T), 277, 285, 293 (L), 310 (L)*

Stephen Featherstone

architectural designer and design
director of Llewelyn-Davies Architects
020 7612 9435
*pp67, 77 (T), 100–1, 121, 131 (D),
172–3, 290–1, 294 (T), 310 (R)*

Christopher Healey Furniture

27–29 Union Street,
London SE1 1SD, 020 7639 4645
also available through Concord
Designs, 01524 412 374,
www.concorddesigns.co.uk
*pp14 (T), 117, 143 (T), 195, 212 (B),
216 (B), 243 (B), 280*

**Karen Howes
at TMH Designs Ltd**

208 The Chambers,
Chelsea Harbour, London SW10 0XF,
020 7349 9017, tmh@dircon.co.uk
*pp20 (T), 61 (T), 76, 80 (T), 86 (R),
109 (D), 122 (T), 132–3, 150 (B),
159, 167 (T), 175, 196, 211, 219 (L),
231 (T), 247 (T&B), 292 (B), 296 (T)*

Interior Design House

The Coach House, 8 Avenue
Crescent, London W3 8EW,
020 8752 8648
(interior designer Fleur Rossdale
and architect Peter Wadley,
020 8752 8642,
wadley@dircon.co.uk)
*pp26, 108 (B), 111, 166 (B), 215 (T),
261 (B), 266–7, 270 (T), 297 (L)*